THE CONSTITUTION OF TAIWAN

In addition to the economic miracle, with surprising growth in the 1970s and 1980s, Taiwan has further shown the world two others. One is the democratic miracle which brought about a silent revolution from notorious authoritarian regime to full democracy in Asia. Intertwined with that miracle is the constitutional one, in which political reform was undertaken in a constitutional manner and through constitutional means. Indeed, Taiwan's transition to democracy was made possible by incremental constitutional revisions, courts responsive to changing dynamics, and a civil society engaged in the project of constitutional transformation. These changes ushered in the unprecedented development of a transitional and transnational constitutionalism.

This volume seeks to explain the drivers and context of these constitutional transformations. Democratisation, indigenisation and globalisation all drove the transformation of an externally imposed constitution into an internally embraced, vibrant constitution. The changes analysed in this volume include institutional shifts from a cabinet system to a semi-presidential one; from three parliaments to one; from manipulated central-local relations to a functional federalism; from a Constitutional Court that merely rubber-stamped to one that is responsive and supports social and political dialogues. More importantly, this volume details how a short list of constitutional rights has been transformed to a burgeoning rights-based discourse engaged by civil society.

Taiwan: Colour Politics of Blue, Green and Red

The three predominant colours in the composition reflect Taiwan's main political parties and influences: blue representing the National Party (Kuomintang), green, the Democratic Progressive Party and red, the spectre of China. The white sun radiating over blue sky and red earth looming in the background represents Taiwan's national flag. The juxtaposition of the red brick Presidential Palace and the iconic Taipei 101 symbolises Taiwan's political power, economic miracle, and modernity. '2005' is etched onto the Presidential Palace Tower to celebrate Taiwan's most significant constitutional reform which took place in that year. An image of Lee Ten-huei, the first native Taiwanese president, hailed as 'Mr Democracy of Taiwan', is depicted on the left side of the Tower. This is flanked by Chiang Kai-shek, whose presidential tenure was dubbed 'White Terror'. In the arch of the palace, a Tsou warrior personifies Taiwan's indigenous tribes. A formosa black bear is depicted as Taiwan's counterpart to China's panda. A singular sunflower recalls the 'Sunflower Movement' led by a coalition of students and civic groups in 2014 in protest against the Kuomintang Party's trade agreement with China. A black figure[1] holding a flower commemorates the 'Wild Lily' student movement of 1990, which became a pivotal turning point in Taiwan's democracy development. The other hand of the figure points to Liberty Square.

Putachad, Artist

---

[1] inspired by Matisse's 'Two Dancers'

Constitutional Systems of the World
General Editors: Peter Leyland, Andrew Harding and Benjamin L Berger
Associate Editors: Grégoire Webber and Rosalind Dixon

In the era of globalisation, issues of constitutional law and good governance are being seen increasingly as vital issues in all types of society. Since the end of the Cold War, there have been dramatic developments in democratic and legal reform, and post-conflict societies are also in the throes of reconstructing their governance systems. Even societies already firmly based on constitutional governance and the rule of law have undergone constitutional change and experimentation with new forms of governance; and their constitutional systems are increasingly subjected to comparative analysis and transplantation. Constitutional texts for practically every country in the world are now easily available on the internet. However, texts which enable one to understand the true context, purposes, interpretation and incidents of a constitutional system are much harder to locate, and are often extremely detailed and descriptive. This series seeks to provide scholars and students with accessible introductions to the constitutional systems of the world, supplying both a road map for the novice and, at the same time, a deeper understanding of the key historical, political and legal events which have shaped the constitutional landscape of each country. Each book in this series deals with a single country, or a group of countries with a common constitutional history, and each author is an expert in their field.

Published volumes
The Constitution of the United Kingdom; The Constitution of the United States;
The Constitution of Vietnam; The Constitution of South Africa; The Constitution of Japan;
The Constitution of Germany; The Constitution of Finland; The Constitution of Australia;
The Constitution of the Republic of Austria; The Constitution of the Russian Federation;
The Constitutional System of Thailand; The Constitution of Malaysia; The Constitution
of China; The Constitution of Indonesia; The Constitution of France; The Constitution
of Spain; The Constitution of Mexico; The Constitution of Israel; The Constitutional Systems
of the Commonwealth Caribbean; The Constitution of Canada; The Constitution of Singapore;
The Constitution of Belgium

Link to series website
http://www.hartpub.co.uk/series/csw

The Constitution of Taiwan

A Contextual Analysis

Jiunn-rong Yeh

·HART·
PUBLISHING
OXFORD AND PORTLAND, OREGON
2016

Published in the United Kingdom by Hart Publishing Ltd
16C Worcester Place, Oxford, OX1 2JW
Telephone: +44 (0)1865 517530
Fax: +44 (0)1865 510710
E-mail: mail@hartpub.co.uk
Website: http://www.hartpub.co.uk

Published in North America (US and Canada) by
Hart Publishing
c/o International Specialized Book Services
920 NE 58th Avenue, Suite 300
Portland, OR 97213-3786
USA
Tel: +1 503 287 3093 or toll-free: (1) 800 944 6190
Fax: +1 503 280 8832
E-mail: orders@isbs.com
Website: http://www.isbs.com

Hart Publishing is an imprint of Bloomsbury Publishing plc.

British Library Cataloguing in Publication Data
Data Available

Library of Congress Cataloging-in-Publication Data

Names: Yeh, Jiunn-rong, 1958– author.

Title: The Constitution of Taiwan : a contextual analysis / Jiunn-rong Yeh.

Description: Oxford : Hart Publishing, 2016. | Series: Constitutional systems
of the world | Includes bibliographical references and index.

Identifiers: LCCN 2015048262 (print) | LCCN 2015048697 (ebook) |
ISBN 9781849465120 (pbk.) | ISBN 9781509905591 (Epub)

Subjects: LCSH: China (Republic : 1949–). Xian fa. | Constitutional
law—Taiwan | Constitutions—Taiwan.

Classification: LCC KNP207.A311946 Y4 2016 (print) | LCC KNP207.A311946
(ebook) | DDC 342.5124902—dc23

LC record available at http://lccn.loc.gov/2015048262

ISBN: 978-1-84946-512-0

Typeset by Compuscript Ltd, Shannon

Lightning Source UK Ltd

Acknowledgements

Since Taiwan's democratic reforms in the late 1980s, presenting Taiwan's constitutional struggles in a book has been at the top of my research agenda. Here is the Taiwan volume in this series 'Constitutional Systems of the World'.

I am grateful to everyone who shared their time in making this volume possible. Andrew Harding and Peter Leyland introduced me to this great series and showed tremendous patience and support. Putachad Leyland's artwork for the cover is truly the pearl of this volume. My colleague Wen-Chen Chang—with great inspiration—generously commented on my manuscript. Various National Taiwan University College of Law graduate students offered their assistance, including but not limited to: Chun-Yuan Lin, Yen-Lun Tseng, In-Lon Lei, Yi-Li Lee, Shao-Man Lee, Szu-Chen Kuo, Pei-Jung Li, Ju-Jing Huang, Jo-Tzu Ma, Ray-Yun Hong and Wayland Chang. I owe deep thanks to Christopher Martin and Roger Dixon for their very helpful proofreading of the final manuscript.

Last but not least, I am grateful to a very large group of people in Taiwan that include: engaged citizens, civil rights advocates, reform-minded intellectuals, as well as judges and justices of the courts. Together they have contributed to Taiwan's democratic and constitutional miracles on which I have elaborated in this volume.

Contents

Acknowledgements v
Table of Abbreviations xiii
Table of Cases xv
Table of Legislation xix

1. **TAIWAN'S CONSTITUTION IN WORLD
   CONSTITUTIONALISM: COMMON
   AND SALIENT FEATURES** 1
   I.   Driving Forces of Profound Transformation:
        Indigenisation, Democratisation and Globalisation...............3
   II. Common Features in Constitutional Perspective 7
        A.   Constitutional Democracy...8
        B.   Fundamental Rights and Freedoms 9
        C.   Separation of Powers and Accountability.....................10
        D.   Rule of Law and the Independence of the Courts 11
   III. Salient Features in Transitional Perspective..........................12
        A.   Incremental Constitutional Revisions...........................12
        B.   The Constitutional Court and Dialectical
             Judicial Review...13
        C.   Quasi-Constitutional Statutes...15
   IV. Salient Features in Transnational Perspective.......................16
        A.   Incorporation of International Human
             Rights Treaties 16
        B.   Transnational Judicial Dialogues....................................17
        C.   Global Convergence of Institutions 18
   V.   Aims and Structure of this Book...19
        Further Reading 21

2. **TAIWAN'S CONSTITUTIONAL JOURNEY:
   IMPOSITION AND INDIGENISATION** 23
   I.   A Tale of Two Foundations: Externally
        Imposed Constitutions..24
        A.   Japanese Colonisation, the Meiji Constitution,
             and the Hybrid Constitutional Foundation....................25

    B.   Regime Relocation, the ROC Constitution
        and Taiwan's Incorporation 28
  II. Pre-democratisation Constitutional
     Manipulation and Authoritarianism 30
     A.   Temporary Provisions and
        Authoritarian Leadership 31
     B.   Old Thieves and the Manipulation of
        Representation 32
     C.   Martial Law and Constitutional
        Authoritarianism..34
  III. Democratisation and Constitutional
     Indigenisation 36
     A.   Democratic Mobilisation and
        Negotiated Change 37
     B.   The Reconstruction of Representation
        and Incremental Constitutional Reform.......................38
        i.   Reinforcing Internal Representation: Down
           with the 'Old Thieves' and Extending Full
           Suffrage to Taiwan's Residents 39
        ii. Reinforcing External Representation:
           The Embarrassing Status of the Taiwan
           Provincial Government 42
        iii. Reinforcing Representation as to
           Constitutional Sovereignty: The Fate
           of the National Assembly and the
           Public Referendum 44
  IV. Conclusion 48
     Further Reading 49

3. **THE EVOLVING PRESIDENCY AND
    THE EXECUTIVE**..51
  I. The Evolution of the Five-power
     Government Scheme..52
     A.   The Development of the Five-power
        Government Scheme..52
     B.   The Road to Semi-Presidentialism 57
  II. The Evolving Presidency..59
     A.   The Changing Role and Extensive
        Powers of the President....................................60

    B.   National Security Council and
        Cross-Strait Policy 63

    C.   Presidential Elections, Powers and
        Political Divisions 65

III.   The Executive Yuan: The Premier and
     Executive Oversight 68

    A.   The Premier, Cabinet Meetings and Policy
        Co-ordination..69

    B.   Ministries and Agencies 71

       i.   The 14 Ministries...74

       ii. The Eight Co-ordinative Councils.........................75

       iii. The Designated Independent
            Commissions...75

    C.   Independent Regulatory Commissions...........................75

IV.   Government Reform..80

    A.   Government Streamlining 81

    B.   The Public–Private Partnership 83

    C.   The Examination Yuan and the
        Civil Service 87

V.   Conclusion 89

     Further Reading 90

**4.   REPRESENTATION AND
       LEGISLATIVE PROCESS** 91

I.   The Transformation of Representative
     Institutions: From Three Parliaments to One......................94

    A.   From Three Parliaments to Two:
        The Transformation of the Control Yuan....................94

    B.   From Two Parliaments to One:
        The Abolition of the National Assembly 97

II.   The Electoral System and Political Parties.......................... 100

    A.   Changes to Legislative Seats and
        Electoral Rules... 100

    B.   Election Institutions and Neutrality........................... 107

    C.   Political Parties and Accountability
        Problems.. 109

III. Legislative Functions and
     Constitutional Control 114

    A.   Legislative Autonomy and Limitations...................... 114

B. Financial Control.. 117
C. Shared Powers and Conflict Resolution 120
IV. The Control Yuan after Transformation............................ 123
V. Conclusion 126
Further Reading 127

5. **MULTI-LEVEL GOVERNANCE AND
    DEVOLUTION** 129
I. Central–local Relations in the
    ROC Constitution.. 131
A. Elections and Accountability...................................... 131
B. Pre-emption and Regulatory Supremacy..................... 133
C. Budgetary Control and Devolution............................. 134
II. Taiwan as a State versus Taiwan as a Province 135
A. Constitutional Amendment and
    Legislative Action.. 137
B. The Rise and Fall of the Taiwan
    Provincial Government.. 140
C. Taipei and the Special Municipalities in
    Transitional Politics... 142
D. The Rise of Mega Metropolitans and the
    Changing Geopolitical Landscape............................... 146
III. Beyond Borderlines: Central–local Relations
    in Regional and Global Perspectives................................ 148
A. Micro Central–local Relations:
    Taiwan and Her Offshore Islands............................... 148
B. Taiwan in Multi-level Governance 150
IV. Conclusion 152
Further Reading 153

6. **JUDICIAL REVIEW AND THE FUNCTION
    OF THE CONSTITUTIONAL COURT** 155
I. Changing Institutions and Processes: From the
    Council to the Court 157
A. Organisational Evolution... 157
B. Appointment Process 160
C. Powers and Jurisdictions 162
D. Adjudication Procedure 165
II. Functional Transformations: From Rubber
    Stamp to Constitutional Guardianship............................. 167
A. Overall Performance.. 168

B.   Changing Functions in Response to
        Changing Contexts.. 171
III. Judicial Strategy and Style of Judgment............................. 174
A.   Pro-dialogue Approach 175
B.   The Variety of Constitutional Declarations
        versus the Politics of Unconstitutionality.................. 178
C.   The Principle of Proportionality............................... 184
D.   Judicial Reference to Foreign Law and
        the Incorporation of International Law..................... 186
E.   A United Court versus a Divided Society 189
IV. Conclusion 191
        Further Reading 192

7.   **RIGHTS AND FREEDOMS**.. 193
I.   Rights Discourse in a Transformative Society 194
A.   Rights Discourse in the Wake of an
        Emergent Civil Society.. 195
B.   Rights Discourse in the Wake of
        Constitutional Reform.. 197
C.   Rights Discourse and Incorporation by
        the Judiciary.. 202
II. Civil and Political Rights... 205
A.   Right of Political Participation.................................... 205
B.   Free Speech and Social/Political Transition 208
III. Socio-economic Rights 214
A.   Health Insurance and the Right to Work 214
B.   Gender Equality and the Changing
        Family Structure 218
C.   Waves of Immigrants and Equality............................ 222
IV. Indigenous Peoples and Collective Rights......................... 224
A.   Historical Discrimination.................................... 224
B.   The Indigenous Movement....................................... 227
C.   Gradual Progress and the Implementation
        of Indigenous Rights.................................... 229
V.   The Incorporation of International
        Human Rights 232
A.   International Human Rights and
        Institutional Capacity-building.............................. 233
B.   The Death Penalty Debate as Example................. 236

VI.   Conclusion 238
        Further Reading 240

8. **CONCLUSION: CHALLENGES
    AND PROSPECTS**.. 241
      I.   Constitutional Footprints: What Taiwan
           Has Achieved.. 242
           A.   Transformative Constitutionalism.............................. 243
           B.   Civic Constitutionalism.. 244
     II.   Facing the Future.. 246
           A.   The Infeasibility of Constitutional Change 246
           B.   A Stalemate-prone System of Government.............. 247
           C.   A Fragile Constitutional Sovereignty 250
    III.   Conclusion 253
           Further Reading 253

Index.. 255

Table of Abbreviations

APEC	Asia-Pacific Economic Cooperation
BOT	build-operate-transfer
CCP	Chinese Communist Party
CEDAW	Convention on Elimination of All Forms of Discrimination Against Women
CRC	Convention on the Rights of the Child
CRPD	Convention on the Rights of Persons with Disabilities
DPP	Democratic Progressive Party
ECFA	Economic Cooperation Framework Agreement
ETC	Electronic Toll Collection
ECPAT	End Child Prostitution in Asian Tourism
FETC	Far Eastern Electronic Toll Collection Co.
ICCPR	International Covenant on Civil and Political Rights
ICESCR	International Covenant on Economic, Social and Cultural Rights
KMT	Kuomintang
MWP	minister without portfolio
MMD	multi-member district
NCC	National Communications Commission
NDC	National Defence Conference
NSC	National Security Council
NT$	New Taiwan dollar
NHI	National Health Insurance programme
OT	operate-transfer
PRC	People's Republic of China

PFP	People First Party
ROC	Republic of China
SNTV	single non-transferable vote
THSR	Taiwan High Speed Rail
TSU	Taiwan Solidarity Union
TAEDP	Taiwan Alliance to End the Death Penalty
UDHR	Universal Declaration of Human Rights
WTO	World Trade Organization

Table of Cases

Japan

Case to Seek Invalidation of Election, 65 Minshu
2 (Supreme Court) 106

South Korea

National Assembly Election Redistricting Plan Case, 2000
Hun-Ma 92, 25 October 2001 (Constitutional Court) 106
National Seat Succession Case, 92 Hun-Ma 153, 28 April 1994 112

Taiwan

JY Interpretations.. 167
   No 3 (1952).. 54, 114
   No 31 (1954) 30, 40, 171
   No 31 (1990) 34
   No 76 (1957) 57, 93, 166
   No 78 (1957) 173
   No 85 (1960) 172
   No 86 (1960) 172, 178
   No 105 (1964) 209
   No 117 (1966) 172
   No 124 (1968) 173
   No 125 (1968) 173
   No 150 (1977) 172
   No 151 (1977) 176
   No 165 (1980) 187
   No 165 (1998) 186
   No 166 (1980) 181
   No 175 (1982) 55, 114
   No 177 (1982) 173
   No 185 (1984) 164, 173
   No 194 (1985) 236–7
   No 210 (1986) 176
   No 211 (1986) 179
   No 217 (1987) 176
   No 218 (1987) 181
   No 242 (1989) 203, 220
   No 247 (1989) 176

No 251 (1990) 181
No 260 (1990) 137–9
No 261 (1990) 2, 11, 40, 58, 101, 173–4, 182, 205–6
No 263 (1990) 202, 236–7
No 268 (1990) 176
No 290 (1992) 206–7
No 293 (1992) 203–4
No 313 (1993) 176
No 315 (1993) 190
No 325 (1993) 95
No 328 (1993) 250
No 329 (1993) 17–18, 120–1, 187
No 331 (1993) 112, 206
No 342 (1994) 115
No 357 (1994) 123
No 362 (1994) 220
No 364 (1994) 211
No 365 (1994) 203, 219
No 367 (1994) 176
No 371 (1995) 163
No 381 (1995) 116
No 387 (1995) 58
No 391 (1995) 118
No 392 (1995) 159, 188
No 399 (1996) 203
No 401 (1996) 117
No 407 (1996) 213
No 410 (1996) 203, 220, 219
No 414 (1996) 184, 212
No 419 (1996) 159
No 428 (1997) 184
No 435 (1997) 117
No 439 (1997) 179
No 443 (1997) 177
No 445 (1998) 210–11
    para 1 210
    para 2 210
    para 2(2)–(3) 210
    para 8 209
No 452 (1998) 203, 220
No 472 (1999) 214–15
    para 2 215
No 476 (1999) 184, 236–7
No 479 (1999) 203

No 483 (1999) 179
No 499 (2000) 14, 45–6, 98, 116, 174
No 509 (2000) 180, 212
    para 3... 212
No 514 (2000) 216
No 520 (2001) 14, 67–8, 118, 175
    paras 2–3.. 119
    para 6... 119
No 535 (2001) 204
No 549 (2002) 188, 218
No 550 (2002) 14, 144, 176
No 552 (2002) 220
No 553 (2002) 15, 145
No 554 (2002) 185, 204, 220
No 577 (2004) 212
No 578 (2004) 188, 201, 218
No 582 (2004) 187
No 584 (2004) 185, 217–18
    para 1.. 216–17
No 585 (2004) 66, 96, 123, 180
No 587 (2004) 204
No 601 (2005) 180
No 603 (2005) 159, 163, 185–6, 204
No 613 (2006) 19, 79–80, 122, 182
No 617 (2006) 203, 213
    paras 1–2.. 213
No 618 (2006) 208, 223
No 623 (2007) 204, 213
No 627 (2007) 62, 66–7, 191
No 632 (2007) 55, 122, 125, 179
    para 4... 122
No 644 (2008) 110, 211
No 645 (2008) 122
No 649 (2008) 217
No 656 (2009) 204, 212
    para 2... 212
No 666 (2009) 182–3
No 678 (2010) 211
No 708 (2013) 223–4
    para 1... 224
No 709.. 187
No 710 (2013) 188, 223
No 711 (2013) 217
No 718 (2014) 211

No 719 (2014) 231–2
No 721 (2014) 14, 107, 206
Taipei Tifang Fayuan (Taipei District Court),
 102 Su-Tzu No 3782 (2013) 113
Taitung District Court Judgment (3 September 2012),
 101-Su-152 230
Taitung District Court Judgment (27 November 2012),
 101-Su-218 230
Taitung District Court Judgment (7 January 2013),
 101-Zhongsu-5 230

Table of Legislation

Republic of China

Constitution of the Republic of
China (1947) 129–30, 137, 148, 152,
155, 157–8, 160, 163
Chapter 10 132–3
Chapter 13 135
Arts 25–34 132
Arts 78–79 156
Art 107 133–4
Art 108 134
Art 109 ....133, 135
Art 110 134
Art 111 133–4
Arts 112–136 132
Art 142 135
Art 147 135
Arts 171–172 156
Five-Power Constitution (1936) 28, 53, 59
Organic Act of the Judicial Yuan (1947) 158, 160–1
Arts 3–4 ....158, 160
Temporary Provisions Effective During the Period
of National Mobilisation for Suppression of the
Communist Rebellion (1948) 1, 5, 31–2, 35–9, 59, 61–3,
115, 168–9, 195

Germany

Basic Law, Art 21 110

Taiwan

Act Controlling Guns, Ammunition and Knives (2001 revision) 230
Art 20 230
Act of Gender Equality in Employment (2002) 220
Act Governing the Punishment of Police Offences 181
Act Governing the Punishment for Violation of
Road Traffic Regulations 217
Act Governing Relations between the People of the
Taiwan Area and the Mainland Area (Cross-Strait Act) 64–5, 121, 208,
222–3
Art 5(2) 121

Act on Public Functionary Disciplinary
  Sanctions (1985), Arts 18–19 124
Act Regarding the Council of Grand Justices (1958) 159, 164–6, 189
  Art 5(2) 159
  Art 17 189
  Enforcement Rules 189–90
Administrative Procedure Act (1999) 85
Anti-Sedition Law 197
Assembly and Parade Act 210–11
  Art 29 210
Basic Code Governing Central Administrative Agencies
  Organisations (2004) (Basic Code) 72, 76–8, 82
  Art 3 .... 72, 76, 78
  Art 6 72
  Art 21 78
Basic Law of the Environment, Art 23 68
Budget Act 119
Central Government Agency Personnel Quota Act 82
Child and Juvenile Sexual Transaction Prevention Act 213
Civic Organisation Act 211
Civil Association Act 194
Civil Associations Act (revised 1992) 110
Civil Associations Act (2011), Arts 44–52 110
Civil Code 203, 219
  Art 1002 220
  Art 1089 219
  Part IV (Family), Enforcement Act, Art 1 220
Constitution of the Republic
  of China (1947) 1–5, 10–13, 16, 24–5, 28–31, 36–7,
                                                    41–2, 44–5, 48–9, 51–4, 56–8, 60–2,
                                                    69–70, 88, 91–3, 95, 98–100, 107, 110,
                                                    114–15, 118–20, 133, 136, 138, 140,
                                                    146, 157–8, 161, 173, 177, 183–4, 187,
                                                    194, 197–8, 202, 209, 214, 221, 228–9, 232
  Preamble 53
  Chapter 13 214
  Art 2 30
  Art 7 .... 177, 193, 197, 236
  Art 8 .... 177, 193, 197–8, 223–4, 237
  Art 9 .... 177, 193, 197–8
  Art 10 .... 177, 193, 197–8
  Art 11 .... 177, 193, 197–8, 212
  Arts 12–14 .... 177, 193, 197–8
  Art 15 .... 177, 193, 197–8, 216
  Art 16 .... 177, 193, 197–8

Art 17..111, 177, 193, 197–8, 205
Art 18.. 177, 193, 197–8, 208
Art 19..177, 193, 197–8
Art 20... 193, 197–8
Art 21...177, 193, 197–8
Art 22.. 177, 193, 197–8, 202
Art 23...177, 184, 236–7
Arts 25–34 ....92, 139
Arts 35–37 60
Art 38...60, 120
Arts 39–42 60
Art 44... 54
Art 52... 67
Art 53... 68
Art 54... 70
Art 55... 62
Art 56... 70
Art 58... 114
Art 58(1)... 70
Art 58(2)... 120
Art 59... 117
Art 61... 71
Art 62...30, 32, 92, 114
Art 63... 92, 114, 117, 119–20
Art 64..92, 100
Arts 65–69 92
Art 70... 92, 117–18
Art 71...54, 92
Art 72...60, 92
Art 73...92, 117
Arts 74–76 92
Art 78... 162
Art 83... 88
Art 87..54, 114
Arts 90–103 92
Art 104 ....92, 123
Art 105 ....92, 117
Art 106 92
Art 118 145
Art 134 221
Arts 137–169 214
Art 171 178
Art 172 ....11, 178
Art 173 11

Additional Articles...13, 216, 222, 239
   forewords 250
   Art 11.. 64
Additional Articles (1991)
   Art 2... 101
   Art 9... 115
Additional Articles (1992)
   Art 7(1) 94
   Art 7(2) 123
   Art 7(3) 124
   Art 7(4) 94
   Art 7(5) 94, 123
   Art 7(6) 94
   Art 9.. 139
   Art 12(2) 41
   Art 13(2)–(3) 110
   Art 15(1) 123
   Art 17.. 43
   Art 18.. 215
   Art 18(6) 228
Additional Articles (1994), Art 9(7) 228
Additional Articles (1997)
   Art 4(1) 101
   Art 10(9) 229
   Art 10(10) 228
Additional Articles (1999), Art 1 98
Additional Articles (2000), Art 1 98
Additional Articles (2005) 72
   Art 1 99
   Art 2 165
   Art 2(4) 63
   Art 2(9) 99
   Art 2(10) 99
   Art 3 ....10, 69, 72
   Art 3(2) 62
   Art 3(3) 10, 61
   Art 4 104
   Art 4(2) 221
   Art 4(5) 99
   Art 4(7) 99
   Art 4(8) 116
   Art 5 ....122, 159
   Art 5(1) 156, 160–1
   Art 5(3) 160
   Art 5(5) 165

Art 6 ....88, 122
Art 7 122
Art 10 199
Art 10(2) 199
Art 10(3) 200
Art 10(5) 200
Art 10(6) 199
Art 10(7)–(8) 200
Art 10(10)–(12) 200
Art 11 13
Art 12 ....10, 13, 99
Art 15 94
Constitutional Interpretation Procedure Act (1993).............................. 159, 163, 165
Art 5...163–4
Art 5(1)(3) 163
Art 5(1)–(2)..106
Arts 10–11 166
Art 13...159, 165
Art 17..167, 190
Control Act (1992)
Art 19 124
Art 24 124
Criminal Code..237
Art 100 197
Customs Smuggling Control Act...179
Drug Control Act during the Period for Suppression of the
Communist Rebellion 236
Art 5(1)...236
Enforcement Act of CEDAW (2012)..234
Gender Equity Education Act (2004) 220
Genetic Health Act (2009), Art 9...220
Government Archive Act..190
Government Information Disclosure Act (2005) 85
Government Procurement Act...231–2
Household Registration Act 185
Implementation Act of the Convention on the Rights
of Persons with Disabilities (2014)..234, 236
Implementation Act of the CRC (2014)..234, 236
Income Tax Act..181
Indigenous Peoples Basic Law (2005)...229
Judge Act (2011) 124
Art 4...124
Art 47...124
Labour Insurance Act..188, 218
Labour Standards Act..188, 218

Law for Encouraging Private Sector Participation in
  Transportation Construction (1996) 85
Law No 63 of 1896 26
Law No 31 of 1906 26
Law No 3 of 1921 26
Local Government Act (1999) 16, 139, 145, 147
  Art 4 147
  Art 7-1 147
Local Government Systems Act 141
Martial Law Decree (1949) 1–2, 36–7, 59, 168, 196,
                                                        207, 209, 222, 237
Meiji Constitution 24–8, 43
Name Act 230
National Health Insurance Act (1994) 144, 215
Offshore Islands Development Act 150
Organic Act of the Executive Yuan (1947) 71, 73, 80, 82
  Art 10(1) 70–1
  Art 14 71
Organic Act of the Judicial Yuan (1947), Art 4 161
Organic Act of the National Communication
  Commission (NCC Organic Act) 79–80
  Art 4 80
Organic Law of the Central Election Commission (2009) 108
  Art 3 108
  Art 5 108
Physically and Mentally Disabled Citizens Protection Act 217
Political Donations Act (2004) 111
Political Donations Act (2015), Arts 7–30 111
Procedural Rules of the Executive Yuan Council (2011), Art 5 70
Provisional Act for Adjustment of Functions and
  Organisations of the Executive Yuan 82
Provisional Act for the Restructuring of the Functions, Business
  and Organisation of the Taiwanese Government (1998) 141
Provisional Constitution for the Period of Political
  Tutelage of the ROC (1931) 28
Public Functionaries Appointment Act 179
Public Functionaries Remuneration Act 179
Public Gathering Act 194
Public Officials Election and Recall Act (1980) 108–9, 112
  Art 8 108
  Art 11 108–9
Public Officials Election and Recall Act (1991)
  Art 35 101
  Art 35(2) 105
Public Referendum Act (2009), Art 30 207

Public Service Election and Recall Law 206
Publication Act 194, 209
Referendum Act 207
Referendum Act (2003) 16
Referendum Act (2004) 114
Revised Act Governing the Allocation of Government
    Revenues and Expenditures (1999) 141
Robbery Punishment Act, Art 2(1)(9) 236
Self-Governance Act for Provinces and Counties (1994) 139
Self-Governance Act for Special Municipalities (1994) 139
Urban Renewal Act 188

United States of America

Administrative Procedure Act 7
Freedom of Information Act 7

International Instruments

American Convention on Human Rights 18
Convention on the Elimination of All Forms of
    Discrimination against Women (CEDAW) 17–18, 235–6
Convention on the Rights of Persons with
    Disabilities (CRPD) 17
Cross-Strait Service Trade Agreement (Taiwan/China) 252
Economic Cooperation Framework Agreement,
    Taiwan/China (2010) 17, 65, 251–2
European Convention on Human Rights 18, 188
ILO Conventions 18
    Convention No 169 (Indigenous and Tribal Peoples) 232
International Covenant on Civil and Political
    Rights 1966 (ICCPR) 7, 17–18, 188,
                                            229–31, 234–7
    Art 1 229
    Art 6 237–8
    Art 14(3)(v) 187
    Art 27 229
International Covenant on Economic, Social and
    Cultural Rights (ICESCR) 7, 17–18, 188, 229,
                                             231, 234–6
    Art 1 229
Treaty of Shimonoseki (1895) 25
United Nations Convention on the Rights
    of the Child (CRC) 17–18, 204, 234–5
United Nations Declaration on the Rights
    of Indigenous Peoples 232
Universal Declaration of Human Rights (UDHR) 18

1

Taiwan's Constitution in World Constitutionalism: Common and Salient Features

———➤•◦◄———

Driving Forces of Profound Transformation – Common Features in Constitutional Perspective – Salient Features in Transitional Perspective – Salient Features in Transnational Perspective – Aims and Structure of this Book

TAIWAN'S DEVELOPMENT OF constitutionalism has fundamentally evolved in the last few decades. This miraculous democratic revolution—albeit a rather quiet and peaceful one—has not occurred in a vacuum. Rather, this fascinating process of transition has occurred in response to local, regional and global dynamics, which, in turn, have further generated a wide array of changing features and functions of constitutionalism in Taiwan and have introduced Taiwan to a wide array of constitutionalism's principles and framework.

With the surrender of Japan in World War II, a half-century of Japanese colonisation between 1985 and 1945 was brought to an end and Taiwan was handed over to the Republic of China (ROC). In the midst of the KMT–CCP civil war, the ROC Constitution, which was promulgated in 1946 and became effective in 1947, was replaced by the Temporary Provisions Effective During the Period of National Mobilisation for Suppression of the Communist Rebellion (Temporary Provisions) in 1948. Then, in 1949, a Martial Law Decree was declared for power consolidation in a time of emergency. Soon after, the ROC government relocated to Taiwan as the ruling Nationalist

Party, Kuomintang (KMT), got defeated by the Chinese Communist Party (CCP), ushering in the dark age of constitutional development in Taiwan: a period marred by authoritarian governance, the suspension of national representative elections, a ban on political parties, and the suppression of free speech and other fundamental rights and freedoms.[1]

Then, in the late 1980s, the dawn of democratic constitutionalism appeared on the horizon. The first glimpses of this new era came in 1986, with the formation of an opposition party called the Democratic Progressive Party (DPP). Then, in 1987, after nearly 40 years in existence, the Martial Law Decree was finally lifted. This period was marked by large-scale political and constitutional reforms in response to the demands of waves of street protests and student demonstrations. In June 1990, the Constitutional Court—exclusively vested with the powers of constitutional interpretation and judicial review of statutes—resolved a constitutional crisis in which the first-term national representatives had stayed in office for more than four decades as the second-term national representatives could not be elected from the Mainland China (the Mainland). In its decision, the Constitutional Court ordered the first-term national representatives to leave office by the end of 1991 and demanded that second-term elections be held in due course.[2] The ROC Constitution was first revised in May 1991. Following this initial pass, six subsequent rounds of constitutional revision occurred from 1991 to 2005.[3] In addition, the first parliamentary and direct presidential elections were held in 1992 and 1996 respectively. Then, in 2000, much to everyone's surprise, the KMT lost the presidential election to the DPP, resulting in the first regime change in Taiwan's democratic history. In 2004, however, the DPP was re-elected to the presidency by a razor-thin margin, only to lose to the KMT in both 2008 and 2012. From 2000 to 2008, Taiwan struggled with a period of serious political confrontation between the DPP executive and the KMT legislative majority. These highly charged political disputes

---

[1] For further discussions on the authoritarian control and human rights suppression during this time, see below ch 2.

[2] *JY Interpretation No 261* (1990). For further discussions on this interpretation, see below ch 2.

[3] For further discussions on these constitutional revisions, see below ch 2.

unequivocally called for constitutional resolution and simultaneously tested the judicial wisdom of the Constitutional Court.[4]

From this turmoil, by all accounts, Taiwan has emerged as a vibrant constitutional democracy, with adherence to the rule of law and a commitment to guarantee the protection of human rights. As is argued elsewhere, the form of modern constitutionalism that originated in the West has undergone drastic changes that reflect the two distinctive models of transitional and transnational constitutionalism.[5] Indeed, Taiwan's constitutionalism, which has developed in the past few decades, reflects the dynamics of transitional and transnational constitutionalism, while its features and functions simultaneously embody an entrenched commitment to modern liberal-democratic constitutional order. This chapter outlines the driving forces and features of Taiwan's profound constitutional transformation, some of which mirror those embedded in modern liberal-democratic constitutionalism, while others more closely reflect those of transitional and transnational constitutionalism.

I. DRIVING FORCES OF PROFOUND TRANSFORMATION: INDIGENISATION, DEMOCRATISATION AND GLOBALISATION

Taiwan's miraculous constitutional transformation has been shaped primarily by three driving forces: indigenisation, democratisation and globalisation, which have also affected constitutional developments elsewhere in the world. Their impact has provided a distinctive contextual framework under which the profound constitutional transformations have taken place in Taiwan.

The indigenisation that occurred over the course of the last several decades—the incremental process by which the Constitution for Taiwan was constructed from the blueprint of the ROC Constitution—represents one of the most difficult challenges in the development of

---

[4] For further discussions on the eight years of divided government and judicial responses to these politically charged disputes, see chs 3 and 6.

[5] J-r Yeh and W-C Chang, 'The Changing Landscape of Modern Constitutionalism: Transitional Perspective' (2009) 4 *National Taiwan University Law Review* 145; J-r Yeh and W-C Chang, 'The Emergence of Transnational Constitutionalism: Its Features, Challenges And Solutions' (2008) 27 *Penn State International Law Review* 89.

Taiwan's constitutionalism. The sovereign people constructed under the ROC Constitution were reconstructed from the Chinese people to the Taiwanese people. The system of representation, which was designed for more than 1 billion people in a vast territory, underwent a massive overhaul to instead serve 23 million people on a small island. Even the organisational structure of the government itself was realigned—horizontally and vertically.

All of these profound, and necessary, changes, however, were undertaken amid the ensuing hostilities between the People's Republic of China (PRC), ruled by the CCP on the Mainland, and Taiwan's ROC government, both of whom sought sole representation of China and treated each other as renegades. Worse still, the reconstruction of constitutional identity in the process of indigenisation was further complicated by the identity struggles of and conflict between those who, with their ancestors, had resided in Taiwan for centuries and had experienced Japanese colonisation, and those who recently immigrated to Taiwan from various provinces of the Mainland with the KMT government. The process of indigenisation was fraught with such struggles as unification with the mainland versus an independent Taiwan, Chinese versus Taiwanese self-identification, and revising and maintaining the ROC Constitution versus drafting a new constitution for Taiwan.

Yet, without war or revolution, in what ways could such a profound and complicated process of constitutional indigenisation succeed under a democratic constitutional framework? It is no surprise that this autochthonous transformation was possible only after countless rounds of incremental constitutional revision coupled with hundreds of instances of judicial interpretation. Chapter 2 delves deeper into the driving force of indigenisation and surveys Taiwan's ensuing constitutional journey. Chapters 3, 4, and 5 explore the strengthening of the presidency, the reformation of parliament, and the evolving relationship between the central and local governments respectively, all of which were fostered by constitutional indigenisation.

The second driving force of constitutional transformation is democratisation. Those who bore witness to the rapid economic growth of the 1960s and 1970s, which bred a strong middle class and an emergent civil society, called for subsequent social and political reforms during the 1980s. Still, under the KMT government, Taiwanese society remained under very rigid social and political control. Those fundamental freedoms of speech, assembly and the press, enjoyed by so many in the modern democratised world, were banned under the KMT regime. Further, although local (city and county) elections were held periodically, national elections were not. In fact, the first-term national representatives had remained in office since 1948, since there was no way to elect the second-term national representatives from the Mainland. Finally, the Temporary Provisions had granted the President unlimited tenure.

By the late 1980s, Taiwanese citizens became increasingly frustrated by their lack of influence on the national government. Inspired by movements spurring democratisation forward from the Berlin Wall, Tiananmen Square, and other demonstrations of 'people's power' elsewhere around the world, Taiwanese citizens took to the streets for demonstrations, which sometimes resulted in bloodshed.

Because of numerous constitutional barriers, democratisation was no easy task. Before second-term national representatives could be elected, the constitution required revision to allow for such elections to occur. Yet, the KMT government was very hesitant about resorting to any solution that required constitutional revision. The KMT government was concerned that amending the ROC Constitution and electing second-term national representatives from Taiwan, rather than the Mainland, would pull back the curtain to reveal that the KMT government effectively ruled only Taiwan, thus undermining its claim to be China's only legitimate government. Nevertheless, the resonating cry for democracy necessitated unconventional approaches and solutions. The very first of these unorthodox solutions came from the judiciary, which rendered a decision ordering the first-term national representatives to leave office. Another exemplar was the establishment of a system of proportional representation, in which national representation could be achieved through the development of political parties. Other democratisation-reform measures included a direct presidential election, stronger democratic controls over the exercise of executive powers, and increasing demand for governmental transparency and accountability. Chapters 3, 4 and 5 discuss these and other changes. Perhaps most noteworthy among the changes sweeping Taiwan were grassroots efforts, begun by human rights groups and non-governmental organisations, aimed at deepening democracy. Through strategic interaction with both political and judicial entities, these groups successfully engaged in the vibrant politics of rights in the wake of rapid social and political transitions. The empowered civil society has become critical, both in Taiwan and elsewhere in the world, to establishing and maintaining effective checks and balances within and on the government. These concepts are further discussed in chapter 7.

The third and final driving force for Taiwan's drastic constitutional change that is explored in this book is one that is shared by all nations—globalisation. Triggered by the technological revolution of recent decades that saw the advent and relative explosion of internet technology and the extension of global market, globalisation has substantially altered the boundaries of nation states and the relationships between states and their citizens. Further, constitutional and quasi-constitutional arrangements have occurred, one of the most prominent aspects of which has been the universal guarantee of fundamental rights and freedoms. In addition, the pressure of global competitiveness has stirred the reinvigoration of public functions, pushing forward government streamlining and the development of new partnerships between public and private sectors. Such new challenges brought by globalisation are particularly difficult for Taiwan, for it had been isolated from the international community since the 1970s. This isolation can trace its roots to 1971, when the United Nations (UN) General Assembly passed a resolution to recognise the PRC government and to expel the representatives of the ROC government from its previously held UN seat and from all UN-related organisations. Following this resolution, many states terminated their diplomatic relationships with Taiwan. The United States—which had previously been Taiwan's strongest ally—terminated its formal diplomatic relationship with Taiwan in 1979. Then, beginning in the 1990s, the rise of the PRC as one of the world's leading economies brought even more steep challenges to Taiwan's international participation. In fact, to date, there are currently only 22 states that maintain formal diplomatic relations with Taiwan.

Taiwan's isolation from the international community, however, has not shielded it from the impacts of globalisation. The areas in which globalisation's impact has been most dramatic include trade, human rights and government reform. First, the need for economic development and the dependence on trade have pushed both governmental and non-governmental actors to seek possible foreign partnerships from all available avenues and to simultaneously remain in close contact with regional and global markets. These efforts gradually crystallised in the form of Taiwan's accession to international economic co-operation and memberships of such entities as the Asia-Pacific

Economic Cooperation (APEC) in 1991, the World Trade Organization (WTO) in 2002, and several others. Second, from lessons learned
from past human rights violations, many civil groups advocated for
Taiwan to incorporate core international human rights treaties in the
hope of strengthening human rights guarantees.[6] Third, the pressure
of global competitiveness triggered the government to launch reforms
to improve its governing integrity, competence and transparency.
Hence, Taiwan adopted a comprehensive plan of government reform
and enacted and implemented legislation similar to the United States'
Administrative Procedure Act and Freedom of Information Act.
Impacted upon by globalisation, these constitutional developments are
discussed at length in chapters 3, 5, and 7, and cursorily throughout as
relevant to other parts of the book.

The three driving forces of indigenisation, democratisation and
globalisation have led to unprecedented constitutional transformation
in Taiwan. These transformative changes—like those that occurred
elsewhere—have embodied prominent features that fit squarely into
liberal-democratic constitutionalism, which traces its origins to the
West. However, at the same time, there are constitutional features
that, rather than simply mirror 'standard constitutionalism', reflect the
development of transitional and transnational constitutionalism against
the contextual dynamics in which these three forces—indigenisation,
democratisation and globalisation—intertwine in Taiwan. These features are discussed in the following section, with those common to
liberal-democratic constitutionalism discussed first, followed by a
discussion of the other salient features that embody transitional and
transnational dynamics.

II. COMMON FEATURES IN CONSTITUTIONAL PERSPECTIVE

Modern constitutionalism, which began in the eighteenth century
in the West, has never been without variations. However, as is often

---

[6] Examples of such treaties and agreements include the ratification of the International Covenant on Civil and Political Rights (ICCPR) and of the International
Covenant on Economic, Social and Cultural Rights (ICESCR) in 2009, as well as the
accession of other similar instruments.

understood, its common core elements, more or less uniform throughout, include constitutional supremacy, rule of law, separation of powers,
checks and balances, popular sovereignty, democracy, and the protection of fundamental rights and freedoms.[7] Constitutional supremacy
requires that the government conform to constitutional prescriptions.
The rule of law demands the government to rule and be ruled by law.
The commitments to separation of powers and checks and balances
exist to ensure that the government's powers remain limited. The
principle of popular sovereignty establishes a thick version of democratic basis for a modern constitution, while, relatedly, the principle of
democracy entails a government based on the consent of the governed.
At the centre of all these tenets and features is a core of fundamental
rights and freedoms that bar government intrusion. After decades of
profound transition, it is evident that constitutionalism in Taiwan has
fully embraced and embodied these generic elements of modern liberal-
democratic constitutionalism.

A. Constitutional Democracy

Driven largely by indigenisation and democratisation, as illustrated
above, Taiwan has undergone seven rounds of constitutional reform
since the 1990s. These revisions were primarily tailored to the reconstruction of political representation that was no longer based on the
Chinese Mainland, but on Taiwan itself and the needs of the Taiwanese
people.

Parliamentary reorganisation and the reform of the representational
system began immediately after the constitutional reforms started in
1991, and were followed by a series of institutional tinkerings in 1992,
1994, 1997, and 2005.[8] In order to strengthen political representation in
Taiwan, the 1994 constitutional revision established a popular election
for the presidency. As a consequence of these reforms, the institutional

---

[7] See, eg, L Henkin, 'A New Birth of Constitutionalism: Genetic Influence
and Genetic Defects' (1993) 14 *Cardozo Law Review* 533, 535–36; AS Rosenbaum,
'Introduction' in AS Rosenbaum (ed), *Constitutionalism: The Philosophical Dimension*
(California, Praeger, 1988) 4.

[8] For further discussion, see below ch 4.

reform of the governmental system itself—from parliamentary to semi-presidential—was eventually addressed by the constitutional revision of 1997.[9]

These revisions of the Constitution have demonstrated a deep commitment to the resolution of political crises through constitutional measures. The elections held as a direct result of the rounds of constitutional revision have also facilitated democratic governance, in which the government ensures that the people enjoy equal suffrage. These factors serve as unequivocal evidence that constitutional democracy has been firmly established in Taiwan.

B. Fundamental Rights and Freedoms

Since the late 1980s, Taiwan has made significant progress towards the protection of the fundamental rights and freedoms discussed above. The burgeoning of a vibrant civil society and functioning courts have contributed to such advancement. In the course of democratic transition and constitutional reform, social groups and human rights organisations have triumphed over rights and freedoms discourses.[10] Although the seven rounds of constitutional revision did not result in the addition of rights or freedoms, numerous policies directed to prescribing the duty of the state to fulfil such pre-existing rights and freedoms were expressly written into laws. More important, constitutional litigation has been strategically used by quite a few social groups and human rights organisations, since the beginning of the reforms, as a way to effectuate rights protection—something that would not have been possible, or at least would have been extremely difficult, beforehand.

The judicial construction of additional rights and freedoms, especially by the Constitutional Court, is also particularly noteworthy. To supplement the rather brief list of rights and freedoms explicitly mentioned in the Constitution, the Constitutional Court has articulated such unenumerated rights as the right to marry, the right of privacy, freedom of contract, the right to reputation, sexual freedoms, and various other

---

[9] For further discussion, see below chs 3 and 5.
[10] For further details, see below ch 7.

'judge-made' rights. Moreover, core international human rights conventions have been both judicially and legislatively incorporated, reflecting the development of transnational constitutionalism discussed below. The articulated evolution of rights and freedoms in Taiwan's transitional context is discussed in detail in chapter 7.

C. Separation of Powers and Accountability

Despite the semi-parliamentary system adopted by the ROC Constitution, prior to democratisation and constitutional reforms, a so-called 'super presidency' was the reality in Taiwan. Presidential powers were expanded and coupled with the creation of extra-constitutional organs, which encroached upon the separation of powers and escaped legislative oversight.[11] It is thus no surprise that constitutional revision has made the governmental system a primary target of the efforts at reform.

Following the rounds of constitutional reform over the last few decades, Taiwan now most closely resembles a semi-presidential system of government. The legislature exercises the powers to legislate and to amend the Constitution.[12] The President is now popularly elected with the exclusive power to appoint the premier, even absent legislative consent.[13] Nevertheless, the premier is still accountable to the legislature, since the legislature is vested with the power to conduct no-confidence votes against the premier.[14] The legislature's 'no confidence' power is kept in check by the premier's power to, in turn, request that the President dissolve the legislature.[15] Despite reforms, criticism remains strong, especially on the President's accountability. In contrast with the premier, who is accountable to both the President and the legislature, the President—once elected—seems relatively autonomous. Therefore, calls for future reforms persist.[16]

---

[11] For further discussions, see below chs 2 and 3.

[12] Art 12, Additional Articles to the Constitution of the Republic of China (2005).

[13] Art 3, Additional Articles to the Constitution of the Republic of China (2005).

[14] Art 3(3), Additional Articles to the Constitution of the Republic of China (2005). For further discussion, see below ch 3.

[15] Ibid.

[16] For further discussion, see below ch 3.

D. Rule of Law and the Independence of the Courts

Constitutional supremacy and the rule of law are expressly guaranteed under the ROC Constitution. The ROC Constitution states that laws in conflict with the Constitution, or rules in conflict with laws or with the Constitution, shall be null and void, and that the Council of Grand Justices—later known as the Constitutional Court—is granted the power to decide the constitutionality of laws or rules if doubts arise as to whether such conflicts exist.[17] Unfortunately, however, the Constitutional Court did not effectively exercise its powers until the late 1980s.

Political liberalisation and democratisation of the late 1980s and early 1990s placed the Constitutional Court at the centre of transitional politics. Most evident was the above-mentioned Constitutional Court decision that ordered the first-term national representatives to leave office and demanded that second-term elections be held in due course.[18] Resolving the constitutional crisis at issue and successfully steering the constitutional-reform agenda forward, the Constitutional Court has since become a leading force in the course of Taiwan's democratic transition and has uninhibitedly safeguarded fundamental rights and freedoms. As chapter 6 illustrates, the number of petitions the Constitutional Court received began to skyrocket in its fifth term (1985–1994). During its sixth term (1994–2003), the Court received an average of about 250 petitions per year. Since 2003, this number has roughly doubled to 500 or 600 petitions per year.[19] The Constitutional Court's assertion of its power is also evident in the number of findings of unconstitutionality. The ratio was 39.3 per cent (75 'unconstitutional' rulings, out of 191 total constitutional interpretations) in the sixth term of the Constitutional Court, and it climbed to 49.6 per cent (67 'unconstitutional' rulings, out of 135 total constitutional interpretations) from 2003 to 2013.[20]

There is no doubt that the Constitutional Court has become a powerful institution in Taiwan. Prudent and skilful, the Constitutional Court

---

[17] Arts 172–173, Constitution of the Republic of China (1947). For further discussions, see below ch 6.

[18] *JY Interpretation No 261* (1990).

[19] See below ch 6.

[20] Ibid.

has proved its capacity in arbitrating political disputes and resolving conflicts of fundamental rights and values.

III. SALIENT FEATURES IN TRANSITIONAL PERSPECTIVE

When analysing the experiences of new global democracies in the 1990s, three distinctive features frequently appear in transitional constitutionalism.[21] First, democracies typically engage in transitory constitutional measures in preparation for, complementary with, or even in lieu of formal constitution making or revision. Second, extraordinary constitutional politics often trigger or necessitate unconventional constitutional adjudication. Third, democracies may enact quasi-constitutional statutes as short-term solutions or expedient responses to the difficulty of constitutional revisions. As is briefly discussed in the following chapter and further elaborated on in subsequent chapters, Taiwan's constitutional development since the 1990s has exhibited each of these transitional constitutional features.[22]

A. Incremental Constitutional Revisions

In the constitutional reform that has occurred in Taiwan since the 1990s, one of the most salient features is the absence of either a brand new constitution or a single large-scale constitutional revision. While the call for a new constitution still resonates, the course of constitutional change followed a pre-ordained model—constitutional revision occurred in step with incremental democratic transition.[23]

Altogether, there were seven rounds of constitutional revision that tackled constitutional issues in a gradual, piecemeal and incremental fashion. Notwithstanding the troubled statehood of the ROC and the questioned identity of the ROC Constitution, the name of the ROC and the main text of the ROC Constitution remained intact throughout

---

[21] Yeh and Chang, 'The Changing Landscape' at 150–55.

[22] Yeh and Chang, 'A Decade of Changing Constitutionalism in Taiwan'.

[23] J-r Yeh, 'Constitutional Reform and Democratization in Taiwan, 1945–2000' in PCY Chow (ed), *Taiwan's Modernization in Global Perspective* (Westport, CT, Praeger, 2002) 47.

the rounds of constitutional revision.[24] The revisions occurred in a separate text annexed to the Constitution, known as the Additional Articles. Designation of the rights and obligations and 'disposition of other related affairs' between citizens of the Mainland and those of Taiwan were designated for stipulation by special laws.[25] The KMT demanded the integrity of the ROC Constitution remain intact in constitutional negotiations with the DPP and other political parties. As the KMT has always had the legislative majority, the DPP—despite its slant toward independence—was forced to accept such a baseline for constitutional reform.

Even with no changes to the main text, however, the parties satisfactorily addressed the issues of governing legitimacy and democratic representation. Perhaps the most noteworthy round of constitutional revision is the seventh—and final—round, completed in 2005. The 2005 revision took a bold step in locking the ROC Constitution into its current iteration. The threshold to pass a subsequent constitutional revision was raised to require that proposals for constitutional amendments be passed by at least three quarters of the members present at a meeting, which is attended by at least three quarters of the total members of the legislature, and further, that upon the expiration of a mandatory six-month period of public announcement of the proposal, a public referendum must be held. Finally, for any amendment proposal to succeed, it must garner the approval of at least one half of the total eligible voters.[26] This high threshold certainly makes constitutional revision difficult, if not impossible, and may render an uncertain future for constitutional reform in Taiwan.

B. The Constitutional Court and Dialectical Judicial Review

The rise of constitutional courts in the assertion of judicial review has become a common phenomenon in recent democratic transitions

---

[24] This is the so-called *Fatung* legacy insisted on by the KMT. For further discussions, see below ch 2.

[25] Art 11, Additional Articles to the Constitution of the Republic of China (2005).

[26] Art 12, Additional Articles to the Constitution of the Republic of China (2005).

worldwide.[27] Taiwan is certainly no exception. Without express authorisation, the Constitutional Court granted itself the power to review and invalidate constitutional amendments it deemed unconstitutional. The first such decision was *JY Interpretation No 499*, in which the constitutional revision of 1999 was held unconstitutional in its entirety as violative of both procedural and substantive limitations of constitutional revision.[28] In a more recent decision, *JY Interpretation No 721*, the Constitutional Court reviewed the constitutionality of the 2005 constitutional revision regarding the legislature's electoral reform.[29] There is little doubt that the Constitutional Court has become *a* powerful, if not *the most* powerful, institution in Taiwan's constitutional development.

During the democratic transition of the 1990s and the period of divided government in the 2000s, the Constitutional Court was often called upon to resolve highly contested disputes or politically charged cases. The Constitutional Court developed various strategies to survive these serious political confrontations. The most noteworthy among these strategies is dialectical judicial review: facilitating political dialogues rather than immediately resolving disputes.[30] For example, in a constitutional dispute regarding the suspension of a nuclear power plant, the Constitutional Court strategically avoided a substantive decision. Instead, it directed the DPP executive to negotiate with the KMT legislative majority to formulate a policy solution acceptable to both parties.[31] In another case that involved a financial dispute regarding the national health insurance programme, the Constitutional Court again stressed that both parties—the central and local governments—bore the duties to support the national health insurance programme, and thus must negotiate with one another to achieve an amiable result.[32] Yet another example of dialectical judicial review involved an election dispute between the central government, which was controlled by the DPP, and the local government, which was controlled by the KMT. Having held that the central government was correct in its decision, the

---

[27] Yeh and Chang (n 5) 150–57.

[28] For further discussions, see below ch 2.

[29] *JY Interpretation No 721* (2014).

[30] See below ch 6. See also Yeh, 'Presidential Politics and the Judicial Facilitation of Dialogue'.

[31] *JY Interpretation No 520* (2001).

[32] *JY Interpretation No 550* (2002).

Constitutional Court nevertheless decided not to entertain the DPP's decision, arguing instead that ultimate solutions should be provided by the administrative court if the issue were litigated further.[33]

Over time, additional dialectic or pro-dialogue strategies have been developed by the Constitutional Court, which are discussed in further detail in chapter 6. For example, to facilitate dialogue between political parties, the Constitutional Court might provide for various constitutional declarations to deal with unconstitutional statutes or ordinances. Instead of immediately invalidating impugned statutes, the Constitutional Court may fashion alternative declarations to give room for political parties to mitigate the practical or political implications of the judicial decisions. As the Constitutional Court finds a way to survive in unconventional transitions and extremely contentious politics, similar such declarations abound.[34]

C. Quasi-Constitutional Statutes

Constitutional revisions usually entail high voting thresholds and are thus more difficult to attain when political consensus is lacking. As a result, statutes passed by the legislature with less strict procedural requirements may fill a constitutional vacuum and satisfy the need for amendment during periods of democratic transition.[35]

In Taiwan, there has been a persistent political division between the *pan-blue* (the KMT and its political alliance) and the *pan-green* (the DPP and its political alliance). The division has resulted in part from individuals tying their identity to when they or their ancestors immigrated to Taiwan. Those who came during the reign of KMT government after 1949 tend to identify with the *pan-blue*, while those whose ancestors have resided in Taiwan for centuries tend to identify more with the *pan-green*. A similar division exists in the citizens' attitudes with the Mainland: the *pan-blue* seem more willing to have closer ties with China while the *pan-green* may assert the independence of Taiwan to a greater extent. At various times throughout Taiwan's history, this persistent

---

[33] *JY Interpretation No 553* (2002).

[34] See below ch 6.

[35] Yeh and Chang, 'The Changing Landscape of Modern Constitutionalism: Transitional Perspective' (n 5) 156–57.

political division has rendered political collaboration and negotiation between the *pan-blue* and the *pan-green* nearly impossible. Against such a political backdrop, statutes that provide short-term solutions with built-in framework for streamlined subsequent amendment have become a popular option.

As discussed above, Mainland China–Taiwan affairs were typically not decided through constitutional revision but rather were left for resolution by statute. Similarly, as most of the provisions in the ROC Constitution that dealt with central–local government relationships were not applicable to Taiwan, the legislature enacted a quasi-constitutional statute—the Local Government Act—as the only feasible solution.[36] The most recent example of a quasi-constitutional statute was the Referendum Act of 2003 and the implementation, at both the national and local levels, of the people's right to referendum where matters regarding constitutional amendments, laws and policies are at issue.

IV. SALIENT FEATURES IN TRANSNATIONAL PERSPECTIVE

Constitutionalism, driven by globalisation, has developed beyond nation states to present both internationalisation of constitutional laws and constitutionalisation of international laws.[37] These new phenomena consist primarily of three distinctive features: (i) domestic incorporation of international treaties (in particular, human rights treaties), (ii) the engagement of transnational judicial dialogues, and (iii) the global convergence of institutions.[38] Since the turn of the century, such features of transnational constitutionalism have appeared in Taiwan's recent constitutional development, in varying degrees.[39]

A. Incorporation of International Human Rights Treaties

Taiwan has been party to the trend towards transnational constitutionalism, in spite of its isolation from the international community

---

[36] For further discussions, see below ch 5.
[37] Yeh and Chang, 'The Emergence of Transnational Constitutionalism' (n 5) at 91–92. See also Chang and Yeh, 'Internationalization of Constitutional Law'.
[38] Ibid.
[39] Yeh and Chang, 'A Decade of Changing Constitutionalism in Taiwan'.

at large. Recently, Taiwan has made a great deal of progress in terms of both trade and human rights. On trade issues, Taiwan has become an avid trade participant, especially in the Asia-Pacific region, obtaining membership of the WTO and signing the Economic Cooperation Framework Agreement (ECFA) with China.

Taiwan has incorporated several international human rights treaties into its domestic legal order. In 2007, Taiwan passed the accession into the Convention on the Elimination of All Forms of Discrimination against Women (CEDAW) by an overwhelming legislative majority. Although the UN ultimately rejected the instrument of accession, Taiwan's government nevertheless passed an Implementation Act to ensure the domestic applicability of women's rights and gender equality that was enshrined in the CEDAW, with the initial state report completed in 2009, and a second report in 2014, both of which were reviewed by independent experts.[40] Similarly, in 2009, the government ratified the International Covenant on Civil and Political Rights (ICCPR) and the International Covenant on Economic, Social and Cultural Rights (ICESCR) and passed an Implementation Act to ensure that all rights protected under the two covenants were applicable domestically. The initial state reports of the ICCPR and the ICESCR were released in 2012, and were followed by a 2013 independent-expert review.[41] At the conclusion of the review, the government adopted concluding observations and recommendations, and has pledged to achieve full compliance and implementation. Then, in 2014, Taiwan passed Implementation Acts which demanded domestic compliance of the relevant provisions of both the Convention on the Rights of the Child (CRC) and the Convention on the Rights of Persons with Disabilities (CRPD).

B. Transnational Judicial Dialogues

Taiwan's Constitutional Court has adopted an open approach towards international human rights law. In *JY Interpretation No 329*, the Constitutional Court paved the way for the domestic application of international treaties through its adoption of a new, relatively monistic view

---

[40] For further discussion, see below ch 7.
[41] The state reports of ICCPR and ICESCR and the information regarding the unprecedented international review are available at www.humanrights.moj.gov.tw/np.asp?ctNode=33565&mp=200.

on the relationship between domestic and international laws.[42] The Court's view is in stark contrast to the dualist norm in most civil law jurisdictions regarding the relationship between such international and domestic legal orders.

Since its first reference to international human rights law in 1995, the Constitutional Court has offered limited, yet gradually increasing, judicial reference to such doctrine.[43] The international human rights treaties the Court has referenced most frequently include the ICCPR, ICESCR, CEDAW, CRC, the European Convention on Human Rights, International Labour Conventions, the American Convention on Human Rights, and the Universal Declaration of Human Rights (UDHR). Notably, the UDHR is the international document most frequently cited in separate opinions. Their non-binding nature notwithstanding, these treaties have been referred to as persuasive, and at times even compelling, legal authority.[44]

C. Global Convergence of Institutions

The third pervasive feature of transnational constitutionalism is the global convergence of institutions. New institutions that are responsible for constitutional guardianship such as constitutional courts, human rights commissions and independent auditors have become increasingly common, as well as indispensable.[45] The empowerment of the Constitutional Court in Taiwan has been part of this global convergence. The constitutional revision of 2005 further increased the scope of the Constitutional Court's power, vesting the Court with the power to adjudicate disputes of presidential impeachment—a change that once again corresponds to the global trend of empowering courts to resolve highly charged political disputes.[46]

---

[42] *JY Interpretation No 329* (1993).

[43] For further discussion, see below ch 7.

[44] See W-C Chang, 'An Isolated Nation with Global-minded Citizens: Bottom-up Transnational Constitutionalism in Taiwan' (2009) 4 *National Taiwan University Law Review* 203, 212.

[45] Yeh and Chang, 'The Emergence of Transnational Constitutionalism' (n 5).

[46] Chang et al, *Constitutionalism in Asia* 338–39.

Another recent global trend has been the establishment of independent regulatory commissions. Taiwan's first independent regulatory commission, the National Communications Commission (NCC), was established in 2006.[47] Not surprisingly, its establishment during the years of divided government triggered contentious political confrontation. Partly as a result of such confrontation, accountability concerns have also surfaced about whether and to what extent the administration's unity could be derogated without suffering deleterious effects. These fears led the Constitutional Court, in *JY Interpretation No 613*, to sanction the creation of the NCC and also to recommend that certain safeguards be implemented to maintain the system of checks and balances.[48] Despite the controversy that accompanied it, the creation of the NCC signified Taiwan's great leap toward a new era of global digital convergence and regulatory reform.

V. AIMS AND STRUCTURE OF THIS BOOK

Taiwan is known across the globe for its 'economic miracle'—the rapid industrialisation that led to profound economic transformation and growth. This book argues that Taiwan has yet another miracle to reveal to the world—Taiwan's peaceful democratic transition that has been marked by sweeping constitutional change. Taiwan's past few decades of constitutional transformation represent a distinctive model of constitutional evolution in the context of indigenisation, democratisation and globalisation. These transformative changes reflect both the generic elements of liberal-democratic constitutionalism and the distinctive features of transitional and transnational constitutionalism that have recently developed. Unequivocally, Taiwan's story of constitutionalism is of great importance and interest to readers and constitutional scholars in Taiwan, China, and numerous countries around the world.

This book analyses Taiwan's recent constitutional transformations from working models of constitutional democracies across the globe

---

[47] Concerning the development of independent commission in Taiwan, see J-r Yeh, 'Experimenting with independent commissions in a new democracy with a civil law tradition: the case of Taiwan' in S Rose-Ackerman and P Lindseth (eds), *Comparative Administrative Law* (MA, Edward Elgar, 2010).

[48] *JY Interpretation No 613* (2006). For further discussions, see below ch 3.

into its own distinctive context and culture and illustrates ways in which the forces of indigenisation, democratisation and globalisation have shaped and reshaped the development of constitutionalism in Taiwan. The book highlights constitutional features common to either liberal-democratic constitutionalism or transitional and transnational constitutionalism. Similar to other works in this series on Constitutional Systems of the World, this book focuses not only on constitutional *text*, but also on constitutional *context*. The sources in which transformative constitutions are articulated are formed not only through the constitution, statutes and court decisions, but also through a region's political history, social movements, actions, and initiatives undertaken by non-governmental actors.

This book comprises eight chapters. Chapter 2 illustrates Taiwan's distinctive constitutional journeys from imposition to indigenisation, with Taiwan's miraculous transformation of constitutional identity as the primary focus. Next, chapters 3, 4 and 5 analyse structural and representational reconstructions of both the government system and political powers. Chapter 3 begins by exploring the evolving presidency and the executive branch. This is followed by a discussion, in chapter 4, of Taiwan's representation and legislative process. Chapter 5 focuses on multilevel governance and devolution. Chapters 3, 4, and 5 illustrate the ways profound constitutional changes have occurred in tandem with constitutional indigenisation and democratisation. Without these necessary structural and representational changes, Taiwan's constitutional evolution would not have succeeded.

Chapters 6 and 7 follow the structural discourse of the earlier chapters and focus on judicial review and the guarantees of fundamental rights and freedoms. These two chapters demonstrate ways in which Taiwan's constitutional transformation has bred a strong civil society that is willing not only to engage in the discourse of rights and freedoms but also to actively participate in constitutional processes by interacting with political and judicial powers. These interactions also exhibit various transnational features of constitutionalism. The book concludes with chapter 8 and a discussion of the challenges and prospects of Taiwan's constitutionalism that lie ahead. While there are certainly daunting tasks on the horizon, the experience Taiwan has gained through its development of transformative constitutionalism over the last several decades will surely serve as a roadmap to navigate the path ahead.

FURTHER READING

Chang, W-C and Yeh, J-r, 'Internationalization of Constitutional Law' in M Rosenfeld and A Sajó (eds), *The Oxford Handbook of Comparative Constitutional Law Comparative Constitutionalism* (New York, Oxford University Press, 2012) 1166–84.

Henkin, L, 'A New Birth of Constitutionalism: Genetic Influence and Genetic Defects' (1993) 14 *Cardozo Law Review* 533–48.

Yeh, J-r and Chang, W-C, 'A Decade of Changing Constitutionalism in Taiwan: Transitional and Transnational Perspectives' in AHY Chen (ed), *Constitutionalism in Asia in the Early Twenty-first Century* (Cambridge, Cambridge University Press, 2014) 141–68.

Yeh, J-r and Chang, W-C, 'The Changing Landscape of Modern Constitutionalism: Transitional Perspective' (2009) 4 *National Taiwan University Law Review* 145–83.

Yeh, J-r and Chang, W-C, 'The Emergence of Transnational Constitutionalism: Its Features, Challenges and Solutions' (2008) 27 *Penn State International Law Review* 89–124.

2

Taiwan's Constitutional Journey: Imposition and Indigenisation

————◆◆◆————

A Tale of Two Foundations: Externally Imposed Constitutions – Pre-democratization Constitutional Manipulation and Authoritarianism – Democratisation and Constitutional Indigenisation – Conclusion

AIWAN'S CONSTITUTIONAL JOURNEY has been one of struggle—beginning with external imposition and gradually progressing to indigenisation. This process of transformation occurred via incremental democratic and constitutional reforms, enacted in the face of historical legacies of foreign colonisation, externally imposed constitutions, constitutional manipulation, and authoritarian governance.

Located off the shore of Mainland China, Taiwan has long been treated as peripheral territory and has suffered from frequent foreign occupations. Among these were the rules of the Spanish and Dutch in the seventeenth century, the rule of the Qing Empire in the eighteenth and nineteenth centuries, and Japanese colonisation from 1895 to 1945. At the end of World War II, Taiwan was turned over to the Government of the Republic of China (ROC), and specifically under the Kuomintang of China (KMT). In 1949, however, the KMT was defeated by the Chinese Communist Party (CCP) on the mainland, and the ROC relocated to Taiwan. Its experience with these forms of colonial rule and externally imposed governance forced Taiwan to undergo an extensive self-positioning and capacity-building process,[1] in which it perennially struggled with its constitutional identity—especially against that of Mainland China. More recently, Taiwan has continued to face challenging cross-Strait relations with the People's Republic of China (PRC) in an age of burgeoning global competition and regional engagement.[2]

This chapter situates Taiwan's constitutionalism in its specific evolutionary context. The historical path of this island nation evokes three main themes: constitutional imposition, constitutional indigenisation, and the reconstruction of the people. After offering a reflection upon Taiwan's legacies of Japanese colonialism and Chinese imposition of a constitutional order, the chapter proceeds to an analysis of Taiwan's dual constitutional foundations, both before and after World War II. The chapter ends with a look at the dynamics of constitutional change over two periods—pre-democratisation and democratisation—each presenting problems associated with constitutional manipulation and the reconstruction of a system of effective representation of the people. Through this rather unique process of indigenisation and democratisation, the citizens of Taiwan have developed a new constitutional identity. The ROC Constitution is now the Constitution of Taiwan, those represented by it the Taiwanese people.

I. A TALE OF TWO FOUNDATIONS: EXTERNALLY IMPOSED CONSTITUTIONS

Taiwan's contemporary constitutional order is supported by dual foundations, evolving as it did during two consecutive constitutional impositions: the Meiji Constitution, brought by Japanese colonists; and the ROC Constitution, imposed under the auspices of the KMT. Taiwan's experience with the former—notwithstanding the debate on applicability[3]—left a significant impact on it in the fight for

---

[1] J-r Yeh, 'Institutional Capacity-Building Toward Sustainable Development: Taiwan's Environmental Protection in the Climate of Economic Development and Political Liberalization' (1996) 6 *Duke Journal of Comparative & International Law* 229.

[2] J-r Yeh, 'Democracy-driven Transformation to Regulatory State: The Case of Taiwan' (2008) 3 *National Taiwan University Law Review* 31.

[3] See section A below.

self-governance during the colonisation. The ROC Constitution, although it garnered very limited support from Taiwanese delegates,[4] has been Taiwan's basic constitutional framework since 1949 when the KMT government relocated to Taiwan.

Taiwan has never considered these two constitutions to be its own creations. Rather, they were external impositions—drafted, negotiated and promulgated in distant places and for disparate purposes. Even the determinations that they had any applicability to the Taiwanese context were decisions made from afar. Yet, from an historical point of view, the two constitutions served as the primary foundations upon which the process of constitutional indigenisation took hold and upon which Taiwan's contemporary constitutionalism was built.

A. Japanese Colonisation, the Meiji Constitution, and the Hybrid Constitutional Foundation

In 1895, after China's defeat in the Sino-Japanese War, Taiwan was ceded to Japan by the Treaty of Shimonoseki. Six years before the treaty, the Japanese imperial government had promulgated the Meiji Constitution and deemed it an iconic part of the modern state's infrastructure.[5] When Japan brought it over, Taiwan had never before encountered a modern constitution.

At the time, however, it was hotly debated whether the Meiji Constitution should even apply to the new colony. Some argued that it should be introduced to Taiwan; others maintained that doing so would hinder colonial governance. The debate was triggered in part by the dismissal of Takenori Takeno, then the Chief Judge of Taiwan (also known as Formosa). Takeno appealed his dismissal on the grounds that, as Chief Judge, his title and service term were guaranteed by the Meiji Constitution. The imperial government refuted his claim, arguing that Formosa was merely a recently acquired colony, and the home country's Constitution should not apply to it.[6]

---

[4] W-C Chang, 'East Asian Foundations for Constitutionalism: Three Models Reconstructed' (2008) 3 *National Taiwan University Law Review* 111, 122.

[5] Ibid.

[6] Y Takekoshi, *Japanese Rule in Formosa* (Taipei, SMC Publishing, 1996) 32–37.

The constitutional debate also raged on the scope of application. Some argued that if the Meiji Constitution's privileges were intended to be provided to all citizens, the imperial government must grant these privileges to Formosans who were naturalised as Japanese citizens—in other words, they insisted that the Constitution's applicability be founded upon equal citizenship. Others, however, contended that the newly acquired colony's inhabitants could not, except in specific controlled circumstances, enjoy the Meiji Constitution's privileges. Under this view, if the imperial government, in disregard of Formosa's actual societal conditions, decided to implement the Constitution, the only result would be disorder.[7] The proponents of this view thus promoted economic and political concerns—the colonial empire's short-term and long-term interests—over constitutional or legal concerns.

This debate illustrates the inexperience of the Japanese government in handling both colonisation and constitutional governance. Remarkably, it was not until a British legal advisor commented on the situation to the Japanese Minister of Justice that Japan finally resolved the applicability question.[8] But even then the imperial government could not reach a clear decision on the matter. In the end, Taiwan was provided a special legal status.[9]

The reality of Japanese colonial governance in Taiwan was nominal constitutional rule. The Japanese Emperor delegated most of his powers, including legislative and executive ones, to the then-Governor of Taiwan through the enactment of special laws such as Law No 63 of 1896, Law No 31 of 1906, and Law No 3 of 1921. Hence, legislative powers were concentrated in the Governor's hands, a development that conflicted with the provisions of the Meiji Constitution. Similarly, representative institutions were not installed in a constitutional manner, and rights and liberties were rigidly constrained and suppressed by the colonial military and state police.[10] Colonial rule was therefore

---

[7] Ibid.

[8] Itō Hirobumi (ed), *Report to minister of the justice by William Montague Hammett Kirkwook*, see T-s Wang, 'The Emergence of Modern Constitutional Culture in Taiwan' in J-r Yeh and W-C Chang (eds), *Constitutional Reengineering in New Democracies* (Taipei, Angle, 2008) 141 (in Chinese).

[9] Takekoshi (above n 6).

[10] J-Y Huang, FF-T Liao, and W-C Chang, *Development of Constitution Law and Human Rights in Taiwan Facing the New Century* (Japan, Institute of Developing Economies, 2003).

quite different from the kind of constitutional governance modern democratic constitutionalism has engendered. Instead of implementing a true constitutional rule, Japan's implementation of the Meiji Constitution in Taiwan was merely an instrument for building a Japanese identity among the Taiwanese people.

The event most revealing of the Taiwanese relationship with the Meiji Constitution was the petition for the establishment of a Taiwanese council. The petition was launched in 1921, nearly three decades after Taiwan came under Japanese rule. In the intervening years, the Taiwanese people had gained their first experience with modern constitutional governance. Although Japan only allowed the Meiji Constitution to be applied in a limited fashion, the Taiwanese people nevertheless began to experience a bit of the very essence of constitutionalism. By 1921, local elites, grounding their claims on the Meiji Constitution itself, sought greater political freedoms. They submitted to the Japanese colonial government a signed petition for the creation of a Taiwanese council. This petition was met with scepticism by the Japanese, who saw it as a direct challenge to the validity of the Meiji Constitution as applied to Taiwan.[11]

In arguing for the petition, the local elites viewed themselves as Japanese nationals, which might suggest a denial of their Taiwanese identity. Yet, as a closer look at the petition reveals, the elites campaigned that 'the people' represented a self-governing entity that was fundamentally imbued in the concepts of modern constitutionalism. The Meiji Constitution's extended imposition in Taiwan might have been intended as an instrument for retaining colonial rule, but the Taiwanese people themselves advocated, on the basis of that very Constitution, for their autonomy and equal status with respect to the Japanese.

The Japanese eventually rejected the petition. In 1945, however, as World War II waned, the Japanese government devised a plan to grant the Taiwanese the right of parliamentary participation as a way to strengthen their allegiance to Japan. But Japan surrendered that August, and the plan was never carried out.

---

[11] T-s Wang, *Legal Reform in Taiwan under Japanese Colonial Rule (1895–1945): The Reception of Western Law* (Seattle, University of Washington Press, 2000) 149–50.

B. Regime Relocation, the ROC Constitution and Taiwan's Incorporation

While the Meiji Constitution's implementation in Taiwan was ambiguous and controversial, the ROC Constitution's was more straightforward. As the largest republic in Asia, the ROC had been struggling with framing a constitution since its inception in 1912. Constitutional negotiations peaked in the early 1930s, but was interrupted by war. Prior to the final constitutional enactment, the fundamental law—promulgated in 1931—was called the 'Provisional Constitution for the Period of Political Tutelage of the ROC'. This KMT-initiated constitutional framework was not a democratic constitution, but was intended as an intermediate step toward constitutional governance. Before World War II, the KMT government commenced a constitutional convention in Nanking and, on 5 May 1936, the so-called 'Five-Five Draft Constitution' was released, followed by the election of delegates in 1936 and 1937. Taiwan, still a Japanese colony, was not represented in the process.

After World War II ended with Japan's surrender in 1945, the KMT government took over Taiwan. Immediately, and before the Constitution's final enactment, Taiwan became an ROC province, and the ROC legal system—implemented in the Chinese mainland—was applied to Taiwan. However, the system's governing powers were centralised in the Governor-General's office, and Taiwan remained without the benefit of any democratic forms of governance. In addition, the initial years of this governance structure was overshadowed by the 228 Incident—a tragedy that began on 28 February 1947, which brought the arrests and killings of many Taiwanese elites. In the view of some, this incident was nothing but a massacre of Taiwanese elites perpetrated by the KMT government.[12]

After World War II, constitution making in Mainland China resumed, and even accelerated. At this time, the political and economic orders governed by the KMT were far from stable; indeed, the CCP had instigated a rebellion and a civil war. But despite this turmoil, the constitution-making process was able to progress. In 1946, the Constituent National Assembly convened, its members the delegates

---

[12] For the details of the 228 Incident, see T-h Lai, RH Myers and W Wei, *A Tragic Beginning: The Taiwan Uprising of February 28, 1947* (Stanford, Stanford University Press, 1991).

elected in 1936 and 1937. Amid political instability and alleged electoral scandals, Taiwan sent 17 delegates to the convention, along with thousands of those from the mainland.[13] Compromises were made, as they needed to be in order to facilitate the constitution-making process in this critical political situation. The ROC Constitution—finally enacted on 25 December 1946, promulgated on 1 January 1947, and enforced on 25 December 1947[14]—was filled with compromises that resulted in mixed power structures and confused institutional designs. This level of ambiguities in the final text of the Constitution had further complicated its implementation in Taiwan.

After the ROC Constitution's promulgation, a debate ensued as to whether it should be implemented in Taiwan at all. The KMT government initially decided not to extend the applicability of the Constitution to Taiwan, on the grounds that the Taiwanese people were deeply influenced by the Japanese colonial rule and were thus ill-prepared for a constitution-style governance. Nevertheless, after losing the civil war to the CCP in May 1949 and subsequently relocating to Taiwan, the KMT brought the Constitution with it along with the declared martial law decree.

Insisting that it was the only legitimate Chinese government, the KMT asserted that the ROC still maintained sovereignty over Mainland China. Accordingly, all people on the mainland and in Taiwan were governed by the ROC Constitution. Thus, a Chinese identity was imposed on the people of Taiwan, and they became the 'compatriots' of the Chinese mainlanders, whom they had never met. Compared with Mainland China's large population, Taiwanese representation remained somewhat diluted: there were only 17 Taiwanese delegates among the thousands in the 1946 Constituent National Assembly. In addition, the people now governed by the ROC Constitution had scant ability to influence the authorship of that very Constitution. These issues called into question both the Constitution and the people's identity, not to mention the state of the ROC, which had already been defeated by the PRC on the Chinese mainland.

Despite this assertion, the KMT government could only effectively govern those residing in Taiwan, including those who had experienced Japanese rule and those mainlanders who had followed the

---

[13] Chang, 'East Asian Foundations for Constitutionalism', above n 4, 121–23.
[14] Ibid.

KMT to Taiwan. Substantiated or not, this contention unequivocally reinforced the decision to impose the ROC Constitution on Taiwan and the Taiwanese populace.

The structure of the national representation reflected the twin issues of constitutional authorship and the people's identity. As Article 2 of the ROC Constitution reads, 'The sovereignty of the Republic of China shall reside in the whole body of the citizenry'. Article 62 further provides that 'the Legislative Yuan[15] shall be composed of members elected by the people and shall exercise legislative power'. As a fundamental element of democracy, representation should properly reflect the people. Yet, as the entire Chinese mainland was under PRC control, national elections were essentially impossible to hold. As a result, the national representatives[16] elected on the mainland in 1947 and 1948 remained in power in Taiwan up until the 1990s. In essence, the structure of representation was distorted, to the detriment of the Taiwanese people. To justify this representational manipulation, the KMT government appealed to *Fatung*, a traditional Chinese justification for power succession,[17] and went so far as to enlist an interpretation by the Constitutional Court.[18]

II. PRE-DEMOCRATISATION CONSTITUTIONAL MANIPULATION AND AUTHORITARIANISM

Since the time of the KMT government's relocation, the ROC Constitution has been the fundamental law in Taiwan. However, during the pre-democratisation era—from 1949 to the late 1980s—constitutional practice in Taiwan remained clouded by the KMT's constitutional authoritarianism.

---

[15] 'Yuan' means 'branch'. The Legislative Yuan is the legislative branch of the central government. For further discussion on the designs and functions of the five Yuans, or branches, of the central government in the ROC Constitution, see ch 3.

[16] According to the 1947 Constitution, national representatives include members of the Legislative Yuan, the Control Yuan, and the National Assembly.

[17] See J-r Yeh, 'The Cult of Fatung: Representational Manipulation and Reconstruction in Taiwan' in G Hassall and C Saunders (eds), *The People's Representatives: Electoral Systems in the Asia-Pacific Region* (NSW, Allen & Unwin, 1997) 1–8.

[18] *JY Interpretation No 31* (1954).

Three measures were implemented in conjunction with this authoritarianism: the Temporary Provisions, tenured representatives, and martial law. Although these were designed to be short-term responses to a constitutional crisis, they lasted for four decades. Paradoxically, while these measures were undertaken primarily in order to consolidate the power of either the President or the KMT, they were nevertheless developed in accordance with the Constitution. For example, the Temporary Provisions, while not necessarily constitutional, were attached to the Constitution; the martial law rule was imposed in a constitutional manner; and tenured representatives were legitimised by a Constitutional Court ruling.

A. Temporary Provisions and Authoritarian Leadership

The path of Chinese constitutional development in the early Republic was not a smooth one. The ROC Constitution was adopted in the midst of the Chinese Civil War. To consolidate power during the war, the first ROC President, Chiang Kai-shek, with knowledge that the President only enjoyed limited power under the young Constitution, sought to revise it.

Sixteen months after the Constitution's promulgation and fewer than four months after it began to be enforced, it was amended. In order to grant special presidential powers beyond the original mandate, the National Assembly—the organ vested with the authority of constitutional revision—was instructed to make a constitutional change.[19] However, instead of undertaking a formal revision, the Assembly decided to bypass the process by adopting a special measure, the Temporary Provisions for the Period of Mobilisation to Suppress Rebellion (Temporary Provisions), as a constitutional addendum. The rationale for using this politically expedient method was that the Temporary Provisions were only meant as a short-term way of coping with emergencies and the fight against Mainland Chinese communists.

The Temporary Provisions were later amended a number of times, infringing upon such basic constitutional principles as separation of powers and checks and balances through the consolidation of

[19] J-r Yeh, 'Changing Forces of Constitutional and Regulatory Reform in Taiwan' (1990) 4 *Journal of Chinese Law* 83, fn 19.

presidential power. Even after its retreat to Taiwan, the KMT government maintained that the 'period of mobilisation to suppress rebellion'
had not yet ended and thus refused to retire the ostensibly 'Temporary'
Provisions,[20] allowing for their enforcement well into the 1990s. This
atypical constitutional practice was formally terminated in 1991 by
President Lee Teng-hui. Altogether, these Temporary Provisions lasted
44 years—43 of which, surprisingly, in Taiwan.

B. Old Thieves and the Manipulation of Representation

To maintain legitimacy in Taiwan, the KMT government exercised
political expediency, such as claiming that the mainland-elected national
representatives residing in Taiwan still represented all of China. This
claim was supported by the KMT government's confident belief that
control over the mainland would soon be re-taken. However, as this
ultimate objective began increasingly to be recognised as impossible,
this particular bit of political expediency found its limits.

The ROC Constitution proclaims that national legislators in the Legislative Yuan represent the whole body of citizens and are vested with
powers that otherwise belong to the whole body.[21] Straightforward as
this may seem, questions remained as to how the Constitution defines
the whole body of citizens and who may legitimately serve as representatives thereof. These questions were complicated by the fact that two
separate authorities, respectively, claimed political representation on
both sides of the Taiwanese Strait[22] and that each of these authorities
held itself out to be the legitimate government of Mainland China and
Taiwan.

The KMT government maintained its sovereignty claim over the
Chinese mainland, but acknowledged the reality that a national election
had been impossible since the relocation to Taiwan. This position posed
two problems: (1) How could the government justify its claim over the
mainland when the people there could not vote for their representatives
in Taiwan? (2) How could the Taiwanese people be convinced that the

---

[20] Ibid, fn 20.
[21] Art 62 Constitution of the Republic of China (1947).
[22] There are Taiwanese delegates in the National People's Assembly of the
People's Republic of China.

ROC-based government's representative structure would appropriately reflect their interests? In the eyes of many of Taiwan's residents, the KMT government was indeed a foreign regime.[23] For those in Mainland China, the KMT consisted of rebels in exile. Thus, since relocation, the KMT government had faced this two-pronged crisis of representative legitimacy.

Over time, the KMT government found the need to enhance its legitimacy, as national recovery and power consolidation could not solve the political crisis. Social theorist Max Weber stressed the necessity of legitimacy for domination. He argued that custom, personal advantage, and the purely effectual or ideal motives of solidarity do not form a sufficiently reliable basis for a given domination. A further element is necessary: the belief of legitimacy.[24] Legitimacy is a must for governance, but how to define the meaning of legitimacy remains an open question for the KMT government. Democratic legitimacy requires not only adherence to the rules of the game by both a majority of the voting citizens and those in positions of authority, but also trust on the part of the citizenry in the government's commitment to uphold them.[25]

Can a regime claim legitimacy when representatives are not subject to re-election? The KMT government answered affirmatively. To support this answer and to serve as the theoretical basis for its rule, the government drew on the concept of *Fatung*, a traditional Chinese canon expression for a political claim based on the authenticity of power succession. Such traditional legitimacy, however, was not sufficient. Additional justification, especially based upon the Constitution, was needed.

Constrained by the Constitution's no-revision policy, the government called upon the judiciary to solve the political crisis. In response, the Constitutional Court endorsed the mainstream position that Mainland-elected representatives would remain in power until re-election became

---

[23] Separationists have argued that the status of Taiwan is still uncertain, perhaps awaiting the self-determination of its residents. See, eg, L-c Chen and WM Reisman, 'Who Owns Taiwan? A Search for International Title' (1972) 81 *Yale Law Journal* 599.

[24] M Weber, *Economy and Society*, G Roth and C Wittich (eds) (Berkeley, University of California Press, 1978) 213.

[25] J Linz, 'Crisis, Breakdown, and Reequilibration' in J Linz and A Stepan (eds), *The Breakdown of Democratic Regimes* (Baltimore, Johns Hopkins University Press, 1978) 17.

an option.[26] The Constitutional Court did not provide sufficient rationale for the ruling and not a single dissenting opinion was filed. Rather than resolving the political crisis, the decision merely rubber-stamped the functions for the KMT government.

Such judicial intervention was not without criticism. Indeed, the issue was highly political, and public opinion should have been the deciding factor. Aware of the inherent political risks in doing so, the KMT government nevertheless decided to strengthen its position using the judiciary. Such practice, in political scientist Juan Linz's view, is typical for a regime confronting political crisis:

> The aim is to gain time, since legal solutions are notoriously slow … The legitimacy of having judicial bodies make what are essentially political decisions in a democracy is always doubtful, and in countries where judicial bodies have been established only recently, their judgment is even less likely to be considered binding … The result is a lessening of the authenticity of democratic institutions, particularly the power and responsibility of parliament.[27]

Linz was correct in pointing out the likelihood of converting a political crisis into a legal or technical issue—and more specifically into a question for the Constitutional Court. However, such efforts were not necessarily made to gain time; the Constitutional Court resolved *JY Interpretation No. 31* quickly, as necessitated by the political climate. But this accommodating stance had side effects, as the judiciary's willingness to bow to the political situation evidenced that institution's fragility. As a result, the then-young Court suffered a serious blow that augured tremendous reputational damage and hampered its ability to channel constitutional change in a time of political crisis.

C. Martial Law and Constitutional Authoritarianism

The representational crisis arising from the regime's relocation to Taiwan was defused by *JY Interpretation No. 31*, at least for the time being. Yet, to satisfy its hunger for power concentration—and specifically, for retaking the mainland and controlling Taiwan more tightly—the KMT government undertook additional measures that cut against

---

[26] *JY Interpretation No 31 (1990).*
[27] J Linz, 'Crisis, Breakdown, and Reequilibration', above n 25, at 69.

the Constitution's spirit and values. Thus, a collaboration of the executive, the legislature, and the judiciary formed a regime of constitutional authoritarianism, the most devastating consequence of which was the enduring martial law rule.

Beginning with constitutional authoritarianism, public sovereignty—in the form of general elections—was sacrificed with the Court's support. In accordance with the Court's ruling, the national representatives, including respective members of the National Assembly and the Legislative Yuan who were all elected on the mainland, were no longer constrained by re-election. Thus, the general public lost its electoral oversight of the governing body, even though the Constitution still guaranteed the right to vote. This perhaps explains how, along with the Temporary Provisions' cessation of the two-term limit for Presidents, the Assembly was able to re-elect Chang Kai-shek as President for five consecutive terms until his death, after 27 years, in 1976.

The Constitution suffered extensive distortions in service of an authoritarian regime, and various constitutional requirements were functionally disabled by the Temporary Provisions. Before political liberalisation set in, the Provisions not only legitimated authoritarian measures, but also deterred necessary constitutional revisions in order to cope with social change. Against this background, martial law decree was declared and various restrictive laws—effective in the 'Period of National Mobilisation Against Communist Rebellion'—were promulgated.[28] In the shadow of the KMT government's power consolidation, economic policies became at best the servant of political mobilisation. The state machine intervened extensively by tightly controlling foreign exchange, imports and exports, and market entry, as well as instituting state ownership of several major industries, including transportation, steel, electricity, water, oil, salt, and sugar.[29] As a result of such intrusive regulatory intervention, the state machine penetrated every sector of society, eventually exercising comprehensive controls over universities, the entertainment community, farmers' associations, fishermen's associations, labour unions, trade unions, and local financial associations.[30]

---

[28] J-r Yeh, 'Constitutional Reform and Democratization in Taiwan, 1945–2000' in PCY Chow (ed), *Taiwan's Modernization in Global Perspective* (Westport, CT, Praeger, 2002) fn 34.
[29] Ibid, fn 35.
[30] Ibid, fn 36.

Civil liberties otherwise guaranteed by the Constitution were severely curtailed by the Martial Law Decree. Civilians were tried by courts-martial for ordinary offences. Emergency laws and regulations restricted the freedoms of association, press, speech, and movement. Local autonomy as guaranteed by the Constitution was substantially limited or completely removed. This was indeed a long, dark period of constitutional authoritarianism.

Despite these infringements of democratic suffrage and human rights, the authoritarian regime nevertheless claimed that it ruled in accordance with the Constitution. Measures aimed at power consolidation or rights infringements, including the Temporary Provisions and the Martial Law Decree, were drafted in constitutional terms and rubber-stamped by the Constitutional Court. It was not until the late 1980s that a strong enough momentum built to finally bring democratisation and constitutional reform.

III. DEMOCRATISATION AND CONSTITUTIONAL INDIGENISATION

In the late 1980s, Taiwan started on its path to political liberalisation and democratic reform, in tandem with constitutional reform. The link between political democratisation and constitutional reform was due in part to the KMT government's manipulation of the ROC Constitution in order to build up the legitimacy of authoritarian rule.

Generally, there were two divergent views of reform. One claimed that, to mark a new beginning for the constitutional order and to break with the authoritarian past, Taiwan as a sovereign state should have a brand new constitution. Such constitution-making sentiment peaked in the late 1980s to the early 1990s as the taboo on advocating for constitutional revision seemed to lift. This development provided momentum for a comprehensive constitutional overhaul.

The other, more dominant view was one of political pragmatism. This camp preferred retaining the ROC Constitution to prevent further complications and making only those changes necessary to satisfy Taiwan's need for democratic transition. Proponents argued that the problem was not the Constitution itself, as it by and large embraced democratic governance and human rights, but the manipulation of the Constitution by the KMT government. Based on this view, renowned constitutional scholars such as Fu Hu advocated for the ROC Constitution's reform. For them, the primary tasks were to repeal the Temporary Provisions and lift the Martial Law Decree.

Given these contrasting views, compromises needed to be made. Over time, Taiwan settled on pursuing constitutional reforms that were piecemeal and incremental.

A. Democratic Mobilisation and Negotiated Change

The democratisation of Taiwan began with soft measures undertaken by President Chiang Ching-kuo, Chiang Kai-shek's son and successor, in the final years of his presidency. The most important of these was the lifting of the Martial Law Decree in July 1987, only months before Chiang's death in January 1988.

Upon Chiang's death, Vice-President Lee Teng-hui succeeded as President, in accordance with the Constitution. Owing to his symbolic status as a native Taiwanese, Lee's succession was met with an undercurrent of opposition from KMT party cadres. Still, Lee navigated through such political turbulence to become the ROC President and the KMT Chairman. He was the first native Taiwanese to occupy both offices.

Lee was determined to respond to the public outcry for political reform. Although the Martial Law Decree had already been lifted, the Temporary Provisions and tenured representatives remained the biggest challenges. Yet, he had to walk a political tightrope as reform measures would have a tremendous impact on the vested interests of KMT party cadres who had received, since the Mainland China days, the support of military leaders loyal to the KMT ideology and Chiang Kai-shek. To the nation's enormous relief, no coup d'état ensued. Had there been one, Taiwan's democratisation would have been delayed for an extended period of time.

The presidential transition from the Chiang family to Lee Teng-hui did not automatically produce substantial reform. Decades-long constitutional authoritarianism would not disappear overnight, even with a leadership change in the government or in the ruling KMT. Unlike other democracies in transition, Taiwan's democratisation did not begin with a regime change. The KMT government still remained in power, and democratisation occurred through a process of negotiated transition among political parties and a growing civil society.

The pinnacle of Taiwan's democratisation was the autonomous citizen uprisings, especially the student movement. On 16 March 1990 students, forming the largest student movement in Taiwan's history, gathered in front of the Chiang Kai-shek monument to chant for political reform. The students requested a reform agenda with four goals: (1) dissolving the National Assembly; (2) abolishing the Temporary Provisions; (3) calling for a national affairs conference; and (4) providing a timeline for political and economic reform. At about the same time, proposals for reform were debated in the KMT and among opinion leaders.

Confronting increased outcries for reform, Lee invited student leaders to the presidential office for discussions. Many of the students' requests were received positively by Lee, who promised reform. A National Affairs Conference, convened by Lee and attended by 141 representatives chosen from all societal corners, was held three months later and entrusted with developing a political and constitutional reform agenda. A major consensus was reached during the National Affairs Conference which eventually paved the way for a series of incremental constitutional reforms. This consensus agreed on the total demolition of the Temporary Provisions, bringing a final end to the mobilisation era. As for the reconstruction of representation, the Constitutional Court issued interpretations that called for the legislature's total dissolution and re-election. Together, these measures laid a foundation for the reforms of the subsequent decade.

B. The Reconstruction of Representation and Incremental Constitutional Reform

Beginning in 1991, Taiwan undertook seven rounds of constitutional revisions: in 1991, 1992, 1994, 1997, 1999, 2000 and 2005. Observing their frequency and often chaotic nature, many may question the wisdom of such piecemeal constitutional revisions: Are these revisions purely incidental and random events? Is there any rationale or paradigm—even a changing one—underlying these rather impressive constitutional transformations?

Over the last two decades, incremental constitutional reform has concentrated on one theme: the representation of the people. The regime's need to respond to representational crises arising from the Mainland-to-Taiwan regime relocation drove consecutive constitutional revisions. Indeed, the major driving force behind Taiwan's constitutional reform has been the need to fix the long-manipulated system of representation. As discussed above, tenured representatives that had faced no re-election contests since 1949 could not represent the Taiwanese population's best interests. Taiwan's political development can be characterised as one of manipulation and then reconstruction of democratic representation, beginning with the legislature and then the presidential election.

The reconstruction of representation has taken three consecutive phases to complete, and its reforms have usually been codified in incremental constitutional revisions and, on occasion, affirmed by rulings of the Constitutional Court. The first phase focused on the full suffrage of Taiwan's residents, with respect to both the election of national representatives and the direct election of the President. The second phase dealt with the representation of Taiwan in the international community through a consolidated presidency. The third phase saw reconstruction end, with the final abolition of the National Assembly and the reinstitution of popular sovereignty through a public referendum on constitutional revision. In hindsight, these three phases focused on the reconstruction of representation in different ways. In the first phase, constitutional revisions were undertaken to build legitimacy for Taiwan's system of domestic representation. The second phase was aimed at the reinforcement of Taiwan's external representation. Finally, the third phase was an attempt to return full public sovereignty to the Taiwanese people. These points are elucidated further in the following.

i. Reinforcing Internal Representation: Down with the 'Old Thieves' and Extending Full Suffrage to Taiwan's Residents

Over the years, the representational crisis worsened as the tenured representatives aged and passed away. The Temporary Provisions added a few seats for local Taiwanese residents to elect their national representatives in supplementary elections. The newly elected representatives—though a small minority—could claim better representation and more legitimacy than tenured representatives, who were defamed as 'old thieves' (as the Confucian Analects explain, those who live to old age but make no contribution to society become old thieves).[31] Despite their political shortcomings, the tenured representatives still refused to step down, believing that they genuinely represented the ROC, and that their absence in the Legislative Yuan and National Assembly would herald the end of that government. At the same time, they were forced to ask how the ROC's legitimacy could continue unabated when, as at some point they must, all the representatives who had been elected more than 40 years before on the Chinese mainland stepped down. It became apparent that the KMT could not solve the problem from within—by simply holding fast to the original ROC constitutional mandate. Rather, two outside forces contributed to a workable solution: one was the opposition party, and the other the same Constitutional Court that had legitimised the tenured representatives.

The passage of time by itself exposed the flaws in the manipulation of representation. Even though tenured representatives were not forced to step down, they could not live forever. When the last tenured representative died, the seats would all be replaced by new blood elected in Taiwan. The issue was therefore not whether the status quo would be changed; it was only a matter of time before change occurred. But time itself was running against the KMT government, which once saw tenured representatives as a token of constitutional legitimacy but now had to deal with the consequences of such manipulation. Eventually a law was passed providing substantial compensation in exchange for the voluntary retirement of tenured representatives. However, for some diehard representatives, their seats were not something to be sold. Unsurprisingly, the Constitutional Court, which had previously created this deadlock, was called upon to resolve the issue.

In the landmark decision *JY Interpretation No 261*, the Constitutional Court ordered all tenured representatives to retire by the end of 1991. Unlike *JY Interpretation No 31*, a previous ruling that, without much analysis, legitimised tenured representatives, this interpretation provided a more sophisticated rationale and contextual reasoning. The Constitutional Court defended its previous decision by arguing that tenure extension had been necessary for maintenance of the constitutional system. It further argued that the previous decision did not fix the

---

[31] *Confucian Analects* 14: 46.

term of national representatives, nor did it intend to endorse a life-long extension. In conclusion, the Constitutional Court ordered tenured representatives to step down and a national election to be held promptly. It was fitting that the same Constitutional Court that had created tenured representatives also resolved the paradox.

Constitutional revisions in 1991, 1992 and 1994 were made in response to the crisis of representation that had begun with the tenured representatives. The 1991 constitutional revision ended the term of tenured representatives and provided for representative elections by the people of Taiwan—the only place where the ROC had ruled since 1949. Ironically, the 1991 constitutional revision, which entailed a termination of tenured representatives, was carried out by the tenured representatives themselves.

The following year, the KMT government launched a second round of constitutional revision, this time to invest presidential elections with greater democratic legitimacy. But the National Assembly had not settled on whether the President should be elected directly, or indirectly through such proxy as a presidential college. This unresolved matter notwithstanding, it was nevertheless agreed upon that the next constitutional revision, to be completed in 1994, would bring a resolution.[32] In this way, the arrangement exemplified the proper functioning of incremental constitutional reform—providing more time for negotiating through differences and building upon what had already been agreed to.

The 1994 constitutional revision proceeded under the shadow of intra-KMT power struggles. As previously mentioned, the 1992 revision had not pinpointed the method by which the President was to be elected. This irresolution was due in part to two intra-KMT factions that held differing views about Chinese identity. On one side, the die-hard KMT faction feared that the ROC would become the Republic of Taiwan once Taiwan's residents began to directly and exclusively elect native Taiwanese Presidents.[33] On the other side, the moderate KMT faction felt that, as long as the ROC Constitution was maintained, the issue of identity was of no concern. With the critical support of the KMT moderates and President Lee, the constitutional revision eventually allowed for the direct election of the President. Nevertheless, this

---

[32] Art 12(2) Additional Articles to the Constitution of the Republic of China (1992).

[33] Yeh, 'Constitutional Reform', above n 28, fn 45.

revision caused a deeper partisan split within the KMT: the pro-China forces consolidated into the New Party, the third largest political party and one that represented the far right of the political spectrum.

With three rounds of constitutional revisions in four years, the Constitution had undergone a 'quiet' reinforcement of representation— necessary for a system of modern Taiwanese democratic governance. Although still regarded as non-native, the KMT government had increased its legitimacy through a process of indigenisation and democratisation that opened up both presidential and legislative elections in Taiwan. This was evident when the opposition Democratic Progressive Party (DPP), in lieu of a more dramatic revolutionary movement, chose to compete in institutionalised elections under the ROC Constitution.

ii. *Reinforcing External Representation: The Embarrassing Status of the Taiwan Provincial Government*

With the authorisation of the 1994 constitutional revision, the first directly elected President, Lee Teng-hui, was inaugurated in 1996. Unlike legislative election, direct presidential election allowed for unprecedented nationwide political mobilisation in Taiwan. It also formed a strong sense of identity among the Taiwanese people that not only strengthened Taiwan's political leadership but also created an image of Taiwanese sovereignty in the eyes of the global community.[34] This partially explains why China launched a missile exercise on the eve of the 1996 presidential election.

The fourth round of constitutional revision was undertaken against the backdrop of Hong Kong's handover to China in 1997, suggesting a move to consolidate representation in the context of diplomacy abroad. Apprehensive of the increasing integrative pressures from the Chinese, Taiwan became acutely aware of the embarrassing status of the Taiwan Provincial Government, as well as of the attenuation of Taiwan's bargaining power with China. With this awareness, most changes made in the 1997 constitutional revision were aimed at increasing the President's power to personify Taiwanese sovereignty in the international community. For instance, one of the amendments revoked legislative approval of the appointment of the premier by the President, which resulted

---

[34] Ibid, fn 46.

in more presidential influence over the cabinet. More important, the revisions authorised a downsizing of the Taiwan Provincial Government in order to downplay Taiwan's provincial status, a position with which both the PRC and the KMT agreed. In addition to this symbolic political effect, provincial downsizing also represented an effort by the government to reorganise and cut bureaucratic red tape.[35]

Taiwan formerly followed a three-tiered central–local relations system specified by the Constitution and divided into national, provincial, and county governments. Upon its relocation to Taiwan, the ROC ruled over only one province: Taiwan. The governor of the Taiwan Provincial Government was appointed by the central government, but the 1992 constitutional revision changed the procedure to a direct election.[36] Remarkably, the Taiwan Provincial Government's territorial scope— excluding only Taipei City and Kaohsiung City, which each enjoyed a status equal to the Taiwan Provincial Government—overlapped significantly with the ROC national government's. Hence, with the introduction of direct elections for both the national President and the provincial governor, over 80 per cent of these positions' constituencies overlapped. Around this time, Taiwan Provincial Governor James Soong was nearly as popular as President Lee, and the political competition between these two figures was fierce. These jurisdictional frictions might have sparked a political controversy: if the PRC had designated Governor Soong, but not President Lee, for political negotiations over Taiwan's future, a significant political crisis would have arisen. Against this background, the proposal to downsize the Taiwan Provincial Government was pushed forward, albeit against the Governor's will.[37]

Downsizing the level of the Taiwan Provincial Government was imperative once Hong Kong's handover to the PRC materialised. The 1997 constitutional revision also saw partisan collaboration toward political change. Dissatisfied with the speed and comprehensiveness of constitutional reforms, the DPP opposed the KMT during the first three rounds of constitutional revision in 1991, 1992 and 1994. Yet, as the KMT government gradually increased representation, the DPP

---

[35] Ibid, fn 47.

[36] Art 17 Additional Articles to the Constitution of the Republic of China (1992).

[37] For further discussions on the downsizing of the Taiwan Provincial Government, see ch 5, II B.

decided to co-operate. In 1997, while the National Assembly drafted the constitutional revision proposal, the DPP worked closely with the KMT in a preparatory roundtable to counter the Chinese threat and address Taiwan's external representation crisis. Thus began to develop a sense of bipartisanship in service of constitutional reform. Nevertheless, citizen groups were still disappointed that the reforms continued to focus primarily on government restructuring and presidential powers—in other words, on the interests of political parties rather than human rights.

iii. Reinforcing Representation as to Constitutional Sovereignty: The Fate of the National Assembly and the Public Referendum

The final stage of incremental constitutional reform was directed at the institutional reorganisation of the National Assembly. Under the ROC Constitution, the National Assembly had the power to elect the President and Vice-President and to revise the Constitution. In contrast, legislative powers were exercised by the Legislative Yuan, to which the Executive Yuan was accountable. As the President and Vice-President were now popularly elected, a heated debate began over whether to maintain the National Assembly. Over time, and through a series of constitutional revisions, the Assembly's powers were relinquished to the Legislative Yuan and to the people. In particular, the people were to vote through public referendum on amendment proposals made by the Legislative Yuan. Completing this reform, however, took three rounds of constitutional revision in 1999, 2000 and 2005.

The fifth round of constitutional revision in 1999 further confirmed that constitutional reform in Taiwan was an endless partisan enterprise. The reasons for this were many, but a compelling explanation could be found in the vested interests of the National Assembly as a monopolistic organ of constitutional revision. Having completed four rounds of revision, the National Assembly now became the target of reform. One radical proposal—offered amid public outcry against the Assembly—would have abolished it altogether. Other more moderate proposals included various reorganisation plans: strengthening the Assembly by giving it more powers, or transforming it into the second chamber of a new bicameral Congress, of which the Legislative Yuan would be the first chamber.

The KMT and the DPP took different positions on these proposals. The KMT preferred moderate proposals, in consideration of the
impact of the possible reforms that may have resulted from the coming
2000 presidential election. The DPP, however, pushed for more radical
proposals, including the total abolition of the National Assembly or
the formation of a brand-new Congress. In any event, self-interested
National Assembly members crossed party lines and agreed to a moderate version of reform. The Assembly ultimately survived a fifth round
of constitutional revision, and retained its exclusive power to amend
the Constitution. Nevertheless, no further election would be held to fill
the next National Assembly, members of which would be appointed
in proportion to the seats of various political parties and independents
allocated in the Legislative Yuan. In addition, in order for the next
National Assembly's term to run concurrently with the Legislative
Yuan's, the terms of existing Assembly members were extended for two
years. This term extension drew harsh criticism from the general public.

Responding to the public outcry, then-Vice-President Lien Chan,
the KMT presidential candidate for the upcoming election, condemned
the constitutional revision as irresponsible. This and other similar con-
demnations resulted in the expulsion of National Assembly Speaker Su
Nan-cheng from the KMT and the loss of Su's Assembly membership.
The New Party took the initiative of appealing to the Constitutional
Court for a constitutional interpretation, and the KMT and the DPP
followed suit, respectively. Worried about the constitutional interpretation's impact on the upcoming election, the parties all urged the Constitutional Court to render judgment promptly.

But the Constitutional Court shied away from taking any action
that would have a significant effect on the election. Therefore, one
week after the election, on 24 March 2000, the Constitutional Court
announced *JY Interpretation No 499*, which declared unconstitutional
the constitutional revision—including both the term-extension and
proportional-appointment clauses. Unsurprisingly, National Assembly
members affiliated with the KMT and the DPP denounced the decision
as a judicial abuse of power.

With respect to proportional appointment, the Court's interpretation necessitated that an election for the next National Assembly be
held soon. However, neither the KMT nor the DPP decided to hold an
election; instead, they began a sixth round of constitutional revision in

April 2000, which produced two important changes. First, the National Assembly was transformed from its previous role as a long-standing constitutional organ into an ad hoc, mission-oriented institution. Thereafter, the three hundred elected members of the Assembly would only convene if the Legislative Yuan proposed a new constitutional amendment. Second, and in retaliation against the Constitutional Court, the pensions were suspended of those justices who had been appointed from scholarly circles. The decision to target only these justices stemmed from political speculation that they more strongly supported *JY Interpretation No 499* and were more likely to resort to judicial activism than those appointed from judicial circles.

These changes to the National Assembly altered both the nature of the government's organisation and the practice of constitutional revision. It was widely expected that the frequent revisions that had occurred since the early 1990s would come to an end after the sixth round in 2000. However, the citizenry's outcry against the legislature fuelled the seventh, and latest, round in 2005.

Of the seven rounds of revisions, the 2005 reform stands as an obvious departure from its predecessors, with respect to both its scope for change and future impact. In brief, two types of change were embedded in the 2005 reform: congressional reform and the introduction of the public referendum for constitutional revision. Regarding congressional reform, three new measures were undertaken: reducing the number of legislative seats from 225 to 113, introducing a single electoral district system, and adopting a dual ballot system.

First, the halving of the number of legislative seats was designed to prevent a politics of localism, as an overabundance of seats may have led to undersized electoral districts and entrenched local interests. Some of the strongest proponents of downsizing were citizen groups that resented the legislature's partisan politics. At that time, public opinion polls rated the Legislative Yuan and the National Assembly among the least satisfactory of Taiwan's public institutions. Second, the introduction of a single electoral district was meant to improve legislative politics. Under the previous system of multiple electoral districts, legislative candidates could be elected relatively easily, so long as they manipulated a specific group of voters. Hence, those with extreme positions might well have enjoyed a fair chance of being elected. A system with a single electoral district would, on the contrary, be more advantageous for moderate candidates, as the winners would have to win a majority of the votes. The thought here was that taking moderate positions would ensure a more peaceful and rational exercise of legislators' mandates. Third, the dual ballot system, in which voters cast one ballot for their favourite candidate and the other for their desired political party, would strengthen party politics under the democratic political system. Under this new system, the election's focus would be likely to shift to policy debates between competing political parties. This, in turn, was expected to substantially improve legislative quality and efficiency.

The changes introduced by the 2005 constitutional revision have had profound and lasting impacts on Taiwan's representative politics. With the introduction of the single district system, it had been widely speculated that small parties such as the New Party, the People First Party, and the Taiwan Solidarity Union were to be marginalised, and that a two-party system between the KMT and the DPP was likely to be formed. In addition, there were also concerns from DPP elites that under the new system, the DPP might no longer be able to win the legislative majority, as the KMT was systematically favoured by the existing districting practices.[38]

The 2005 constitutional revision's other major change involved two steps: the abolition of the National Assembly and the introduction of a public referendum in the constitutional revision process. As discussed above, the National Assembly's self-interest and the partisan politics embedded in incremental constitutional revisions had infuriated the general public. The Assembly's total abolition was therefore widely expected and supported by Taiwan's political parties. Further, the Assembly's self-dissolution paved the way for a second step: the establishment of a public referendum to approve constitutional amendment proposals passed by the Legislative Yuan.

This new procedure's most salient feature, however, is the extremely high threshold it enforces for further constitutional revisions. To illustrate, it requires a three-quarters legislative majority to pass a constitutional amendment proposal. This requirement is considered to amount to no less than a consensus resolution in the Legislative Yuan. In addition, a new proposal has to be publicised and subject to citizen deliberation for at least six months before a public referendum may be held. Lastly, for a proposal to successfully be ratified, half or more of

---

[38] For further discussions on the electoral system and political parties, see ch 4.

Taiwan's eligible voters must participate and cast a vote of approval. It is speculated that these high thresholds will make future constitutional revisions extremely difficult, if not impossible.

Notwithstanding the sheer procedural difficulty in effecting future constitutional revisions, this final phase of revision has profoundly transformed the ROC Constitution in Taiwan. First, the National Assembly, which had historically been seen as an institution critical to the flourishing of the ROC Constitution, was abolished. This significant institutional alteration, along with the other aforementioned reconstructions of representation in previous rounds of revision, has generated a very different institutional structure from that of the original ROC Constitution. Second, and even more important, the power to revise the Constitution—a most symbolic sovereign power of a constitutional form of government—is now returned to the people. Without majority approval, no further constitutional change can be made. For the first time in history, public sovereignty truly resides in the Taiwanese people.

IV. CONCLUSION

Taiwan's constitutional journey bears a strong resemblance to the fundamental features of modern constitutionalism. The dramatic shift in context from Mainland China to Taiwan, where the constitutional text became gradually indigenised, has challenged the very concepts of sovereignty, the people, and constitutional identity.

During the Japanese colonial era, local Taiwanese elites embraced their identities as Japanese subjects and sought political freedoms. The imposition of a foreign constitution did not foreclose the dream of developing into an autonomous people whose identity depended upon a constitution. Likewise, the implementation of the ROC Constitution in Taiwan, although partly due to the imposition of the KMT government, was accepted and later transformed into a system of full, autonomous self-governance.

Although Taiwan did not experience revolution and never drafted a new constitution, 'the people' and their constitutional identity emerged over time as a result of the incremental changes that developed a new constitutional order. Thus formed a new collective identity of Taiwanese people under democratic governance, in which they passionately and genuinely participated in the process of constitutional reform. This identity was further reinforced by the reconstruction of representation that occurred through various rounds of constitutional revision.[39] By these incremental processes of constitutional reform, the ROC Constitution simultaneously underwent a process of indigenisation and democratisation, thereby firmly establishing a new constitutional identity for the Taiwanese people.

FURTHER READING

Chang, W-C, 'East Asian Foundations for Constitutionalism: Three Models Reconstructed' (2008) 3 *National Taiwan University Law Review* 111–41.

Chu, Y-h and Lin, J-W, 'Political Development in 20th-Century Taiwan: State-Building, Regime Transformation and the Construction of National Identity' (2001) 165 *The China Quarterly* 102–29.

Wang, T-s, *Legal Reform in Taiwan under Japanese Colonial Rule (1895–1945): The Reception of Western Law* (Seattle, University of Washington Press, 2000).

Yeh, J-r, 'Constitutional Reform and Democratization in Taiwan, 1945–2000' in PCY Chow (ed), *Taiwan's modernization in global perspective* (Westport, CT, Praeger, 2002) 47–77.

[39] See Yeh, 'Constitutional Reform', above n 28, 55–59.

3

The Evolving Presidency and the Executive

The Evolution of the Five-power Government Scheme – The
Evolving Presidency – The Executive Yuan: The Premier and
Executive Oversight – Government Reform – Conclusion

A LTHOUGH IT WAS structured around the same principle of
separation of powers that we typically associate with governments divided into three branches—executive, legislative and
judicial—which are compartmentalised yet interrelated through checks
and balances, the ROC Constitution is unique in its establishment of
a five-power, semi-parliamentary government. This design, borne of
political compromise, is based on the teachings of Sun Yat-sen and
exhibits a striking resemblance to various Chinese imperial systems.
However, the transition from an authoritarian rule to a democratic one
has necessitated various reforms from Sun Yat-sen's model, including
the evolution to a semi-presidential system in which presidential powers
extend to broad categories of national security and cross-Strait policies.
As a result, the key to understanding this rather complex governmental
structure lies in an understanding of the interrelationships it creates,
from the President and the premier, to the accountability and integration of the respective branches of government.

Notwithstanding the evolution that has already occurred, continuing
concerns which stem from the cumbersome and ambiguous nature of
Taiwan's governmental structure abound. However, due to the high
threshold for constitutional revision implemented following the 2005
round of amendment, a sweeping overhaul of the government's structure through constitutional reform seems very unlikely. Nevertheless,
incremental government reform has been possible through statutory

measures. These changes, driven by the impetus of global competitiveness, have resulted in government streamlining and the creation of public and private partnerships.

This chapter presents the structural evolution of both the government and the state itself in the context of democratisation and constitutional change, focusing on the institution, power and operation of the executive branch, particularly the presidency. As this governmental transformation has been driven by indigenisation, democratisation and globalisation, contextual dynamics that were present at different stages of this evolution are also highlighted. This chapter is divided into four sections. The first explains the five-power government model and its transformation during the periods from authoritarian rule through democratic transition. The next section focuses on the presidency and its evolving powers. The third section discusses the executive power of the premier. The last section highlights recent government reforms driven by globalisation.

I. THE EVOLUTION OF THE FIVE-POWER GOVERNMENT SCHEME

A special feature of the 1947 ROC Constitution is the embodiment of a five-power government (that is, the separation of government powers into five branches or powers, as opposed to the somewhat more typical three-branch structure). In addition to three branches that we typically associate with—executive, legislative and judicial—the five-power government scheme includes control and examination branches as well. The constitutional design of a five-power government, though originally designed for China, has existed in Taiwan since 1949. However, this five-power constitutional scheme has undergone institutional reform through negotiation within Taiwan's contextual realities, moving away from the drafters' original intent toward a special semi-presidential system.

A. The Development of the Five-power Government Scheme

The development of the five-power government could be analysed in three stages: from revolutionary idyllic notion, to formal constitutional enactment, and finally to practical implementation.

The five-power constitution is a government system proposed by revolutionary leader Sun Yat-sen in 1906, and served as the democratic governmental formula for the new republic after the overthrow of the imperial Qing regime. It established a central government composed of five Yuans, or branches. In addition to the traditional three branches—executive, legislative, and judicial—the five-power system also contains the Examination Yuan, to administer the selection of candidates for the bureaucracy, and the Control Yuan, to monitor the honesty and efficiency of the government. Sun advocated for these two additional branches to safeguard the rights of the people and the integrity of the government through the repair of abuses he viewed as caused by the long-held division of three powers. Though Sun's model may be seen as revolutionary, it was not entirely new—rather, it was derived from traditional Chinese administrative components.

Sun argued that the division of three powers, as it exists in the West, suffers from two problems. First, the administrative institute oversees public employment, so it is susceptible to abuse. Second, granting parliament, alone, the power of supervision could similarly lead to abuse of this power. Sun sought solutions to these two potential problems from two traditional Chinese imperial systems: the imperial examination (kē jǔ) and imperial censor (yù shǐ). These additional elements led to his five-power government scheme. Further, in an effort to curb the patronage of public appointments, Sun advocated mandatory exams to determine qualifications for all government officials. To prevent the legislators from acting solely for personal interests, the powers of public oversight and impeachment should be removed from the auspices of the legislature. Doing so, Sun reasoned, would promote governmental efficiency. The essence of a five-power division does not stem merely from the difference of the number of branches, but from the principle that the addition of the powers of examination and supervision would lead to a boon in governmental efficiency, enabling the government to more effectively work for the well-being of the people.

Although the KMT honoured Sun's five-power constitution, the principle was both debated and modified by other political parties during the constitution-drafting process. In the end, though the idea of a five-power government was codified in the 1947 ROC Constitution, it was greatly modified through political negotiations. Still, the

Preamble to the ROC Constitution honours Sun Yat-sen's teachings and their impact on the founding and shaping of the republic. Further, the Constitution sets forth the five-power scheme sequentially, with chapters 5 to 9 regulating each of the government's five powers (Yuans). This sequential layout of the five powers in the Constitution embodies Sun's original concept, and, to an even greater extent, manifests the KMT's political ideology—an ideology that would not be altered without an arduous fight. The government's five-power scheme, as stipulated in the Constitution, has been implemented in Taiwan, with the current government divided according to the five powers.

To pre-emptively address conflict among the five Yuans, Article 44 of the Constitution authorises the President to convene mediation meetings when there are inter-Yuan disputes that stem from constitutional matters. By this design, the President essentially serves as the superior mediator in political conflict or gridlock among the five government powers. Although the use of this 'mediation power' is rare, the President has exercised it a few times. This power is not, however, unchecked. Recently, the speaker of the Legislative Yuan rejected the presidential call for such a mediation meeting over the political crisis triggered by the student occupation of the legislative floor. This occupation incident began over controversies arising from the legislative review of the service trade agreement with mainland China.[1]

The five-power government and interactions between and among the powers are further exemplified by certain practices authorised by the Constitution and confirmed by the Constitutional Court. For example, additional powers (or Yuans), aside from the Executive, are entitled to propose and present legislative bills to the Legislative Yuan. *JY Interpretation No 3* reasons that

> [s]ince the Examination Yuan may propose bills of act to the Legislative Yuan for matters within its authority in accordance with Article 87 of the Constitution, based upon the system of the separation of the five powers and equal interdependence, [further] in reference to the legislative history of that Article and Article 71, it is in compliance with the spirit of the Constitution that the Control Yuan may propose bills of act to the Legislative Yuan concerning matters within its authority.

---

[1] For further discussion on this incident and other related conflicts between the Executive and Legislative Yuans, see ch 4.

Similarly, *JY Interpretation No 175* states as follows:

> Because the Judicial Yuan is the supreme judicial agency of the country, it naturally has the authority to propose and present statutory bills to the Legislative Yuan with regard to matters within its authority based on the constitutional system of 'separation of powers' and 'checks and balances' among the five branches of the Central Government to enact proper laws and regulations.

Despite the attractiveness to constitutional drafters of Sun Yat-sen's theory of the five-power government, in practice, it has two inherent problems. First, these five powers are not equal. Impressive as it may first appear, a five-power government is susceptible to corruption and through a party or dictatorship under a strong leader that gains a majority and thus leaves one or two small Yuans with little independent power. This worst-case scenario has been realised in practice, particularly as the Control Yuan and Examination Yuan have, at times, been rendered effectively unable to perform their equal-footing function in Taiwan's five-government scheme.

One example of this 'hand-tying' is reflected against the backdrop of *JY Interpretation No 632*. In 2000, the five-power government suffered its biggest humiliation in Taiwan's contentious political history after the first regime change, when the DPP President, for the first time, had the power to nominate the members of the Control Yuan since, according to the 2000 constitutional revision, members of the Control Yuan were to be nominated by the President and approved by the Legislative Yuan. During DPP President Chen Shui-bian's second term, the appointment of members to the Control Yuan became a point of serious political confrontation between the DPP government and the KMT legislative majority. President Chen submitted a list of nominees for legislative confirmation in 2004, as the tenure of the third term members of the Control Yuan were set to expire at the end of January 2005. However, the KMT legislative majority blocked the nomination from entering into floor discussion. Afterwards, in February 2005 a newly elected legislature, in which the KMT still enjoyed a majority, was inaugurated. President Chen again submitted his list, but the KMT continued its boycott for another three years.

It ultimately took the Constitutional Court to emphatically denounce this boycott as unconstitutional in *JY Interpretation No 632*. The Constitutional Court stated that the Constitution would not allow for the event in which either the President or the Legislative Yuan failed to nominate or consent to the nomination of candidates. To allow otherwise would prevent the Control Yuan from exercising its power or function and thereby jeopardise the integrity of the constitutional system. Notwithstanding the ruling, the KMT legislative majority continued to block the nomination until 2008, when the KMT won the presidential election and the KMT President nominated a new slate. Though this turmoil was not resolved until the same party wrested control of both the Legislative and Executive Yuans, it did illustrate that the government could still operate without the Control Yuan, calling into question the integrity of the five-power government scheme.

The second problem with the five-power government is the extent to which each of the Yuan's powers under the system of checks and balances pervade the powers and authority of each of the different branches. Separation of powers exists not only to protect citizens from the government, but also to protect the government from itself, and to facilitate effective and efficient governance. Yet, the separation of the powers in a five-power government scheme may ultimately result in less efficient governance. This tends to occur because there are more relationships that must be defined between and among the powers, and the degree of complexity and number of linkages in these relationships represents a drastic increase over its three-branch counterparts, with only three relationships the drafters must contend with among the entities in a three-branch system and 10 such relationships among the entities under a five-power system, such as the one practised in Taiwan. However, if we scrutinise the original ROC Constitution, there are surprisingly few provisions that directly address these 10 relationships. While it is certainly understandable that it is both impractical and arguably unnecessary to cover all potential relationships and interworkings among the entities in the Constitution, their omission has given rise to many grey areas that have contributed to conflicts among these five powers, in operation.

Before the 2005 abolition of the National Assembly, there were two additional powers—the National Assembly and the President—in addition to the five-power government scheme, which effactually resulted in 21 relationships among the powers governed by the Constitution. As previously explained, the National Assembly existed to elect the President and to amend the Constitution, while the President served as a ceremonial head under the parliamentary system. Even after the abolition of the National Assembly, however, potential conflicts between or among five Yuans plus the President may and do still arise, and typically require judicial intervention.

For example, in *JY Interpretation No 76*, the Constitutional Court faced the controversy of identifying the legislative branch(es) of the ROC government. The Constitution stipulated that the Legislative Yuan should be the highest legislative organ; however, the National Assembly and the Control Yuan separately exerted their constitutional competences similar to powers exercised by legislative bodies under Western constitutional systems. Like the Legislative Yuan, which is composed of elected national representatives, the National Assembly was directly elected by the ROC citizens to exercise its powers to elect the President and to amend the Constitution. The Control Yuan, also a citizen-elected body, had investigatory, impeachment, and consent powers over key government posts. Eventually the Constitutional Court decided to appease all three branches, holding that the National Assembly, the Legislative Yuan and the Control Yuan, 'from the perspective of the nature of their statuses and functions in the Constitution, should all be considered as equivalent to the parliaments of democratic nations'. The Legislative Yuan's position as Taiwan's only true legislative branch was not ultimately affirmed until the constitutional revisions of the 1990s, which made incremental adjustments and reductions to the composition and powers of the National Assembly and the Control Yuan.

B. The Road to Semi-Presidentialism

Not surprisingly, the choice of the ideal government system and its composition have been at the forefront of issues hotly debated by the framers of the ROC Constitution for the new Republic. One of the key questions that plagued the drafters of the Constitution soon after the emperor-based system was discarded, and which continues to puzzle the reformers to this day, is whether the new Republic would operate better as a parliamentary system or a presidential system. Yet in the seemingly perpetual struggle to draft and reform the Constitution since the Republic's beginning, issues regarding Taiwan's ideal government structure were mingled in the flux of borrowed Western ideas, partisan interests and personal ambition, without a clearly defined structure emerging from the fray. Still, many believe that the structure as penned in the Constitution is most nearly a parliamentary system with mixed elements, including a not-so-ceremonial presidency and tripartite parliamentary institutions—the National Assembly, the Legislative Yuan and the Control Yuan. This built-in ambiguity has given rise to quite a few political manipulations within and transcending the constitutional context.

One such conflict that arose from the ambiguity of Taiwan's government structure occurred soon after the landmark *JY Interpretation No 261*, when a new legislature emerged on the political horizon which created an unexpected constitutional controversy. Originally based on a parliamentary system, the ROC Constitution stipulated that the premier, the President of the Executive Yuan, is accountable to the Legislative Yuan. Yet, since the most recently elected legislature was inaugurated in 1948, it was not clear whether the premier should submit his or her resignation to the President when the newly elected legislators were sworn in office. The Constitutional Court answered in the affirmative in *JY Interpretation No 387*, stating that 'since the premier had to receive consent from and be politically accountable to the Legislative Yuan, the premier had to resign before the first session of each new Legislative Yuan so as to fulfil the doctrine of government by the people and his or her political accountability'. However, one dissenting opinion contended that 'the issue cannot be solved before the type of government system is defined'.[2]

Though the Office of the President was initially designated as a ceremonial head, it had become a powerful institution during the period of authoritarian rule. However, when the Legislative Yuan became a full-fledged representative body in 1992, political conflicts began to erupt between the President and the Legislative Yuan. The Legislative Yuan began to challenge the increasingly powerful President's legitimacy. With such a strong presidency—especially after the strongman Chiang Kai-shek—the idea of formally establishing a presidential system and having a direct presidential election was at the forefront of the political agenda, though it ultimately took two rounds of constitutional revision (in 1992 and 1994) to initiate a full-fledged, direct presidential election. Yet, even this and the other changes implemented through these rounds of revision did not clear up the ambiguity of Taiwan's governmental structure, nor did they resolve the debate regarding the proper framework—parliamentary or presidential system.

---

[2] Dissenting opinion of Justice Geng Wu, *JY Interpretation No 387* (1995).

In the first direct presidential election, held in 1996, then-premier Lien Chan was on the same ticket as the incumbent President, Lee Teng-hui. The Lee-Lien ticket won by a landslide. Soon after the inauguration of the new President and Vice-President, the premier's role became the subject of controversy. Newly elected President Lee Teng-hui refused to appoint a new premier for parliamentary approval, insisting that Vice-President Lien Chan could simultaneously serve as both Vice-President and premier. This proposition was met with a strong outcry from the parliamentary opposition. Premier Lien (also the Vice-President Lien) was designated, through legislative resolution, as *persona non grata* in the Legislative Yuan, and was not even allowed to enter the parliamentary floor for debates. This situation served as the backdrop for the 1997 constitutional revision and led to the removal of legislative approval for the premier. Owing in part to this and other revisions, a semi-presidential system of government has evolved in Taiwan.

II. THE EVOLVING PRESIDENCY

After the 1911 revolution, the presidency was essentially a new concept to the Chinese citizens. Political leaders desired a strong President, while ordinary citizens abhorred the idea, due to its resemblance to a discarded emperor. Thus, the constitutional embodiment of the presidency over the last six decades in Taiwan has been nothing short of evolutionary. The Constitution had originally intended the President of the Republic to perform largely ceremonial roles as a head of state, while leaving most of the actual powers to the premier and the cabinet (called the Executive Yuan). However, with the Chinese Civil War and subsequent imposition of martial law, the President was vested, through the Temporary Provisions to the Constitution, with comprehensive and substantial power over the military as well as over civil administrative matters.[3] These grants of power, in large measure, paved the way for the expansion of presidential power ever since.

The constitutional revisions of the 1990s made significant changes to the government system by, among other measures, codifying into

---

[3] For a discussion of the enactment of the 1948 Temporary Provisions and their subsequent revision prior to the lifting of the Martial Law Decree and democratisation, see ch 2.

the Constitution the President's expanded powers exercised during the period of authoritarian rule. Although these revisions changed the government system from quasi-parliamentary to semi-presidential, key institutional features embodied in a parliamentary system remained intact. This led to the carry-over of a considerable amount of institutional ambiguity, which ultimately bred a series of constitutional controversies, particularly during the period immediately following the first regime change from the KMT to the DPP, in 2000. As expected, the judiciary played an important role in strategically adjudicating these disputes.

A. The Changing Role and Extensive Powers of the President

Though the framers of the 1947 ROC Constitution envisaged a parliamentary system, they felt the need to simultaneously provide for the Office of the President for the new Republic. With this compromise, the President of the Republic was designated as the ceremonial head of state while the President of the Executive Yuan, the premier, served as the head of government, accountable to the Legislative Yuan. However, as a result of residual institutional ambiguity, the reformers ultimately conferred substantial power upon the presidency.

The President's ceremonial powers include the power to confer honours and decorations,[4] and to issue and promulgate laws and regulations made by concerned authorities.[5] As stated above, the President also enjoys certain powers that appear ceremonial, yet, in practice, allow the President to wield substantial authority. For instance, the President may appoint and remove civil and military officials,[6] and grant amnesty, pardons, remission of sentences and restitution of civil rights.[7] In addition, the President serves as the Commander in Chief of the armed forces[8] and may declare martial law with the approval of the Legislative Yuan.[9] Finally, the President may enter into treaties and international agreements and may declare war.[10]

---

[4] Art 42 Constitution of the Republic of China (1947).
[5] Arts 37 and 72 Constitution of the Republic of China (1947).
[6] Art 41 Constitution of the Republic of China (1947).
[7] Art 40 Constitution of the Republic of China (1947).
[8] Art 36 Constitution of the Republic of China (1947).
[9] Art 39 Constitution of the Republic of China (1947).
[10] Arts 35 and 38 Constitution of the Republic of China (1947).

Chiang Kai-shek, shortly after serving his first presidential term and finding the ceremonial presidency unappealing, decided to expand the presidential powers via constitutional and political means. Through the enactment and subsequent revisions of the Temporary Provisions, presidential powers were expanded substantially under Chiang Kai-shek from the original design. Further, President Chiang was able to consolidate power through both the KMT's party apparatus and military force. As a result, both of the Chiang presidencies—Chiang Kai-shek and his son Chiang Ching-kuo—expanded presidential powers well beyond those originally found in the Constitution.

Notably, the Constitution also stipulates that the President serve as an intermediary between the Executive and Legislative Yuans. According to the Constitution as amended, should the Executive Yuan deem a statutory, budgetary or treaty bill passed by the Legislative Yuan difficult to execute, the Executive Yuan may, with the approval of the President of the Republic and within 10 days after its transmission to the Executive Yuan, remit the bill to the Legislative Yuan for reconsideration. Within 15 days of such a request, the Legislative Yuan must convene and reach a resolution.[11] Should the Legislative Yuan not reach a resolution within the prescribed period, the original bill is declared invalid. Should more than one half of the total legislative members uphold the original bill, however, the premier shall immediately ratify the bill.[12] In this process of checks and balances between the executive and legislative powers, the role of the President remains pivotal. Without his or her approval, the premier would be unable to exercise countermeasures against the Legislative Yuan. Although some have interpreted this intermediate role as largely ceremonial, the majority has viewed it as a substantive and influential presidential power. Regardless whether one views the power as one of form or function, however, the power to serve as gatekeeper or backstop has significantly transformed the structure of executive powers and the relationship between the President and the premier.

With the end of the two Chiang presidencies in the late 1980s and the suspension of the Temporary Provisions in the early 1990s, previously

---

[11] Should the Legislative Yuan be in recess, it shall convene of its own accord within seven days and reach a resolution within 15 days after the session begins.

[12] Art 3(3) Additional Articles to the Constitution of the Republic of China (2005).

expanded presidential powers were expected to be revoked or reshaped by subsequent constitutional revision. However, not only were the powers as expanded under the Temporary Provisions not revoked, they were, in fact, codified and often even further expanded in later revision cycles. Thus, in spite of speculation to the contrary, presidential powers that were expanded throughout the periods of authoritarian rule and democratic transition were ultimately codified in the years that followed.

As noted in chapter 2,[13] direct election of the President and Vice-President from the citizens of the ROC's 'free area', namely Taiwan, was established by the 1994 constitutional revision. This measure was enacted to grant the President democratic legitimacy, and to establish, with Taiwan's democratically elected legislature, a dual democracy. The 1994 revision also extended the President's power by removing the requirement for presidential appointments and dissolution of the Legislative Yuan to be approved by the premier. In addition, the 1997 constitutional revision further augmented presidential powers by removing the requirement of legislative consent to the President's appointment of the premier.[14] Since this revision, the premier has served at the will of the President and gradually become a Chief Executive Officer under the President. Though not all of the expanded presidential powers were stipulated in the Additional Articles, most of the additional powers that previously existed were, in fact, confirmed by the Constitutional Court. In *JY Interpretation No 627*, the Constitutional Court stated: '[S]ubject to the scope of his executive powers granted by the Constitution and the Amendments to the Constitution, the President is the highest executive officer and has a duty to preserve national security and national interests.'[15] Evidently, after the incremental changes made to the presidency through the constitutional revisions, the President under the ROC Constitution was no longer a ceremonial head in a parliamentary system as the drafters initially intended, but rather was gradually transformed into a Chief Executive under a semi-presidential system.

---

[13] For the discussions of constitutional revisions related to direct presidential elections, see ch 2.

[14] This can be compared with Art 55 of the ROC Constitution, which provides that the premier shall be nominated and, with the consent of the Legislative Yuan, appointed by the President of the Republic.

[15] Art 3(2) of the Additional Articles reads: 'The President of the Executive Yuan shall be appointed by the President.' *JY Interpretation No 627* (2007), reasoning para 10.

B. National Security Council and Cross-Strait Policy

By imposing the Temporary Provisions in 1948 and subsequent constitutional amendments, Chiang Kai-shek expanded presidential powers by establishing the National Security Council (NSC) in the Presidential Office, among other changes.

The NSC has since aided the President in exercising his powers. The organisation and authority of the NSC was basically an extension of the National Defence Conference (NDC), which was established by Chiang Kai-shek in 1952 and became operational in 1954. The NDC reviewed all foreign and domestic affairs, including the economy, finance, education, culture and transportation plans and measures, if such measures were deemed by the President or premier to have 'a major national defence or military affairs component'. Moreover, the NDC reviewed the Executive Yuan's budget for the central government prior to its submission to the Legislative Yuan for resolution.

In March 1966, the National Assembly revised the Temporary Provisions to authorise the President to 'establish organs for mobilisation to suppress the Communist rebellion, to determine policies relating to the period of mobilisation and to deal with battlefield politics'. Soon after a small preparatory group drafted an organisational programme, the President promulgated 'the Organizational Outline for a National Security Council during the Period of National Mobilisation in Suppression of Communist Rebellion' in 1967, thereby marking the official establishment of the NSC. Prior to the termination of the Temporary Provisions in 1991, the NSC had functionally replaced the cabinet, the Executive Yuan, and served as the key administrative arm of the President. Ironically, these atypical constitutional arrangements were retained even after the termination of the Temporary Provisions in 1991, and were formally incorporated in the Additional Articles that were appended to the Constitution in 1994.[16]

The President serves as the chair of the NSC, which comprises other members including the Vice-President, presidential office chief of staff, the President's chief military aide, chairman and vice-chairman of the

---

[16] Art 2(4) Additional Articles to the Constitution of the Republic of China (1994): 'To determine major policies for national security, the President may establish a national security council and a subsidiary national security bureau. The organization of the said organs shall be stipulated by law.'

strategic advisory committee, the premier and vice-premier, minister of national defence, minister of foreign affairs, minister of economic affairs, minister of finance, chief of the general staff, NSC secretary-general, and any other personnel designated by the President. Through his control over the NSC, the President can develop and promote policies that relate to national security. Due in part to the breadth of offices and organisations represented in its membership, the NSC has become a powerful institution, known as the 'Upper Executive Yuan', surpassing the Executive Yuan in terms of its perceived influence and power.[17]

In addition to the fact that its members represent from key ministries and institutions, the NSC draws power from the definition of 'national security' itself and the NSC's exercise of control over all things related to national security. A loose definition of national security could result in the NSC's ability to claim dominion over nearly every government function. For instance, in 2014, the NSC addressed loosely defined 'national security issues' ranging from food safety to the Ebola outbreak—crises that tended to fall under the auspices of various ministries which are supervised by the premier. Yet, by labelling those issues as relevant to national security, the President wrested control over those issues. More importantly, once a policy is categorised as a matter of national security, the legislature no longer has any control over the matter, since it is the premier's decisions, not the President's, that are subject to the Legislative Yuan's review.

While the President may easily draw extra-constitutional powers from the 'black box' of national security, he or she may also extend the presidential powers through actions related to cross-Strait matters and policy. Article 11 of the Additional Articles to the Constitution provides that 'Rights and obligations between the people of the Chinese mainland area and those of the free area, and the disposition of other related affairs, may be specified by law'. The current law is the Act Governing Relations between the People of the Taiwan Area and the Mainland Area (the Cross-Strait Act) which, among other things, mandates the establishment of the Mainland Affairs Council, responsible for comprehensive research, planning, review, co-ordination of Mainland policies and affairs, and partial implementation of inter-ministerial programmes. The Act also mandates the establishment of

---

[17] National Security Council, Encyclopedia of Taiwan, available at taiwanpedia. culture.tw/en/content?ID=3855.

a private body, the Straits Exchange Foundation, to handle cross-Strait negotiations, exchanges and service affairs authorised by the public authority.

According to the Cross-Strait Act, the Legislative Yuan is to monitor cross-Strait policies and engagements, and the Mainland Affairs Council, under the Executive Yuan, is to formulate and oversee the implementation of cross-Strait policies. However, the President has, in fact, exercised strong leadership on such matters through both NSC meetings and via direct instruction to various ministries (and even to the premier). This phenomenon can be highlighted in the Economic Cooperation Framework Agreement (ECFA), which was negotiated and enacted in 2010 between China and Taiwan. Negotiations and implementation were driven in large part by the President through the NSC, notwithstanding the Cross-Strait Act's delegation of power over such affairs to the Legislative and Executive Yuans.

C. Presidential Elections, Powers and Political Divisions

The semi-presidential system as it developed in Taiwan's democratic context is prone to contentious partisan confrontations. The President is often involved in controversy over issues such as transitional justice, political parties, the contested powers and jurisdictions of national and local governments, and national identity. Such unyielding partisan differences are intensified where tremendous political stakes further entrench the political divisions between competing political parties in winner-take-all presidential elections. Further, the constitutional ambiguity surrounding presidential powers only exacerbates the tension. Although constitutional revisions resulted in direct presidential elections, the President's role and relationship with the premier and the Legislative Yuan remain ambiguous, even after several rounds of incremental constitutional revisions that have changed Taiwan's form of government from a parliamentary system to a semi-presidential system.

Political conflicts that arose in times during which the branches of government were controlled by a heterogeneous mix of political parties were further intensified. This scenario led to many serious constitutional disputes regarding not only presidential powers and the separation of powers, but also disputes borne of political divisions either reflecting or stemming from historical ethnic or social cleavage.

In 2000, when the DPP won the presidency but the KMT enjoyed a majority in parliament, heightened partisan politics resulted in many politically charged issues surrounding the President's role—issues ripe for resolution by the Constitutional Court, such as issues over disputes regarding presidential elections, the exercise of presidential powers and the separation of powers, and presidential involvement in conflicts between national and local governments.

For example, on the eve of the 2004 presidential election, there was an unsuccessful yet controversial assassination attempt on incumbent President Chen Shui-bian, who was seeking re-election. The opposition party, the KMT, suspected Chen of orchestrating the incident to draw voter sympathy and electoral support. The KMT-controlled legislative majority quickly passed a special law creating an investigative commission, whose membership consisted mostly of extremely partisan members of the KMT. According to this special law, the commission's findings could overrule judicial decisions relating to electoral disputes. The DPP, contending that the special commission was unconstitutional, engaged in a parliamentary fight with the KMT and referred the issue to the Constitutional Court. In *JY Interpretation No 585*, the Court stated that establishing a special commission, if established as part of parliament's powers of conducting a parliamentary investigation, was within the legislative ambit and was, therefore, constitutional. However, the Court noted that given its status as a parliamentary organ, the special commission could neither command nor supervise prosecutors or other judicial personnel during the course of its investigation, and further, the commission's findings on the assassination attempt could not result in the revocation of judicial decisions. In the Constitutional Court's view, while the parliamentary investigation could proceed, the certification of an official recount and the resolution by the lower courts and confirmation by the Supreme Court would officially resolve the controversy over the 2004 presidential election. The Court held that no findings by a subsequent parliamentary investigation would affect these results. Though the KMT legislative majority was very dissatisfied with the Constitutional Court's decision, it accepted the ruling and revised the law to allow the commission to work within its narrowly defined jurisdiction.

In a divided government, in which no single party controlled the executive and legislative branches, the President was often under intense scrutiny. *JY Interpretation No 627* illustrates a case in which the

Constitutional Court circumvented presidential immunity and privilege under certain circumstances during an active criminal investigation. In 2006, during his second term in office, President Chen faced an immense political crisis. In 2006, the President and members of his family were accused by muckrakers of various corrupt acts. Protests ensued, which lasted for months in front of presidential buildings, with protesters demanding President Chen's resignation. Prosecutors soon launched investigations into the case. Yet the investigation was mired by questions of its constitutional legitimacy, since Article 52 of the Constitution grants the President immunity from criminal investigation. As a result, the investigation was redirected toward the First Lady, who was suspected of embezzlement regarding a special presidential fund that provides for the President's undisclosed activities concerning national security and diplomacy.

The investigation resulted in embezzlement charges against the First Lady. President Chen, though not formally charged, was indicated as an accomplice in the prosecutorial motion. President Chen questioned the prosecution's constitutionality, arguing that prosecution, even against his wife, should have been suspended due to his constitutionally accorded immunity, and that the disclosure of details regarding the special fund in the prosecution's motion violated presidential privilege. Eventually the Constitutional Court decided in *JY Interpretation No 627* that 'presidential criminal immunity does not extend to the evidentiary investigation and preservation directed at the president for a criminal case involving another person' and that 'if, as a result, the president is suspected of having committed a crime, necessary evidentiary preservation may still be conducted although no investigation may be commenced against the president, regarding him as a suspect or defendant'. While the Court seemingly green-lighted the prosecutorial motion, it simultaneously cautioned the prosecution to take all necessary measures to prevent presidential esteem and authority from being undermined.

Also, the President's policy-fuelled aspirations and actions must often weather the political storm in a contentious polity. *JY Interpretations No 520* involved the President's role in a constitutional controversy over the suspension of a nuclear power plant installation. This controversy arose when President Chen suspended the installation of the fourth nuclear power plant initiated during the KMT Administration, though the plant's utility had been debated for years prior to the suspension. After six months of assessment, President Chen announced the decision to suspend the construction of the fourth nuclear power plant. In response, the KMT legislature filibustered nearly every government budget proposal and piece of legislation. The KMT argued that the decision-making power regarding the construction of nuclear power plants fell within the ambit of the legislature, to which the premier was accountable, and blamed the President for constitutional violations—even calling for his impeachment and recall. This controversy was compounded by the fact that, although the constitutional revisions of the 1990s stipulated presidential election by popular vote and allowed the President to appoint the premier without legislative approval, they did not provide guidance concerning the relationship among the President, the premier and the Legislative Yuan. The Executive Yuan petitioned the Constitutional Court for resolution, and in *JY Interpretation No 520*, though the Court did not specify whether the government system was parliamentary or presidential, it stated that, once elected, the President 'may change previously existing policies or orientation not necessarily consistent with his political views'. However, the Court also ruled that the Legislative Yuan maintained co-decisional power over major government policies. As a result, the Court directed the premier to report to the Legislative Yuan and explain the decision to cancel the plant construction, and compelled the legislature to be receptive to the premier's rationale for the decision and to formulate a mutually agreeable policy solution. Finally, pursuant to the Court's ruling, the Executive and Legislative Yuans issued a joint declaration, affirming the long-term goal of a nuclear-free homeland while agreeing that construction of the fourth plant should resume. The declaration's concept of a nuclear-free homeland was eventually codified,[18] and the installation of the fourth nuclear power plant remains a politically divisive issue in Taiwan.

III. THE EXECUTIVE YUAN: THE PREMIER AND EXECUTIVE OVERSIGHT

According to the Constitution, the Executive Yuan is the highest administrative organ of the State,[19] and the President of the Executive Yuan, the premier, is the head of the government, with paramount

---

[18] Art 23 Basic Law of the Environment.
[19] Art 53 Constitution of the Republic of China (1947).

decision-making power though still accountable to the Legislative Yuan. Following constitutional revisions with a slant toward expanding the President's power, the premier has functionally become the President's CEO, with the President arguably usurping the Executive Yuan as the most powerful administrative organ of the State. Thus, the roles of the premier and his or her Executive Yuan should be defined in relation to the role of the President.

Despite these embedded constitutional ambiguities, the premier still exerts control over Taiwan's government ministries, save for matters relating to personnel policy, which control is vested with the Examination Yuan under the five-power government scheme.

A. The Premier, Cabinet Meetings and Policy Co-ordination

Since the 1997 constitutional revision, the premier has been appointed by the President without the need for legislative consent, yet the premier is still ultimately accountable to the legislature. According to the Constitution and subsequent revisions, the Executive Yuan has a duty to present a statement of its administrative policies and a report on its administration to the Legislative Yuan. Members of the Legislative Yuan may then question the premier and the ministers and chairmen of commissions of the Executive Yuan. In case of law or policy disagreements, the Executive Yuan may, with presidential approval, request legislative reconsideration of challenged resolutions. If more than half of the legislators uphold the resolution, the premier must abide by it.[20] This system of checks and balances between the Executive and Legislative Yuans reflects the institutional framework of a parliamentary system in which the legislature ultimately decides laws and policies. Yet, as previously mentioned, with the expansion of the President's powers and the emergence from the office's role as a figurehead to a much more substantive role, the premier has been subject to the President's control. In other words, though the premier remains answerable to the Legislative Yuan, he or she is effectively also under the President's thumb.

The premier's paradoxical position stems from the hodgepodge design of a government system borne of political compromises. Such

---

[20] Art 3 Additional Articles to the Constitution of the Republic of China (2005).

institutional inconsistency or ambiguity has typically resulted in political conflict. In some cases, the premier faced an uphill battle executing the President's orders, since the premier would first have to sway the Legislative Yuan. This was especially true between 2000 and 2008, during which time the DPP controlled the Executive Yuan while the KMT held a majority in the Legislative Yuan. A vast majority of such conflicts ultimately required judicial resolution.[21] The nuclear power plant case discussed above is one such instance.

The composition and function of the Executive Yuan are set forth in both the Constitution and the Organic Act of the Executive Yuan. According to the Constitution, the Executive Yuan comprises a President of the Executive Yuan (or premier), a Vice-President (vice-premier), a preset number of ministers and chairmen of commissions, and a specified number of ministers without portfolio (MWPs).[22] These cabinet members are appointed by the President upon the premier's recommendation.[23] Under the Organic Act of the Executive Yuan, the premier manages, directs, and supervises all the subordinate organisations and personnel under the Executive Yuan.[24] The Executive Yuan's decision-making occurs via the Cabinet Meeting (often called the Executive Yuan Council), which is, according to the Constitution, made up of all the cabinet members and is chaired by the premier.[25] Statutory and budgetary bills, bills regarding martial law, amnesty, war declarations, conclusions of peace and treaties, and other important affairs are all discussed at weekly Cabinet Meetings. All of the bills are subsequently submitted to the Legislative Yuan. In addition, matters of common concern to various ministries and commissions are also discussed at Cabinet Meetings.

The Procedural Rules of the Executive Yuan Council dictate the operation of the Executive Yuan Council. Per these rules, decision-making at the Cabinet Meeting is conducted by a single majority vote. However, if the premier or the minister in charge of the discussed affair dissents, the premier may veto a decision of the members of the Cabinet Meeting.[26]

---

[21] W-C Chang et al, *Constitutionalism in Asia: Cases and Materials* (Oxford, Hart Publishing, 2014) 127.

[22] Art 54 Constitution of the Republic of China (1947).

[23] Art 56 Constitution of the Republic of China (1947).

[24] Art 10(1) Organic Act of the Executive Yuan (2012).

[25] Art 58(1) Constitution of the Republic of China (1947).

[26] Art 5 Procedural Rules of Executive Yuan Council (2011).

In addition to the Cabinet Meeting, the premier co-ordinates government policies through MWPs and co-ordinative councils. The Constitution specifies that there are a number of MWPs in the Executive Yuan, and the Organic Act of the Executive Yuan designates interministerial policy co-ordination as the MWPs' major function. Often, the premier co-ordinates and oversees policies through the designation of the responsible MWP on the matters. Also, co-ordinative councils, some of which are chaired by an MWP, assist the premier in policy co-ordination, review and evaluation, aiming at executive oversight for government integrity and efficiency. The foremost example of such a council is the National Development Council, which is responsible for innovation and policy co-ordination within the Executive Yuan.

B. Ministries and Agencies

The Constitution provides only that the organisation of the Executive Yuan shall be prescribed by law, leaving the details of the Cabinet's composition open to legislative determination.[27] Therefore, the Legislative Yuan exercises a great deal of control over the structure and make-up of the Executive Yuan's various ministries. For a long time, the Organic Act of the Executive Yuan fixed the cabinet at eight ministries, two commissions, a Directorate-General of Budget, Accounting and Statistics, and five to seven MWPs. The eight ministries were the Ministry of the Interior, Ministry of Foreign Affairs, Ministry of National Defence, Ministry of Finance, Ministry of Education, Ministry of Justice, Ministry of Economic Affairs, and Ministry of Transportation and Communications. The two commissions were the Overseas Compatriot Affairs Commission and the Mongolian and Tibetan Affairs Commission.

Despite this rather rigid legal framework, the law permitted the Executive Yuan discretion to set up cabinet-level organs.[28] To expand the structure of the government and meet growing societal demands, the Executive Yuan created 19 such entities, including the Council of Agriculture, Council of Labour Affairs, Financial Supervisory

---

[27] Art 61 Constitution of the Republic of China (1947).
[28] Art 14 Organic Act of the Executive Yuan (1947).

Commission, Mainland Affairs Council, National Youth Commission, Veterans Affairs Council and Atomic Energy Council, among others. Altogether the Executive Yuan consisted of 37 cabinet-level organs. Governmental organisation was confusing and fostered inefficiency, due in part to the sheer number of composite parts, coupled with the fact that the terms 'commission' and 'council' were used loosely and without a consistent organising principle.

To resolve such organisational chaos, the Constitution was further revised in an effort to loosen the Legislative Yuan's tight control over government organisation. The Additional Articles stipulate that the powers, procedures of establishment, and total number of personnel of national organisations are subject to statutory standards, and are governed by each organisation's guiding policies and operations.[29]

Meanwhile, more sweeping government reforms were on the horizon. Though it had been on the agenda for years, it took the first regime change, which occurred in 2000, to bring about the first true government reform programme. Four years later, in 2004, the Basic Code Governing Central Administrative Agencies Organisations (Basic Code) was finally enacted, and served as the blueprint for the rearrangement of the central government. Under this law, organisations established in accordance with organic laws or decrees that exercise public authority within the scope of its defined functions were designated 'agencies'. There are three levels of agency whose functions and organisational structure are dictated by law. The Executive Yuan is a first-level agency. Ministries, councils, and commissions are second-level agencies.[30] Departmental agencies set up under ministries, councils or commissions are third-level agencies. The different agencies, even within each level, have different responsibilities. For example, ministries dictate policy and form regulatory authorities, while councils serve mainly co-ordinative functions. The 2004 Basic Code removed a great deal of ambiguity from the structure of the government. Prior to the Basic Code, the term 'commission' could even be used to refer to a cabinet-level ministry. However, following the promulgation of the Basic Code, commissions are clearly defined as independent agencies that act in a collegial manner and independently exercise regulatory functions.

[29]   Art 3 Additional Articles to the Constitution of the Republic of China (2005).
[30]   Arts 3 and 6 Basic Code Governing Central Administrative Agencies Organizations (2004).

Furthermore, in 2010, the Organic Act of the Executive Yuan was revised to clearly define the various types of government agency. Pursuant to the Act, an agency of ministerial level was required to be a line ministry, co-ordinating council or independent regulatory commission. This reorganisation, which occurred from 2012 to 2014, led to a reduction in the number of ministerial-level organisations from 37 to 29. Following this restructuring, the Executive Yuan now consists of 14 ministries, eight councils, three independent commissions and four additional organisations (see Table 3.1).

Table 3.1: The Number of Cabinet-level Organisations before and after the Government Reform

Cabinet-level Organisations before Government Reform (until 2012)	Cabinet-level Organisations after Government Reform (since 2014)
Ministry of the Interior	M1: Ministry of the Interior
Ministry of Foreign Affairs	M2: Ministry of Foreign Affairs
Ministry of National Defence	M3: Ministry of National Defence
Ministry of Finance	M4: Ministry of Finance
Ministry of Education	M5: Ministry of Education
Ministry of Justice	M6: Ministry of Justice
Ministry of Economic Affairs	M7: Ministry of Economic Affairs
Ministry of Transportation and	and Energy
Communications	M8: Ministry of Transportation and
	Construction
Mongolian and Tibetan Affairs	M9: Ministry of Culture
Commission	M10: Ministry of Health and Welfare
Overseas Compatriot Affairs	M11: Ministry of Labour
Commission	M12: Ministry of Science and
	Technology
Veterans Affairs Council	M13: Ministry of Environment and
Mainland Affairs Council	Natural Resources
Fair Trade Commission	M14: Ministry of Agriculture
Council of Indigenous Peoples	
Hakka Affairs Council	C1: Overseas Compatriot Affairs
Financial Supervisory Commission	Council
Central Election Commission	C2: Veterans Affairs Council
National Communications	C3: Mainland Affairs Council
Commission	C4: Council of Indigenous Peoples

(continued)

Table 3.1: *(Continued)*

Cabinet-level Organisations before Government Reform (until 2012)	Cabinet-level Organisations after Government Reform (since 2014)
Co-ordination Council for North American Affairs	C5: Hakka Affairs Council
National Science Council	C6: Financial Supervisory Commission
Council of Agriculture	C7: National Development Council
Council of Labour Affairs	C8: Ocean Affairs Council
Council for Economic Planning and Development	
Research, Development and Evaluation Commission	I1: Fair Trade Commission
Atomic Energy Council	I2: Central Election Commission
Public Construction Commission	I3: National Communications Commission
National Youth Commission	
Council for Cultural Affairs	A1: Directorate-General of Budget, Accounting and Statistics
Sports Affairs Council	A2: Directorate-General of Personnel Administration
Consumer Protection Committee	A3: Central Bank
Aviation Safety Council	A4: National Palace Museum
Department of Health	
Environmental Protection Administration	
Coast Guard Administration	
Government Information Office	
Central Personnel Administration	
Directorate-General of Budget, Accounting and Statistics	

M: Ministries; C: Councils; I: Independent commissions; A: Additional organisations

i. The 14 Ministries

As part of an effort to empower the traditional eight ministries in response to the changing nature of traditional administrative affairs, the Ministry of Economic Affairs absorbed Energy Affairs, and the Ministry of Transportation absorbed Construction. In response to mounting challenges, various organs were reorganised and elevated to form such new ministries as the Ministry of Culture, Ministry of Health and Welfare, Ministry of Labour, Ministry of Science and Technology, Ministry of Environment and Natural Resources, and Ministry of Agriculture. In all, six ministries were added to the original eight to fill voids that previously existed in various areas of governmental policy. The institutional reorganisation of these new ministries marks the shift in government focus from overarching managerial concerns to issue-specific designations in the context of both democratic transition and social change.

ii. The Eight Co-ordinative Councils

Each council covers an area of policy requiring inter-ministerial coordination. Either representation-oriented or special-mission tasked, each council was strengthened according to its respective capacity to co-ordinate policy. For instance, the National Development Council consolidates comprehensive powers in policy planning and evaluation for social and economic developments. In contrast to special-mission tasked councils such as the National Development Council, whose establishment met with little resistance, representation-oriented councils, established to serve designated sectors of the population and special interest groups, have been more controversial. Examples of such councils include the Overseas Compatriot Affairs Council for overseas Chinese citizens and compatriots, the Veterans Affairs Council for the veterans, the Council of Indigenous Peoples for the aborigines, and the Hakka Affairs Council for citizens of Hakka descent. Many of these councils were created after the start of democratisation in the 1980s, in response to interest group politics.

iii. The Designated Independent Commissions

Examples of independent commissions that cover designated regulatory areas include the Fair Trade Commission, the Central Election Commission, and the National Communications Commission. The Central Bank was not designated an independent agency, though in light of the global financial crisis, the independence of such institutions and whether, perhaps, it should be created as an independent agency, have been hotly debated. In the aggregate, Taiwan's governmental organisation and reorganisation has been conducive to autochthonous social and political transformation and global convergence.

C. Independent Regulatory Commissions

Creating independent agencies has been a common practice in new democracies, and Taiwan is certainly no exception. Independent agencies under the 2004 Basic Code are created for various purposes such as enhancing technical professionalism, pacifying political confrontation, and boosting administrative efficiency. Above all, they are usually established to ensure that administrative affairs are immune from unduly political intervention and that policies are implemented in a more professional, neutral and efficient manner. By design, this commission-type agency conducts its affairs in a collegial manner and exercises its regulatory functions without intervention from other agencies or supervision from the premier.[31]

The concept of independent agencies originated in the United States,[32] but has been introduced and institutionalised in various other legal and political contexts around the world. Outside the United States, independent regulatory commissions are typically created to foster greater accountability in transitional politics, or to bring about internal co-ordination in response to global convergence.[33] However, accountability concerns are not completely placated, since independent regulatory commissions are left somewhat unchecked by ordinary administrative organs due to their insulation from oversight and management of the hierarchical administrative bureaucracy. Besides the potential to derogate the administrative unity,[34] challenges inherent in the creation of independent agencies can be nearly insurmountable for a new democracy that lacks a robust and established system of checks and balances, and whose judicial system and civil society are not as ingrained as those of constitutional systems that have operated over many generations.[35]

Taiwan's development of independent regulatory commissions marked a paradigm shift from authoritarian rule to transitional politics.[36]

---

[31] Art 3 Basic Code Governing Central Administrative Agencies Organizations (2004).

[32] See, eg, G Breger and MJ Edles, 'Established by Practice: The Theory and Operation of Independent Federal Agencies' (2000) 52 *Administrative Law Review* 1111.

[33] J-r Yeh, 'Globalization, Government reform and the Paradigm Shift of Administrative Law' (2010) 5 *National Taiwan University Law Review* 113.

[34] J-r Yeh and W-c Chang, 'A Decade of Changing Constitutionalism in Taiwan: Transitional and Transnational Perspectives' in AHY Chen (ed), *Constitutionalism in Asia in the Early Twenty-First Century* (Cambridge, Cambridge University Press, 2014) 161.

[35] J Kornai, B Rothstein, and S Rose-Ackerman (eds), *Creating Social Trust in Post-socialist Transition (Political Evolution and Institutional Change)* (New York, Palgrave Macmillan, 2004).

[36] J-r Yeh, 'Experimenting with Independent Commissions in a New Democracy with a Civil Law Tradition: The Case of Taiwan' in S Rose-Ackerman and P Lindseth (eds), *Comparative Administrative Law* (Northampton, MA, Edward Elgar, 2010) 246–64.

Establishing a 'commission' in charge of certain administrative affairs was not uncharted territory for the ROC government; however, there were notable differences between the commissions created before and after the promulgation of the 2004 Basic Code. As discussed earlier, the Executive Yuan created—through legislative authorisation—a number of organs, including several commissions, which were responsible for important administrative affairs (see Table 3.1). Though the entities created by the Executive Yuan were commissions by name, they lacked the legal and operational independence of the commissions created under the Basic Code. Instead, these commissions were created for such purposes as representation, foreign intervention, political strategy, and expediency. Further, most of them were created for the express political purpose of instilling stricter government control. Examples of such commissions include the Mongolian and Tibetan Affairs Commission and the Overseas Compatriot Affairs Commission. These commissions were created to facilitate the KMT government's attempt to represent 'the entire China'.

In the 1950s and 1960s, special-mission-oriented commissions such as the Council for United States Aid and the Joint Commission on Rural Reconstruction were created to act as bridges for foreign aid. It was not until the 1980s that representation-oriented commissions were created in response to growing social and political demands. That decade brought both a rapidly expanding economy and drastic changes to the nation's social and political dynamics to Taiwan. Demands for health care, environmental protection, consumer protection and social security resulted in a drastic increase in the number of statutes enacted and regulatory agencies formed, including such professional technique-oriented commissions as the Fair Trade Commission, the Financial Supervisory Commission and the Atomic Energy Council. In addition, commissions to deal with sensitive political issues or incorporate social forces were created, including the Mainland Affairs Council, National Youth Commission and Veterans Affairs Council. Although the number of commissions steadily rose during this period, the commissions and councils lacked a consistent or coherent organising principle, which led to cries for an overhaul of governmental organisation.

With the first regime change, which occurred in 2000, the creation of an independent regulatory commission was finally possible. As a long-time opposition party, the DPP placed the issue of government reform at the forefront of its action items upon assuming power, despite the fact that the KMT still held the legislative majority. This led, four years later, to the promulgation of the 2004 Basic Code, which, as discussed above, provided guidelines for the creation of government organisations, thus laying the legal foundation to create a truly independent regulatory commission. Under the 2004 Basic Code, an independent agency is defined as 'a collegial commission that acts independently in accordance with the law and without subject to supervisions of other organs', and is composed of five to seven full-time commissioners with fixed terms, each appointed by the premier, with legislative approval. In addition, the commission cannot comprise more than a certain percentage of members that belong to the same political party (generally 50 per cent).[37]

Established in 2006, the National Communications Commission (NCC) was Taiwan's first ministerial-level independent regulatory commission. The NCC was created first, in large part, as a result of the perceived convergence of radio, television and the Internet, which has prompted governments around the world to undertake or at least explore organisational reform directed at the integration of existing fragmented regulatory units into unified independent regulatory commissions. Communication regulation was of great interest to the prior ruling KMT, but its commitment to free speech—one of the cornerstones of a new democracy—was in doubt.

In Taiwan, the KMT's ownership and operation of the radio, television networks and newspapers presented unique hindrances to regulatory reform, even after the regime change in 2000. These obstacles and the lack of transitional justice in partisan politics led the public to place great hope in the inception of the NCC. The NCC was designated an independent commission in response to increased competition between the political parties, rather than to wall off the commission from intervention by either branch in particular.[38] Yet, the establishment of the NCC triggered intense political confrontations, partisan fights, and a ruling by the Constitutional Court. While both the DPP and the KMT were in favour of the establishment of the NCC, the KMT, which

---

[37] Arts 3 and 21 Basic Code Governing Central Administrative Agencies Organizations (2004). This Act was later amended in 2010: Art 21 was amended so as to allow the independent regulatory commission to be composed of five to eleven members.

[38] Yeh, 'Experimenting with Independent Commissions' 246–64.

enjoyed a majority in the Legislative Yuan, sought to appoint commissioners in proportion to legislative seats of Taiwan's major political parties, leaving the premier with little more than the ceremonial power of appointment from those pools.

In 2005, the Organic Act of the National Communication Commission (the NCC Organic Act) was passed, in spite of the serious political standoff that surrounded it. Amid protests, the commissioners were appointed in accordance with the KMT's partisan formula, since, as a minority party in the Legislative Yuan, the DPP's hands were tied. Though the NCC was formally established in 2006, the controversy surrounding the appointment structure did not end there.

The DPP petitioned the Constitutional Court, challenging the proportional appointment of commissioners. In 2006, the Constitutional Court rendered *JY Interpretation No 613*, holding that the appointment of commissioners as set forth under the NCC Organic Act was unconstitutional, as it effectively deprived the premier of his power to appoint commissioners.[39] The Court reasoned that 'under the principle of administrative unity, the Executive Yuan must be held responsible for the overall performance of all the agencies subordinate to it, including the NCC'. Further, because of the administrative unity principle, the establishment of an independent agency must be regarded as exceptional and can be justified 'only if the purpose of its establishment is indeed to pursue constitutional public interests'. The Court derived the exceptionality aspect of creating independent commissions from the text of the Constitution, the administrative unity principle, and the principles of democracy and accountability. The Court additionally found that the method of selecting and appointing NCC commissioners 'deprive[d] the premier of the power to decide on personnel affairs of the Executive Yuan substantially' and therefore 'violat[ed] the principles of politics of accountability and separation of powers'. Overall, the Court criticised the partisan proportional representation system as cutting against the NCC's intended impartiality and neutrality. Despite finding the practice unconstitutional, the Court did not immediately void the relevant provisions. Rather, the Court declared that these provisions would remain in effect until the earlier of the date of any revision and 31 December 2008. The Court further added that, the

---

[39] *JY Interpretation No 613* (2006).

scheduled nullification of the appointment provisions notwithstanding, 'the legality of any and all acts performed by the NCC will remain unaffected'.

With the release of *JY Interpretation No 613*, many of the DPP leaders urged the NCC commissioners to resign immediately to facilitate prompt legislative action to amend the appointment procedures. However, the chief commissioner of the NCC refused to do so. Instead, he stated that he and his colleagues would continue to serve until January 2008, when the term of the current legislature would expire, and urged the legislature to complete revisions no later than that date. The revised NCC Organic Act was completed near the end of 2007. The revised Act stipulated that the NCC comprise seven members, each of whom is appointed by the premier, with legislative approval, and is appointed to a four-year term. Further, no party may hold a majority of the seats.[40]

Over the course of the next several months, the KMT was victorious in several key elections. In January 2008, the KMT won the first legislative election held under a new constitutionally amended electoral rule. In March, the KMT presidential candidate, Ma Ying-jeou, won the election; he assumed office in May. In August, the premier nominated the NCC's second-term commissioners, easily gaining the approval of the Legislative Yuan, where the KMT held roughly three quarters of the seats.

Though the NCC's independent status following the revisions is a laudable accomplishment, questions remained regarding agency accountability and the true degree of independence from political influence of the other two independent agencies created by the revised Organic Act of the Executive Yuan: the Fair Trade Commission and the Central Election Commission.

IV. GOVERNMENT REFORM

Since the 1990s, government reforms have been focused on changing core government functions and enhancing administrative efficiency for global competitiveness.[41] These reforms call for organisational,

---

[40]   Art 4 NCC Organic Act (2008).
[41]   E Kamarck, *Government Innovation around The World* (JFK School of Government, Harvard University, Occasional Paper, 2003) 5.

operational and procedural changes to establish a government rooted in integrity, competence and quality of performance in discharging public functions.[42] Government reform during times of transitional constitutionalism is as important for cultivating trust among the citizens and strengthening the government's capacity to rule as it is for taking strides toward meeting global governance dynamics.

Both globalisation and democratic transition have pushed Taiwan toward a comprehensive reform of government. Beginning around 2000, Taiwan began to reap the fruits of its labours over years of pushing for sweeping government reform. Goals of this movement included streamlining government function to improve efficiency and facilitating improved public–private partnerships with industry and society. Meanwhile, issues arising from the basic structure of Taiwan's constitutional framework remain unresolved (for example, the Examination Yuan's power over the personnel system).

A. Government Streamlining

While there had been plans for government reform during different stages of Taiwan's democratic development, actual steps toward reform did not occur until the 2000s, when the first regime change occurred. During the 1950s and 1960s, the KMT government occasionally adjusted government organisation by creating special commissions in charge of matters of high political importance. These undertakings primarily served the government by maintaining its legitimacy, strengthening its social control, or strengthening foreign relations.

Since the 1990s, Taiwan has engaged in seven rounds of constitutional reform, but much of the agenda was focused on rearranging constitutional institutions. Though Taiwan's period of democratic transition led to burgeoning constitutional revisions, hollow support for regulatory reform produced few meaningful results.[43] In fact, though the KMT government, succumbing to pressure from the opposition, proffered several proposals to reorganise the central government, none resulted in legislative action.

---

[42] Yeh, 'Globalization', above n 33, 113–41.

[43] J-r Yeh, 'Changing Forces of Constitutional and Regulatory Reform in Taiwan' (1990) 4 *Columbia Journal of Chinese Law* 83.

Although constitutional reform failed to bring about substantial government reform, the constitutional revision of 1997 paved the way for future changes by providing a great deal of flexibility for reorganising central government and by lessening legal restrictions on establishing administrative agencies. Above all, the momentum of democratic transition carried on into 2000, and culminated in the first regime change. Upon assuming office, the DPP, which had long served as the opposition party, offered an ambitious agenda of government reform. President Chen Shui-bian established and chaired a committee on government reform in November 2001. The committee adopted four pivotal goals as its guiding principles for government reform: deregulation, decentralisation, administrative corporatisation, and outsourcing. In 2002, another committee for the implementation of government reform was established in the Executive Yuan and began to push major legislation aimed at government reform. One of the most important action items was enacting the Basic Code, which occurred in 2004 and, as discussed above, provided a design for government organisation. The Basic Code represented the realisation of the constitutionally mandated framework for arranging central government agencies. Government streamlining was deemed the quintessential metric for improving government effectiveness and enhancing flexibility. The Cabinet further proposed several government-restructuring bills to the Legislative Yuan, including amendments to the Organic Act of the Executive Yuan, the Central Government Agency Personnel Quota Act and the Provisional Act for Adjustment of Functions and Organisations of the Executive Yuan.

With a KMT legislative majority, the DPP knew that such an ambitious reform agenda was an uphill battle. Ultimately, the DPP was unable to obtain the necessary support in the Legislative Yuan. Tensions and distrust under the divided government resulted in insurmountable obstacles, and the opportunity to carry out government reform slipped away. In the eight years of DPP rule, few legislative acts aimed at government reform were passed, in spite of the DPP's comprehensive agenda. When the KMT eventually regained control of the Executive Yuan and the presidency in 2008, it was able to push through its own agenda for reform, albeit one of a much smaller scale than the DPP's. The post-reform organisational structure of the Executive Yuan was discussed in the previous section.

B. The Public–Private Partnership

With the global trend towards new governance, the boundary between the government and non-governmental entities—as well as the distinction between public and private entities—has eroded and become blurred.[44] Facing unprecedented global competition, governments must be capable of adjusting their size, capacity, function and focus through various reform programmes.[45] One such adjustment that has become more commonplace is the migration of many formerly public functions to the private sector. Decision-making processes now frequently involve interaction between public and private actors. One result of this blurring between public and private bodies is the government's increased utilisation of civil and social organisations, think tanks, and special interest groups to promulgate regulatory measures, which has resulted in the emergence of a new form of governance.[46]

This phenomenon is not unique to Taiwan. The transformation from developmental to regulatory state has occurred in different forms in many emerging democracies. Overall, in the 1960s and 1970s, modernisation efforts contributed to the formation of a developmental state that favoured economic growth to the rule of law, and social stability to open democracy.[47] In such a developmental state, national development was primarily government-driven.

It is a common government practice in the developmental state to monopolise or exercise major control over businesses that are central to the delivery of public goods in the transportation, water, electricity, social security, education and related sectors. Though private business certainly exists during this period, it is often subject to influence from bureaucrats in an effort to steer growth.[48] Some of the main attributes of a developmental state are development-oriented policies, government enterprises, and close or tightly controlled government–business relationships.[49]

---

[44] Yeh, 'Globalization', above n 33, 130; see also C Harlow and R Rawlings, *Law and Administration* 3rd edn (Cambridge, Cambridge University Press, 2009).

[45] Yeh, 'Globalization', above n 33, 125.

[46] Ibid, 118.

[47] J-r Yeh, 'Democracy-driven Transformation to Regulatory State: the Case of Taiwan' (2008) 3 *National Taiwan University Law Review* 31, 33.

[48] Ziya Öniş, 'The Logic of the Development State' (1991) 24 *Comparative Politics* 109, 111.

[49] Yeh, 'Democracy-driven Transformation', above n 47, 35.

When democratisation leads to organisational and procedural changes in the search for efficiency, legitimacy and accountability, government reform measures are initiated and usually entail changes in the operation of regulatory functions. In a regulatory state, the private sector typically leads development, while the government maintains a free and fair market through legal enforcement.[50] Thus, governance in a regulatory state depends on a more transparent, open and fully participating partnership between the government, the market and society.[51]

To reduce governmental control over industry, liberalising and privatising government monopolies is a typical first step in progressing from a developmental to a regulatory state.[52] Measures such as outsourcing public services, Build-Operate-Transfers (BOTs) and Operate-Transfers (OTs) are usually undertaken to boost efficiency and improve allocation of public assets and resources. These measures also serve to build up new types of public–private partnership and further empower the private sector and civil society.[53]

However, the development of public–private partnerships is not without its share of problems. The transfer of public power into private hands has been challenged as violative of the non-delegation doctrine.[54] Also, the inclusion of interest groups, non-governmental organisations, community leaders and experts in the decision-making process is challenged as violating the neutrality principle by permitting ex parte contacts.[55] The transfer of government functions into private hands is further criticised as surrendering public responsibility.[56] Indeed, government accountability has become a grave concern in the process of outsourcing and privatisation. By redistributing certain government functions into the private sphere or allowing interest groups to participate in decision making, the government may effectively shield itself

---

[50]   Ibid, 40.
[51]   For public and private flow, see AC Aman, 'Globalization, Democracy, and the Need for a New Administrative Law' (2002) 49 *UCLA Law Review* 1687.
[52]   Yeh, 'Globalization', above n 33, 120.
[53]   Ibid, 123.
[54]   See JL Mashaw, RA Merrill and PM Shane, *Administrative Law: The American Public Law System* (Minnesota, West Publishing, 1985) 2–6.
[55]   Yeh, 'Globalization', above n 33, 127.
[56]   See A Blackett, 'Global Governance, Legal Pluralism and the Decentered State: A Labor Law Critique of Codes of Corporate Conduct' (2001) 8 *Indiana Journal of Global Legal Studies* 401.

from political accountability. To avoid such potential pitfalls, transparency and public trust must be firmly in place.

Like other new democracies, Taiwan experienced a stereotypical developmental path from a 'milch cow' base for launching national recovery in the 1950s, through the economic development of the 1970s and 1980s, finally progressing to a period of democratic transition since the 1990s.[57] It was during the period of democratic transition that major legislation directed at procedural and substantive rationality began shaping a regulatory environment that leaned toward increased transparency, participation and deliberation.[58] This formative piece of legislation was the Administrative Procedure Act, enacted in 1999, in which administrative contract was stipulated as one type of administrative action, thus paving the way for the government to initiate various mechanisms to foster public–private partnerships. The 2005 Government Information Disclosure Act further increased the level of transparency in the government's decision-making process.

The BOT mechanism has been widely utilised in Taiwan, especially for undertaking public construction projects, because it encourages the private sector's participation and direct investment in long-term governmental infrastructure projects. Implementing BOT projects has not only forced the government to examine and modify its existing legal and administrative public contract framework, but also challenged both the public and private sectors to learn to co-operate in a highly dynamic administrative and legal environment—co-operation illustrated by the following examples.

The Taiwan High Speed Rail (THSR) is the biggest BOT project, and was initiated by the Law for Encouraging Private Sector Participation in Transportation Construction in 1996. The THSR union acquired the right to negotiate with the government by offering terms of 'zero government capital'. The government awarded the union the contract in June 1996; however, many controversies occurred in the process of fulfilling this contract. In 2005, the THSR announced that the launch of the service would be delayed for one year as a result of construction

---

[57] J-r Yeh, 'Institutional Capacity-Building toward Sustainable Development: Taiwan's Environmental Protection in the Climate of Economic Development and Political Liberalization' (1996) 6 *Duke Journal of Comparative and International Law* 229, 233–35.

[58] Yeh, 'Democracy-driven Transformation', above n 47, 34.

delays, further citing fundraising difficulties, which have led them to seek government aid on several occasions. Despite public criticism that the THSR was a BOT project and should not involve funds from the government or taxpayers, the government infused roughly NT$12.5 billion into the project through state-run enterprises. The THSR began operation in 2007, but has been facing financial crises ever since. Ultimately, the government elected to keep the THSR operational and profitable by agreeing to refinance the terms of its loans.

The Electronic Toll Collection (ETC) system is another example of a controversial BOT project.[59] BOT funded the ETC project to provide a speedy toll system for road users. Though the project had previously been stalled, upon the DPP's loss of control to the KMT in 2008, the KMT again renewed efforts to proceed with the BOT system and signed a contract with Far Eastern Electronic Toll Collection Co. (FETC). After more than a decade since the plan's inception, the ETC was finally launched in 2014, and brought with it continued controversy. Bribery, lawsuits, and accusations of collusion between the company and the government have overshadowed the ETC and its services.[60] The government also faced intense public criticism due to an insufficient number of users and overpriced installation fees. Above all, the BOT model has generated concern regarding the FETC's windfall from the project. Besides reaping a staggering NT$200 million (US$6.6 million) in profits, the company was also spared a penalty of more than NT$220 million in 2012 for failing to reach a 60 per cent ETC usage rate, after the government attested to the company's efforts to find a solution. Further, the company later failed to achieve a subsequent benchmark ETC usage rate of 70 per cent, but refused to pay the contractually stipulated NT$440 million penalty. Despite the system's poor quality and usage statistics, the government continued to pay the company NT$2 billion each year under the contract.

Worse still, the Supreme Administrative Court approved a lower court's ruling that the public selection process was flawed and voided the decision by the selection committee in commissioning FETC to set up the system for the Taiwan Freeway Bureau. The embattled government neither anticipated nor endorsed the decision. Still, by focusing more on

[59] See www.Taipeitimes.Com/News/Editorials/Archives/2014/01/12/2003581095.
[60] See Vulcanpost.Com/3696/Taiwan-Bids-Goodbye-To-Its-Toll-Booth-System-Amidst-Protest-From-Locals/.

procedural, rather than substantive, errors in the selection process, the decision afforded the government the opportunity to correct its errors by reopening the process. As the media speculated, the Court did not reopen the selection process to choose from the rival companies, but rather directed the government and the contractor on the project going forward, thus defusing the potential for a political crisis. Finally, as the government and the contractor struggled to implement the Court's improvements to the ETC system, more flaws were found, resulting in a protest that called for a national boycott of the eTag system, urging over 5 million eTag users to withdraw from the programme to force the government to end its co-operation with FETC. The company, while promising to fix the errors as soon as possible, did not show much sincerity as it refused to disclose the system's errors and asserted that termination of the contract and a complete overhaul of the system were unnecessary. Nevertheless, after a painstakingly long and drawn-out process, the ETC system seems to be functioning well.

These BOT controversies highlight several difficult challenges brought by reform initiatives such as outsourcing or privatisation of public services. The concerns regarding the capacity of private business and government accountability cannot be overstated. These challenges reflect the fact that government reform aimed at increasing efficiency through public–private partnerships continues to beget institutional capacity building in both the public and private sectors to foster a more transparent and trustworthy environment.

C. The Examination Yuan and the Civil Service

The constitutional revisions of the 1990s made sweeping constitutional changes, yet made only relatively few changes to the structure of the ROC government. Since roughly 2000, significantly more government reforms have occurred, yet the bureaucratic system still confronts major challenges. One of the most significant problems is that the Examination Yuan's sector of responsibility intersects with the policy-making and management sectors of the civil service—an integral part of the Executive Yuan. As previously mentioned, a constitutionally mandated branch in charge of the public personnel system is unique to Taiwan. The idea, drawn from Chinese tradition, was established by Sun Yat-sen. The Chinese custom of a public servant recruitment system can be dated back to the Tang Dynasty (AD 618–907), when intellectuals joined the government service via fair competition through imperial examinations. Since then, staffing through open and fair examinations has become a feature of the Chinese political system.

The ROC adopted such civil service examinations, similar to those that originate from the imperial examinations in ancient Chinese dynasties, to achieve an effective, rational public administration that is based on a merit system. Under the ROC Constitution, the Examination Yuan was formally established to oversee the national examinations, recruit public functionaries, and manage the personnel system. Yet, this organ's history predates even that of the Constitution itself. In 1930, before the 1947 Constitution was drafted, the Examination Yuan had already been established to carry out largely the same functions set forth in the Constitution, laying the foundation for subsequent civil service development.

The Constitution stipulates that the Examination Yuan is the highest examination organ of the State and is in charge of matters relating to examination, employment, registration, performance rating, salary scales, promotion and transfer, security of tenure, commendation, pecuniary aid in cases of death, retirement and old age pension for civil servants.[61] Unlike more traditional separation-of-powers arrangements in which the executive branch exerts complete power over the bureaucratic system, the ROC Constitution delegates such powers to the Examination Yuan, effectively splitting the management of the civil service from the Executive Yuan. Even after several constitutional revisions between 1991 and 2005, the Examination Yuan remains Taiwan's highest examination body.[62]

The Examination Yuan's structure nearly parallels that of the Executive Yuan. The Examination Yuan has a President, a Vice-President, and 19 members, all of whom are special appointees, nominated by the President with legislative approval. Upon confirmation by the Legislative Yuan, these members serve six-year terms. They deliberate all policies and major related issues, and make resolutions at Examination Yuan Council meetings. In addition to the main body, the Examination

---

[61] Art 83 Constitution of the Republic of China (1947).
[62] Art 6 Additional Articles to the Constitution of the Republic of China (2005).

Yuan has four subordinate agencies—the Ministry of Examination, the Ministry of the Civil Service, the Civil Service Protection and Training Commission and the Public Service Pension Fund Supervisory Board.

According to the Organic Provisions of the Central Personnel Administration under the Executive Yuan, the Examination Yuan oversees recruitment and civil service affairs. The civil service system, as mentioned above, is based on examinations and professional training programmes, in which several key government organs under the Examination Yuan provide notable functions. The Civil Service Protection and Training Commission is in charge of policies and legal matters concerning the protection of civil servants' rights and interests, as well as providing courses on administrative neutrality and training for newly promoted public servants as well as those newly qualified through written examinations. The National Academy of the Civil Service was set up under the Commission to train civil servants and to upgrade their skill sets. The Public Service Pension Fund Supervisory Board coordinates review, oversight and evaluation of the civil service retirement pension fund.

In spite of Taiwan's attempts at compartmentalisation, there have been insurmountable co-ordination problems between the Executive Yuan and the Examination Yuan. In a time when states are competing for talents from around the world, this rigid and disintegrated civil service system stands as a barrier to national competitiveness—remnants of the Republic's early period of form over function.

V. CONCLUSION

The five-power government scheme was plagued by inefficiency and institutional conflicts in the early years of its implementation in Taiwan. Over the course of democratisation and constitutional reform, this five-power scheme has been gradually transformed into a semi-presidential system.

With the rise of the presidency during the authoritarian rule and democratic transitions, the President's role moved from ceremonial figurehead to Taiwan's chief executive, through a vast expansion of the office's scope of powers. The President has exerted great influence over national security and cross-Strait matters in addition to his role as intermediary among the five powers. Yet, the expansion of presidential powers has not been without cost. Given the institutional ambiguity or inconsistency that still persists in the evolving government system, presidential accountability has drawn serious attention and concern.

In contrast with the rising powers of the presidency, the premier, the President of the Executive Yuan, has stood in a paradoxical position. Although the premier has become a veritable CEO under the President, he or she is nevertheless accountable to the Legislative Yuan. This institutional dilemma has generated quite a few constitutional conflicts between the Executive and Legislative Yuans—conflicts that have often required judicial resolution.

Owing to unprecedented global competition, the campaign for government reform was on the agenda for years. Yet, for many years, the seeds of reform bore no fruit. Independent regulatory commissions were created, yet questions of administrative unity and accountability of these commissions still pose challenges to be tackled. Meanwhile, government streamlining has progressed slowly. The projects of outsourcing or privatisation have generated public concerns and distrusts, resulting in serious concerns about the capacity of private business and government accountability. As global competitiveness and democratic accountability drive further reform, more dialogue between the public and private sectors and greater degrees of transparency and public trust must ensue.

FURTHER READING

Linz, J, 'The Perils of Presidentialism' (1990) 1 *Journal of Democracy* 51–69.

Yeh, J-r, 'Changing Forces of Constitutional and Regulatory Reform in Taiwan' (1990) 4 *Columbia Journal of Chinese Law* 83–100.

Yeh, J-r, 'Experimenting with Independent Commissions in a New Democracy with a Civil Law Tradition: The Case of Taiwan' in S Rose-Ackerman and P Lindseth (eds), *Comparative Administrative Law* (MA, Edward Elgar, 2010) 246–64.

Yeh, J-r, 'Globalization, Government reform and the Paradigm Shift of Administrative Law' (2010) 5 *National Taiwan University Law Review* 113–41.

4

Representation and Legislative Process

The Transformation of Representative Institutions: From Three Parliaments to One – The Electoral System and Political Parties – Legislative Functions and Constitutional Control – The Control Yuan after Transformation – Conclusion

R EPRESENTATIVE GOVERNMENT AND electoral democracy unequivocally assume the centre stage of demo-cratic constitutionalism.[1] Modern constitutions usually adopt the concept of representative democracy, in which everyone is guaranteed the right to elect their preferred representatives in forming the government. Representatives are typically chosen in open, free and periodic elections rooted in the ideal of equal suffrage on behalf of atomic individuals rather than racial, ethnic or religious groups, or any special communities.[2] In a parliamentary system, in which the primary legitimacy of governance lies with the parliament, elected members exercise legislative powers and entrust a few to execute laws and regulations. In many presidential systems, on the other hand, in which both the executive and members of parliament are elected, parliament exercises legislative powers and functions—on the people's behalf—as a check on executive power.[3]

Intriguingly, the concepts and institutions of representative govern-ment embraced by the ROC Constitution in 1946 were not entirely

---

[1] W-C Chang et al, *Constitutionalism in Asia: Cases and Materials* (Oxford, Hart Publishing, 2014) 463–64.

[2] Ibid, 467.

[3] Ibid, 143–44.

consistent with these categories.[4] As chapter 2 highlighted, the ROC Constitution established a rather complex system of political representation. In Sun Yat-sen's view, political powers ought to be distinguished from governing powers and both should be represented by different institutions.[5] Political powers are those derived from the people as represented by the National Assembly, which ultimately operates as a check and balance against the exercise of governing powers. Conversely, governing powers are those exercised by the government, which consists of five discrete roles—executive, legislative, judiciary, examination and control—plus the President. According to Sun, this political system was designed to ameliorate the institutional deficiencies of modern western representative governments while preserving some of the characteristics of Chinese governance.[6] Nevertheless, Sun's ideas were not fully reflected in the text of the 1947 ROC Constitution.[7]

In attempting a compromise between the modern representative government and Sun's political invention, the 1947 ROC Constitution created a complex set of representative institutions. First was the National Assembly, whose members were elected for six-year terms by the people directly. The Assembly was vested with the powers to elect the President, to amend the Constitution, and to exercise initiatives and referenda on the people's behalf.[8] Second was the Legislative Yuan, elected by the people and entrusted with legislative powers similar to those exercised by the parliaments of modern constitutional governments.[9] Third was the Control Yuan, whose members were elected for six-year terms by provincial and municipal councils. Members enjoyed a mandate to exercise the powers of consent, impeachment, censure and auditing.[10] The Control Yuan thus exhibited a mixture of parliamentary powers, powers typically exercised by ombudsmen in the West, and powers based on Chinese bureaucratic

---

[4] J-r Yeh, 'The Cult of *Fatung*' in G Hassall and C Saunders (eds), *The People's Representatives: Electoral Systems in the Asia-Pacific Region* (Sydney, Allen & Unwin, 1997) 23–37.

[5] WL Tung, *The Political Institutions of Modern China* (The Hague, Nijhoff, 1964) 95–105.

[6] Ibid, 96–97.

[7] See C-M Chang, *Ten Lectures on the Democratic Constitution of the Republic of China* (Shanghai, The Commercial Press, 1947) preface (in Chinese).

[8] Arts 25–34 Constitution of the Republic of China (1947).

[9] Arts 62–76 Constitution of the Republic of China (1947).

[10] Arts 90–106 Constitution of the Republic of China (1947).

tradition.[11] Chang Chun-mai, a figure central to the drafting of the ROC Constitution, maintained the position—albeit taken from the ideas of Sun Yat-sen—that the Control Yuan was designed to function as an upper house, with the Legislative Yuan as a lower house.[12]

After the implementation of the ROC Constitution, debates arose about which institution or institutions represented the people and which embodied a parliament. As indicated in chapter 2, the Constitutional Court clarified that, 'from the perspective of the nature of their statuses and functions in the Constitution',[13] all three institutions—the National Assembly, the Legislative Yuan and the Control Yuan—'should be considered as equivalent to the parliaments of democratic nations'.[14] Consequently, 'three parliaments' were built and became novel features of the ROC's constitutionalism. Yet, with 'three parliaments' embodying different kinds of representation, invested with piecemeal parliamentary powers, and having distinctive relations with other branches of the government, institutional conflicts naturally arose. Thus, the constitutional reforms of the 1990s and 2000s centred on democratic representation and the parliament(s). In essence, the rearrangement of parliamentary powers has condensed the 'three parliaments' into one.[15]

This chapter has four parts. The first focuses on the transformation of parliamentary institutions and the rearrangement of related powers. The second part covers the electoral system and political parties, highlighting in the process electoral rules, election commission functions, and political party accountability. The third part offers an analysis of legislative privilege, autonomy and functions, along with its respective constitutional limitations. Specifically, this part details the global financial crisis's impact, constitutional limits on legislative spending power, and the nuances of fiscal control mechanisms. The fourth and final part covers the Control Yuan and other functions, with a special emphasis on the abolition of the National Assembly, the transformation of the Legislative Yuan into a single parliament, and the uncertain future of the Control Yuan—bringing the need for further reform.

---

[11] See Chang, *Ten Lectures* 74–75.

[12] Ibid.

[13] *JY Interpretation No 76* (1957).

[14] Ibid.

[15] J-r Yeh, *Democratic Transition and Constitutional Change* (Taipei, Angle, 2003) 393–428 (in Chinese).

I. THE TRANSFORMATION OF REPRESENTATIVE
INSTITUTIONS: FROM THREE PARLIAMENTS TO ONE

Taiwan's representative institutions were transformed in two stages: first in 1992 and again in 2005. In the first, the Control Yuan's reform reduced the number of parliaments from three to two. The second transformation, associated with the abolition of the National Assembly, brought that number down to one.[16] With these institutional changes, related parliamentary powers also shifted around until they were eventually placed under the Legislative Yuan as the nation's single parliament.

A. From Three Parliaments to Two: The Transformation of the Control Yuan

The second round of constitutional revision, in May 1992, fundamentally changed the nature of the Control Yuan, as all members were since required to be nominated and, with the National Assembly's consent, appointed by the President.[17] In addition, the Control Yuan was deprived of its consent powers over such appointments as those of the justices of the Constitutional Court. In the end, the Control Yuan was left with the powers of impeachment, censure and audit.[18] Effectively an ombudsman-like body, the Control Yuan is now legally required to be politically neutral and independent in the exercise of its powers.[19] Unlike their Legislative Yuan counterparts, Control Yuan members are subject to impeachment by their own initiative,[20] and no longer enjoy any parliamentary immunity or privilege.[21]

---

[16] Ibid, 393–450.

[17] Art 15 Additional Articles of the Constitution of the Republic of China (1992).

[18] Art 7(1) Additional Articles of the Constitution of the Republic of China (1992).

[19] Art 7(5) Additional Articles of the Constitution of the Republic of China (1992).

[20] Two members must initiate an impeachment and nine members must pass it. Art 7(4) and 7(6) Additional Articles of the Constitution of the Republic of China (1992).

[21] Ibid.

The Control Yuan's profound changes were formally recognised in a Constitutional Court ruling,[22] in which the Court held that the Control Yuan was no longer a 'central representative authority'[23]—in other words, the three parliaments had become two. The case arose out of a constitutional dispute over this very institutional change. The specific question before the Court was whether some of the Control Yuan's powers should be transferred to the Legislative Yuan, or whether alternative powers should be accorded to the Legislative Yuan instead.

The Court held that the Constitution's five-Yuan system had not changed. Although the Control Yuan was deprived of its powers of consent, it continued to exercise the powers of impeachment, censure and audit. Thus, all the powers conferred to the Control Yuan were to be retained by it alone and not transferred to the Legislative Yuan.[24]

In a novel construction, the Court decided to accord an investigative power to the Legislative Yuan. The Court ruled that, upon making a resolution at a general or committee meeting, the Legislative Yuan may request the relevant officials to provide reference materials on particular issues. As necessary, the Legislative Yuan may request a review of the original documents during the general or committee meeting.[25] Any official receiving such request may not decline it except in accordance with the law or for another justifiable reason.[26]

By giving the Legislative Yuan an investigative power that the ROC Constitution never provided, the Constitutional Court undoubtedly recognised the greater parliamentary authority of the Legislative Yuan over the Control Yuan. It was evident that, despite the Court's insistence that the five-Yuan system was still in effect, its decision altered that system. In 1999, the new investigative power was formally written into the law governing the exercise of parliamentary powers, and others—such as the power to consent to judicial appointments—conferred upon the Legislative Yuan.

---

[22] *JY Interpretation No 325* (1993).
[23] Ibid.
[24] Ibid.
[25] Ibid.
[26] Ibid.

This new power was further strengthened by a constitutional interpretation that arose out of an incident in the 2004 presidential election.[27] On the election's eve, as they visited a re-election campaign rally, both the incumbent, President Chen, and Vice-President, Annette Lu sustained minor injuries from an assassination attempt on their vehicle. Although they won the election by a razor-thin margin (after several rounds of recounting), the KMT alleged that Chen had staged the assassination attempt in order to solicit voter sympathy. The KMT parliamentary majority quickly passed a special law creating a commission with sweeping power to investigate the incident. The commission, whose members were extreme KMT partisans, potentially had the ability to make findings that could revoke judicial decisions regarding electoral disputes. As a result, the DPP petitioned the Constitutional Court to rule on the special law's constitutionality.

By the year's end, the Court in *JY Interpretation No. 585* had confirmed the Legislative Yuan's new power by partially approving the investigative commission—but with the caveat that such a commission must be set up to exercise a parliamentary investigation.[28] According to the Court, the Legislative Yuan, 'consisting of members elected by the people, is the highest legislative body of the State and shall exercise the legislative power on behalf of the people, and for the purpose of effectively exercising its constitutional powers, the Legislative Yuan may exercise a certain power of investigation, which is inherent in its legislative powers'.[29] The Court emphasised that the investigative power enjoyed by the Legislative Yuan is not limited—as suggested by its earlier decision discussed above—to the authority to request files. 'If and when necessary, the Legislative Yuan may also, by resolution of its plenary session, request the presence of a civilian or government official related to the matter under investigation to give testimonies or express opinions, and may impose reasonably compulsory measures upon those who refuse to fulfil their obligations to assist in the investigation.'[30] The Court even permitted, in extraordinary cases, the delegation of parliamentary investigation to those

---

[27] J-r Yeh, 'Presidential Politics and the Judicial Facilitation of Dialogue', 920, 932.

[28] *JY Interpretation No 585* (2004).

[29] Ibid.

[30] Ibid.

not in the parliament.[31] On the other hand, based upon separation of powers principles, the Court also recognised a limit to the exercise of parliamentary investigative power: it should not extend to those bodies who independently exercise governmental power, such as courts, and should not be applied against executive privilege. Further, when disputes arise with respect to the investigative power, they are the judiciary's to resolve.[32] Finally, although the commission's findings cannot bind the judiciary or other bodies that independently exercise governmental powers, they are binding on the parliament itself.

The KMT legislative majority was not entirely satisfied with the Court's decision to only partially uphold the constitutionality of the investigative commission, but the KMT nevertheless agreed to revise the special law and work within the parameters of its newly construed power. As for the question of the assassination attempt, the Court's decision sustained the presidential election results in spite of the parliamentary investigation. Though politics eventually returned to normal,[33] it is undisputed that the Court's ruling had further extended the investigative power of the Legislative Yuan.

B. From Two Parliaments to One: The Abolition of the National Assembly

After the Control Yuan's 1992 functional transformation, the National Assembly and the Legislative Yuan essentially existed as 'two parliaments'.[34] However, as constitutional reforms continued to modify the structure of government institutions, the relationships

---

[31] According to the Court, 'In extraordinary cases, should there exist any necessity of mandating those other than members of the Legislative Yuan to assist in the investigation as to any particular matters, special laws must be enacted, setting forth in detail the purposes of the mandate, the scope of the investigation, the matters relating to personnel and organization, including, without limitation, the qualifications, appointment, term of the mandated persons, the authorities, methods and procedures for the special investigation, which would also serve as the basis of supervision. The organizations and meeting procedures prescribed under the respective laws must conform to the principle of democracy' (ibid).

[32] Ibid.

[33] Yeh, 'Presidential Politics', above n 27.

[34] Yeh, above n 16, 399.

between these two parliaments—and their respective functions—were inevitably altered.

The 1994 constitutional revision mandated that the President and Vice-President should be elected by the people directly.[35] Thus stripped of its electoral power, the National Assembly was left primarily with the power to amend the Constitution. Subsequent constitutional reforms were expected to shift focus to the following topics: the arrangement of the 'two parliaments' and their respective powers;[36] the high costs of electing and maintaining the 'two parliaments'; and the potential for the National Assembly to abuse its monopolistic power to revise the Constitution.[37]

As detailed in chapter 2, the fifth round of constitutional revision in 1999 sought to reform the 'two parliaments'. It was decided that the next (that is, the fourth) National Assembly would not be elected by the people directly—instead, members would be appointed from among the political parties in proportion to the ratio of votes received by each party in the Legislative Yuan elections.[38] Yet, the Constitutional Court found this reform to be unconstitutional and invalidated it. In April 2000, the sixth round of constitutional revision was undertaken.[39] This reform transformed the National Assembly from a perpetual governmental body into an occasional one oriented toward particular missions.[40] For example, the 300 National Assembly delegates would be elected (by proportional representation) only after such events as the proposals of constitutional amendments, territorial changes, or the Legislative Yuan's impeachment of the President or Vice-President.[41] After 2000's constitutional revision, the Legislative Yuan became Taiwan's leading—if not yet only—representative institution. Unsurprisingly, the next round of constitutional revision would abolish the National Assembly altogether.

---

[35] The first direct presidential election was held in 1996. The KMT President Lee Teng-hui, the first native-born Taiwanese to take that position, won the election by a landslide. See engweb.cec.gov.tw/ezfiles/30/1030/img/144/1996.htm.

[36] Yeh, above n 16, 400.

[37] Ibid, 410–16.

[38] Art 1 Additional Articles of the Constitution of the Republic of China (1999). See also *JY Interpretation No 499* (2000).

[39] See generally Secretariat of National Assembly (ed), *The Fourth Meeting of The Third National Assembly Archives* (2000) (in Chinese).

[40] Art 1 Additional Articles of the Constitution of the Republic of China (2000).

[41] Art 1 Additional Articles of the Constitution of the Republic of China (2000).

The 2005 constitutional reform took aim at the Legislative Yuan. Frustrated by endless political confrontations between the KMT-dominated legislature and the DDP-controlled executive, citizen groups strongly campaigned for large-scale constitutional reforms, demanding—among others things—the downsizing of the parliament and the empowering of the citizenry. Crossing the aisle, the DPP and the KMT negotiated a package of constitutional reforms in which the National Assembly would be abolished, the Assembly's powers would be returned to the Legislative Yuan or the people, and the number of Legislative Yuan seats would be cut in half by altering the electoral rules. In May 2005, these proposals were passed in the seventh round of constitutional revision and new amendments were promulgated in the following month.

Following its abolition, the National Assembly's powers devolved primarily to the Legislative Yuan. With respect to the power to amend the Constitution or alter the national territory, it was stipulated that these actions require the Legislative Yuan to pass a proposal by a three-quarters majority which is then affirmed by a public referendum in which the number of valid votes in favour of the proposal must exceed half of the total number of electors.[42] With respect to the power to recall the President and Vice-President, a recall motion must be passed by a two-thirds vote of the Legislative Yuan, followed by a public vote in which more than half of the total number of electors take part and half of the valid votes are in favour thereof.[43] Lastly, with respect to the power to impeach the President and Vice-President, impeachment motions must be initiated by a two-thirds majority of the Legislative Yuan and referred on to the Constitutional Court for adjudication.[44]

With nearly all of the parliamentary powers consolidated, the Legislative Yuan became the only parliament under the ROC Constitution. However, it remained to be seen whether the Legislative Yuan would develop into an effective representative institution, as additional factors

---

[42] Arts 1, 4(5) and 12 Additional Articles of the Constitution of the Republic of China (2005).
[43] Art 2(9) Additional Articles of the Constitution of the Republic of China (2005).
[44] Arts 2(10) and 4(7) Additional Articles of the Constitution of the Republic of China (2005).

influencing legislative functioning, such as electoral design and checks and balances with the President and cabinet—that is, the Executive Yuan—had not yet been fully settled.

II. THE ELECTORAL SYSTEM AND POLITICAL PARTIES

Representatives are chosen directly by the people through open, free and periodic elections. Thus, the design of Taiwan's electoral system is central to the effective functioning of representative democracy. Regarding the election of the Legislative Yuan, the ROC Constitution initially adopted a district-based system which also reserved seats for ethnic minorities, overseas Chinese citizens and occupational organisations.[45] However, the 1991 constitutional revision created—in addition to the district-based system—a certain number of seats for the proportional representation of political parties. The 2005 constitutional revision undertook further comprehensive electoral reform and ushered in the adoption of a two-vote system—one vote for individual candidates in district-based elections and another for political parties via proportional representation. With these electoral changes, the role of political parties has gradually strengthened, both as to electoral competition and to political representation.

This section first discusses the changes that the constitutional reforms of the 1990s and 2000s made to legislative seats and electoral rules. Next, the discussion moves on to the functions of the election commission, whose independence and neutrality are vital to electoral competition and representative democracy. Lastly, the section offers an analysis of the changing roles of political parties, including some related issues.

A. Changes to Legislative Seats and Electoral Rules

As mentioned in chapter 2, in order to resolve the representational crisis and to allow for a second group of national representatives to be elected in Taiwan, the Constitutional Court initiated a proportional

---

[45] Art 64 Constitution of the Republic of China (1947).

representational system.[46] That initiative was implemented by the 1991 constitutional revision, which set aside 30 seats for national representatives on a proportional basis, six seats for overseas Chinese citizens, six seats for aboriginals, and a number of seats for population-based district elections.[47]

For population-based district elections, it was further stipulated that two legislative members should be elected from each province and special municipality. If the population exceeded 200,000, one member would be added for each additional 100,000 people; and if the population exceeded 1 million, one member would be added for each additional 200,000 people.[48] In accordance with Taiwan's population in 1991, 165 seats were allocated for the district elections of both the 2nd and 3rd Legislative Yuans.

The electoral districts were subsequently drawn chiefly on the basis of administrative regions such as provinces, special municipalities, cities and counties. According to the Public Officials Election and Recall Act of 1991, municipalities, cities or counties with one legislative seat would employ the administrative regions as the electoral districts, and those with two or more seats would divide the same electoral districts within the administrative regions.[49] When drawing electoral districts, the following had to be considered: the number of legislative members to be elected, administrative regions, population allocation, geographical location, traffic conditions and historical origins. Ultimately, the Central Election Commission drew 29 districts for the election of the 2nd Legislative Yuan, a number which persisted for subsequent elections.

The 1997 constitutional revision further expanded the number of legislative seats from 165 to 225. Among these, 41 seats were allocated for proportional representation, eight seats for overseas Chinese citizens, eight seats for aboriginals, and 168 seats for district elections in which each city or county would be guaranteed one seat, regardless of the size of its population.[50] This revision applied to the elections of the 4th, 5th, and 6th Legislative Yuans.

---

[46] *JY Interpretation No 261* (1990). See ch 2.
[47] Art 2 Additional Articles of the Constitution of the Republic of China (1991).
[48] Ibid.
[49] Art 35 Public Officials Election and Recall Act (1991).
[50] Art 4(1) Additional Articles of the Constitution of the Republic of China (1997).

The electoral rule for the 2nd to 6th Legislative Yuans was based on a single non-transferable vote (SNTV) under multi-member districts (MMDs).[51] In such a system, voters are provided with a single vote in a district election, and multiple members are to be elected from large-to-medium-sized districts. Seats characterised by proportional representation are allocated to political parties in accordance with their respective percentages of votes passing the 5 per cent threshold. Under such a system, small political parties or independent candidates can meet with some success, as a majority is not necessary for gaining a seat in a district election. Often, candidates who take extreme positions or who appeal to specific groups do better than other more moderate candidates. At the same time, this system can disadvantage larger political parties, as often-intense competition among intraparty candidates results in incidental seat losses.[52] In addition, this electoral rule may also foster vote-buying or electoral corruption:[53] because votes are cast to individual candidates rather than to political parties, candidates in multi-member districts—especially those in rural areas—may face the temptation to buy votes.[54]

Table 4.1 shows the votes and seats held by the KMT and the DPP since the 2nd Legislative Yuan. From the 2nd to the 4th Legislative Yuans, the KMT was the largest political party, followed by the DPP. Seats allocated to the two largest political parties reflected, to a considerable extent, the votes won in the district elections. In the 5th and 6th Legislative Yuans, the People First Party's (PFP's) split-off from the KMT caused the KMT to fall in position to the second-largest political party, while the DPP became the largest. However, the KMT–PFP coalition still beat the DPP's coalition with the Taiwan Solidarity Union (TSU).[55] Ever since the 2nd Legislative Yuan, the DPP has obtained

[51]   T-Y Lin et al, *Constitutional Law: Separation of Powers*, rev edn (Taipei, New Sharing, 2008) 273 (in Chinese).

[52]   Ibid 273.

[53]   J-w Lin, 'Vote Buying vs Noise Making: Two Models of Electoral Competition under the Single Non-transferable Vote—Multimember District System' (1998) 30 *Chinese Political Science Review* 93, 102–05, 116–17, 122.

[54]   Y-h Chu, 'Democratic Consolidation in the Post-KMT Era: the Challenge of Governance' in M Alagappa (ed), *Taiwan's Presidential Politics: Democratization and Cross-Strait Relations in the Twenty-First Century* (New York, Routledge, 2001) 95.

[55]   For the statistics of the 2008 Legislator Election, see engweb.cec.gov.tw/ezfiles/30/1030/img/145/2008.html. For the statistics of the 2012 Legislator Election, see engweb.cec.gov.tw/ezfiles/30/1030/img/145/2012.htm.

Table 4.1: Votes received and seats held by the KMT and the DPP in Legislative Yuan elections

	KMT			DPP		
One Vote / SNTV–MMD						
	District election	**Proportional/ Overseas seats**	**All seats**	**District election**	**Proportional/ Overseas seats**	**All seats**
2nd LY 1993–1996 165 seats	53.02% (votes) 62 (seats)	33 seats	95 seats (57.6%)	31.03% (votes) 32 (seats)	19 seats	51 seats (30.9%)
3rd LY 1996–1999 165 seats	46.1% (votes) 67 (seats)	18 seats	85 seats (51.5%)	33.2% (votes) 41 (seats)	13 seats	54 seats (32.7%)
4th LY 1999–2002 225 seats	46.4% (votes) 96 (seats)	27 seats	123 seats (54.7%)	29.6% (votes) 52 (seats)	18 seats	70 seats (31.1%)
5th LY 2002–2005 225 seats	28.6% (votes) 53 (seats)	15 seats	68 seats (30.2%)	33.4% (votes) 69 (seats)	18 seats	87 seats (38.7%)
6th LY 2005–2008 225 seats	32.83% (votes) 61 (seats)	18 seats	79 seats (35.1%)	35.72% (votes) 70 (seats)	19 seats	89 seats (39.6%)
2005 Constitutional Reform of Electoral Rule **Two Votes / SMD**						
	District election	**Proportional election**	**All seats**	**District election**	**Proportional election**	**All seats**
7th LY 2008–2012 113 seats	53.50% (votes) 61 (seats)	51.23% (votes) 20 (seats)	81 (seats) (71.7%)	38.17% (votes) 13 (seats)	36.91% (votes) 14 (seats)	27 (seats) (23.9%)
8th LY 2012–2016 113 seats	48.18% (votes) 48 (seats)	44.55% (votes) 16 (seats)	64 (seats) (56.6%)	43.80% (votes) 27 (seats)	34.62% (votes) 13 (seats)	40 (seats) (35.4%)

Source: Election data from the Central Election Commission, db.cec.gov.tw/histMain.jsp?voteSel=20080101A2.

steadily more votes and seats, but it has never entered the majority—even when joining forces with the TSU. In the 6th Legislative Yuan, the KMT–PFP coalition held 50.2 per cent of the legislative seats, whereas the DPP–TSU coalition held only 44.9 per cent.

The 2005 constitutional revision overhauled the electoral system outlined above. Owing partly to citizens' demands for parliamentary reform and partly to the increased intensity of electoral challenges by smaller political parties, the KMT and the DPP decided to co-operate to reform the electoral rules. This resulting revision cut the number of legislative seats in half: from 225 seats to 113. Of these 113 seats, the revision allocated 34 for proportional representation, six for aboriginals and 73 for district elections in which each city or county would be guaranteed one seat, regardless of population size.[56] It was also stipulated that the number of elected female members on each party's list for proportional representation should not be fewer than half of the total number.[57]

This new electoral rule gave electors two votes in single-member districts (see 'Two Votes / SMD', in Table 4.1).[58] One vote was to be cast for individual candidates in district elections, the other one for political parties. For the 73 seats elected by districts, only one member could be elected within a single medium-to-small-sized district. Further, proportional representation seats were distributed according to the respective percentages of votes won by political parties. And a party had to obtain a minimum of 5 per cent of the total votes before its votes would count.[59]

The 2005 reform specifically targeted the institutional weaknesses of the previous SNTV-MMD system, in which candidates who took extreme positions stood a better chance of winning. The new SMD rule, as applied to the 73 district-elected seats, was expected to facilitate a two-party system—to the relative advantage of both the KMT and the DPP—since single-member district elections offered better odds for candidates in strong political parties or with moderate platforms, while it reduced the chances of candidates in smaller political parties or with extreme platforms. The new rule, as applied to the 34-seat proportional representation, was designed to accommodate smaller political parties.[60]

---

[56] Art 4 Additional Articles of the Constitution of the Republic of China (2005).
[57] Art 4 Additional Articles of the Constitution of the Republic of China (2005).
[58] Lin et al, *Constitutional Law*, above n 51, 273–74.
[59] Art 4 Additional Articles of the Constitution of the Republic of China (2005).
[60] Lin et al, above n 51, 273.

However, the 2005 reforms did not escape strong criticism. One such criticism concerned the disadvantage suffered by smaller political parties. As discussed previously, the new SMD system facilitated the development of a two-party system by reinforcing the unity and voting concentration in the largest political parties. Consequently, it was quite a challenge for smaller political parties to reach the 5 per cent threshold to secure its votes. Thus, these parties' ability to obtain legislative seats was substantially undermined.[61]

A second—and perhaps the strongest—criticism concerned the vote disparity in relation to the drawing of electoral districts. With 73 seats elected from single-member districts, the drawing of these districts was indeed a difficult task. Aside from the guarantee that each city or county would receive one seat regardless of its population, the 2005 revision provided no further guidance. According to Article 35(2) of the Public Officials Election and Recall Act, after setting aside the indigenous population, the remainder was divided into 73 districts, each with an average of 308,000 residents. A city or county with a below-average population became one electoral district with a single seat. Alternatively, a city or county with an above-average population would be divided into multiple districts.

In August 2005, in order to implement the redistricting plan, the Central Election Commission promulgated a rule in which each local election commission would invite experts and representatives from various groups to hold public hearings in order to propose redistricting draft plans to the central Commission. The Commission would organise a special committee to draft the comprehensive redistricting plan, which the Commission would then submit to the Legislative Yuan for review.[62] After lengthy discussion, the 73 electoral districts were eventually drawn.

Nevertheless, given the guarantee that each city or county would receive at least one seat, voting disparities were expected to be high. For example, the smallest electoral district—Taitung County, with 159,717 residents—had one seat. But the electoral district of Hsinchu County, with 460,667 residents, also had one seat. Thus, the voting disparity

---

[61] F-s Hsieh, 'The Origins and Consequences of Electoral Reform in Taiwan' (2009) 45 *Issues & Studies* 1, 13–15.

[62] The Central Election Commission, Constituency Plan for the seventh election of the Legislative Yuan (in Chinese).

between Hsinchu County and Taitung County was nearly three-to-one. The voting disparity was even higher between offshore islets (such as Kinmen and Matsu) and Taiwan's smallest electoral district. Matsu, the smallest district outside Taiwan, had as few as 10,130 residents. The voting disparity between Taitung County in Taiwan and Matsu was therefore 15.77:1. Comparable cases of voting disparity were ruled violations of voting equality in Japan, South Korea and elsewhere.[63] In Taiwan, what is worse, the KMT has long enjoyed political dominance in the more sparsely populated districts (for example, the offshore islands and aboriginal areas).

In any event, the 2005 constitutional revision was agreed to as a package deal between the KMT and the DPP, for neither political party could reject any particularly unfavourable item. Unsurprisingly, in the 2008 election of the 7th Legislative Yuan, the DPP's share of parliamentary seats was substantially reduced. As Table 4.1 shows, the KMT obtained 71.7 per cent of the parliamentary seats by winning 53.5 per cent of the vote in district elections and 51.2 per cent of the vote by political parties. Conversely, having won 38.17 per cent of the vote in district elections and 36.91 per cent of the vote by political parties—results consistent with its historical performance—the DPP nevertheless secured fewer than a quarter of the total parliamentary seats (23.9 per cent). This small number of seats was not sufficient for the DPP to exercise any oversight powers, and was even below the one-third threshold required before minority legislators could file petitions with the Constitutional Court.[64]

The DPP members of the 6th Legislative Yuan quickly filed a petition with the Court to challenge the constitutionality of both the new electoral rule and the one-third threshold for petitions. However, the Court stalled for over two years, ultimately dismissing the petition as premature in July 2009[65] and offering no explanation for its belated response. In the Court's view, if the new electoral rule's alteration of the

[63] See the *Case to Seek Invalidation of Election*, 65 Minshu 2 (Supreme Court, Japan); *National Assembly Election Redistricting Plan Case*, 2000 Hun-Ma 92, 25 October 2001 (Constitutional Court, South Korea). For further discussion, see Chang et al, *Constitutionalism in Asia* 467–77.

[64] Arts 5(1) and 5(2) Constitutional Interpretation Procedure Act (1993).

[65] *JY Dismissal Resolution No Hui-Tai 8732*, 1343rd Meeting of the Constitutional Court (2009).

2005 constitutional revision caused a voting disparity in the election of the 7th Legislative Yuan, minority legislators must seek constitutional revision before petitioning the Court. Only when revision attempts fail may the Court look into the matter.[66] The Court relied on the same rationale in rejecting the challenge to the one-third threshold.[67] Notably, in June 2014, the Court rendered *JY Interpretation No. 721* in response to a similar challenge brought by the two smallest political parties in the 2008 election of the 7th Legislative Yuan. However, the Court in that decision sustained the electoral rule on the ground that it did not encroach upon democratic principles or any procedural or substantive limits of constitutional revisions.[68]

In 2012, the DPP fought hard to gain legislative seats. As Table 4.1 shows, having won 43.8 per cent of the vote in district elections and 34.62 per cent of the vote by political parties, the DPP obtained 40 seats (35.4 per cent of the total) in the 8th Legislative Yuan. The KMT continued as the legislative majority with 64 seats (56.6 per cent) by winning 48.1 per cent of the vote in district elections and 44.5 per cent of the vote by political parties. These results showed that voting disparity remained a serious issue. Yet, owing to the 2005 constitutional revision's requirement that a high threshold be passed to amend the Constitution, and the Court's reluctance to tackle the issue, no sensible constitutional solution was in sight.

B. Election Institutions and Neutrality

Given the centrality of elections in a representative democracy, their fair administration is of significant importance. Many contemporary democracies have created independent election commissions responsible for electoral administration. Such commissions are set up either by constitution or by statute. Members, who are expected to be impartial and non-partisan, are typically appointed by the executive (with parliamentary consent) and serve for a fixed term. In service of non-partisanship, it is often required that half of a commission's members

---

[66] Ibid.
[67] Ibid.
[68] *JY Interpretation No 721* (2014).

may not be in the same political party. A commission's functions usually include the administration of elections, the regulation of electoral matters—such as drawing electoral districts—and even the settlement of electoral disputes.

Taiwan did not formally establish an independent election commission until the promulgation of the Organic Law of the Central Election Commission in 2009. Prior to that, the Central Election Commission, created by the Public Officials Election and Recall Act in 1980 to administer and supervise elections, had been placed under the Executive Yuan,[69] which often resulted in jurisdictional conflicts with the Ministry of the Interior. Worse, the Commission's impartiality and neutrality had been fiercely criticised, and its members were alleged to be dominated by the ruling political party of the time. In 2009, a bold step to reform the Commission was finally taken when the Organic Law of the Central Election Commission was passed. The Commission has since been reorganised as one of three independent agencies in Taiwan.

As an independent regulatory commission, the Central Election Commission has a chairperson, a vice-chairperson and seven to nine members, each of whom sits for renewable four-year terms.[70] The chairperson, vice-chairperson and members are appointed by the premier, the President of the Executive Yuan, with the consent of the Legislative Yuan. To ensure impartiality and independence, more than one-third of the commissioners may not be members of the same political party and commissioners, while in office, are prohibited from participating in party activities.[71]

As mentioned earlier, one of the Commission's primary functions is to draw electoral districts for national elections. Other functions include the following: issuing public notice for elections and recalls; planning for elections and recalls; examining candidates' qualifications; supervising and inspecting elections and recalls; establishing and administering polling stations and ballot-counting stations; examining and certifying election results; and issuing certificates to elected representatives.[72] The Commission is also responsible for prescribing measures governing

---

[69] Art 8 Public Officials Election and Recall Act (1980). This act was amended in 2014.

[70] Art 3 Organic Law of the Central Election Commission (2009).

[71] Art 5 Organic Law of the Central Election Commission (2009).

[72] Art 11 Public Officials Election and Recall Act (2014).

campaign propaganda and political parties' activities via television or other broadcast media.[73]

Although the Commission was reformed into an independent regulatory commission, local election commissions were not. According to the Public Officials Election and Recall Act, local commission members are still appointed by the executive. The impartiality and neutrality of these commissions continue to be criticised. In 2014, the Deputy Mayor of Taichung City, who also served as the local election commission's chairperson, was accused of abusing his authority by rephrasing an opponent's policy statements in the official election bulletin.[74] Thus, continuing reform efforts should target the organisation of these local commissions to ensure there is a fair process for appointing commission members.

C. Political Parties and Accountability Problems

Political parties form a crucial bridge between citizens and their representatives. Parties have several major functions: linking political elites with the common goals of society; helping to shape and supervise public policies; and, most important, persuading citizens to vote for candidates who would run the government. Prior to the late 1980s, Taiwan banned the formation of new political parties. The only dominant party then was the KMT, which embodied a Leninist style by entrenching its influence in the executive, legislative and military aspects of government. Strict party discipline was the norm. The first opposition political party, the DPP, was formed in 1986, followed by the burgeoning of new parties such as the PFP and the TSU, both mentioned above.[75] As of this writing, there are 268 registered political parties in Taiwan, representing a wide spectrum of affiliations, interests and advocacy.[76]

---

[73] Art 11 Public Officials Election and Recall Act (2014).

[74] '2014 ELECTIONS: Hu abused official resources: Lin', 22 November 2014 *Taipei Times*, at http://www.taipeitimes.com/News/taiwan/archives/2014/11/22/2003605029.

[75] For a discussion of Taiwan's party politics in the 1990s and 2000s, see D Fell, *Party Politics in Taiwan: Party change and the democratic evolution of Taiwan, 1991–2004* (London, New York: Routledge, 2005).

[76] Available at www.moi.gov.tw/dca/02people_005-1.aspx?sn=10.

As stated previously, the importance of political parties to constitutional operations was substantially enhanced after the 1991 constitutional revision adopted a system of proportional representation by party. Yet the ROC Constitution had not contemplated any regulation of political parties. Inspired by a similar German constitutional provision,[77] the 1992 revision added that a political party would be considered unconstitutional if its goals or activities endangered the ROC's existence or the nation's free and democratic constitutional order.[78] The revision also assigned the Constitutional Court the task of dissolving unconstitutional political parties.[79] Thus far, no such case has appeared on the Court's docket.

In addition to constitutional provisions, a few statutes regulate the formation and activities of political parties. Perhaps most important is the Civil Associations Act, which was substantially revised in 1992 when Taiwan began to democratise and has provided fundamental rules for occupational, social, and political organisations, including political parties. According to the Act, government approval is required in order to form most organisations, but notification is all that is necessary in order to form political organisations. After a year-long notification period, political parties—defined as those with more than five members elected to public office in the central or local governments and with assets worth more than NT$10 million—may seek incorporation and register with the courts. Incorporated or not, all political parties that have properly notified can nominate candidates for public office. It is further provided that a political organisation's structure and operation must abide by democratic principles, and that no political party can create any branch or body within universities, courts or the military.[80] Prior to 2008, the Act prohibited any organisation from advocating communism or secession. However, that prohibition was invalidated by the Court, which based its ruling on the freedoms of association and expression.[81] From this, it is evident that, since Taiwan's

---

[77] Art 21 German Basic Law. English translation available at www.iuscomp.org/gla/statutes/GG.htm#21.

[78] Art 13(3) Additional Articles of the Constitution of the Republic of China (1992).

[79] Ibid, Art 13(2).

[80] Arts 44–52, Civil Associations Act (2011).

[81] *JY Interpretation No 644* (2008).

democratisation, political parties have been accorded greater freedom to participate in democratic politics.

The Political Donations Act, promulgated in 2004 and substantially revised in 2008, regulates campaign finance for both political parties and individual electoral candidates. Under the Act, individuals may not contribute more than NT$300,000 annually to any one political party; for-profit corporations are limited to NT$3 million, and non-profit organisations to NT$2 million. Likewise, candidates may not receive more than NT$100,000 per designated election period from any individual, more than NT$1 million annually from any one for-profit, or more than NT$500,000 annually from any one non-profit. Parties and candidates must report all donations to the Control Yuan, or risk confiscation or fines.[82] Although the Act increased the transparency of campaign finance, allegations of unreported political donations have persisted—especially during presidential elections, in which KMT and DPP candidates are often alleged to have received large sums of unreported money.

In Taiwan, the most serious problem affecting the fair competition of political parties is the KMT's enormous wealth and asset base, both legacies of the era of the state party before the nation's democratisation. Even discounting political donations, the KMT and its candidates are financed far better than others. Although proposals targeting the KMT's wealth and assets have been put forward over the years, the KMT-dominated legislature never allows them to reach discussion on the floor. For a similar reason, the KMT also opposed the drafting of a special law on political parties that could have limited the party's resources. In 2012, such a draft law was sent to the Legislative Yuan for consideration, although no progress has been made.

As far as the case law on this issue is concerned, the Constitutional Court received an initial case after the adoption in the 1991 constitutional revision of proportional representation. In it, the Control Yuan presented the question of whether citizens had the right, under Article 17 of the Constitution, to recall representatives elected proportionally.[83] With respect to district-elected representatives, local

---

[82] Arts 7–30, Political Donations Act (2015). The official title is the Political Donations Act.

[83] Art 17 of the Constitution guarantees that the people shall have the rights of election, recall, initiative and referendum.

eligible voters could exercise the right to a recall in accordance with the requirements set forth in the Public Officials Election and Recall Act. However, with respect to representatives elected from proportional lists provided by political parties, no rule concerning recall existed— an oversight which potentially violated the constitutional guarantee of the people's recall rights. In response, the Constitutional Court published *JY Interpretation No 331*, holding that it was constitutional to preclude recall on party-list proportional representatives.[84] The Court stated that the introduction of 'party-list proportional representation for the election of congressmen who represent overseas Chinese and the National Sector' was meant 'to ensure that a certain portion of congressmen … may learn the genuine will of the people as a whole and preserve national interests', and 'to prompt political parties to nominate the most talented, virtuous and reputable members'.[85] The Court noted that if a party-list proportional representative lost his or her membership in the party from which he or she was elected, he or she would certainly be deemed ineligible for the seat, having forfeited any legal foundation for it.[86]

JY Interpretation No 331 was a reasonable decision.[87] At the same time, it gave political parties greater control over party-list proportional representatives, who have become accountable to political parties and defended party interests rather than being accountable to the people and defending national interests. This scenario is made worse by the paucity of legislation on political parties, as discussed above. Recently, as the confrontation between parties has intensified in the Legislative Yuan, parties and their caucus leaders have begun to exercise even greater control over their party members. At times, parties have imposed disciplinary measures—including even the suspension of party membership—against those representatives who failed to vote with the party line. In short, although no anti-hopping laws or floor-switching rules exist, internal party discipline can be quite harsh.

---

[84] *JY Interpretation No 331* (1993).
[85] Ibid.
[86] Ibid.
[87] Nevertheless, counterexamples do exist. For example, the South Korea Constitutional Court decided otherwise in a similar case. See *National Seat Succession Case*, 92Hun-Ma153, 28 April 1994 (Constitutional Court, South Korea).

In September 2013, a politically charged case arose that illustrated the complexities of party discipline and proportional representation. Wang Jin-pyng, President of the Legislative Yuan, a position functionally equivalent to the Legislative Speaker, was accused of being involved in a scheme to illegally lobby the judiciary regarding a case about the DPP caucus leader.[88] Speaker Wang, a senior and influential KMT leader, had for many terms been elected from a district in the south of Taiwan. Owing to his seniority, he was placed at the top of the KMT's proportional list for the current 8th Legislative Yuan, from 2012 to 2016. The criminal allegation, and power struggles with President Ma Ying-jeou (who served as KMT party chairman), resulted in the revocation of Wang's party membership a week later, jeopardising his seat in the Legislative Yuan and his status as the Speaker. This politically manipulative move by the President and the KMT was highly criticised as it could have directly resulted in a change of congressional leadership—a potentially serious interference with the parliament.[89]

Wang quickly sought an injunction from the district court, temporarily retaining his party membership and his leadership of the legislature.[90] On 19 March 2014, the district court handed down a decision in favour of Wang, ruling that the KMT's revocation of Wang's party membership was illegal and in violation of due process.[91] The KMT appealed this ruling to the court of appeals on 10 April.[92] After a five-month trial, the court of appeals upheld the district court's ruling. The KMT further appealed to the Supreme Court on 22 October.[93] However, in 2015, after the KMT's landslide defeat in local elections, President Ma Ying-jeou resigned as KMT party chairman. The new party chairman

[88] M Hay, 'Ma Orders Wang to Return to Taiwan', 8 September 2013 *Taipei Times*, at www.taipeitimes.com/News/front/print/2013/09/08/2003571611.

[89] Y-l Chiu and S Hsu, 'Ma-Wang Showdown: Netizens Criticize Ma "persecution" of Wang Jin-Pyng', 12 September 2013 *Taipei Times*, at www.taipeitimes.com/News/taiwan/print/2013/09/12/2003571949.

[90] C Wang, 'Court Rules in Favor of Wang Jin-Pyng', 14 September 2013 *Taipei Times*, at www.taipeitimes.com/News/front/print/2013/09/14/2003572092.

[91] Taipei Tifang Fayuan [Taipei District Court], 102 Su-Tzu No 3782 (2013) (Taiwan).

[92] 'KMT to Continue Legal Battle Against Legislative Speaker', 10 April 2014 *Focus Taiwan News Channel*, at focustaiwan.tw/news/aipl/201404100020.aspx.

[93] 'High Court backs Wang in KMT membership fight', 27 September 2014 *Taipei News*, at http://www.taipeitimes.com/News/taiwan/archives/2014/09/27/2003600689.

decided not to continue the lawsuit and the case was finally put to rest, with Wang still guaranteed his post as Legislative Yuan Speaker.

The expanded role that political parties have taken in representative politics displays how urgently a comprehensive statutory scheme of party regulation is needed. As Speaker Wang's case has shown, now may be the time for all parties to collaborate on such a law and for the Constitutional Court to reconsider decisions made on the basis of parties' political accountability alone.

III. LEGISLATIVE FUNCTIONS AND CONSTITUTIONAL CONTROL

According to the Constitution, the Legislative Yuan is the highest body of the state that may exercise legislative powers on behalf of the people.[94] Such powers include the approval by resolution of statutory bills, budgetary bills and bills concerning martial law, amnesty, treaties, the declaration of war and conclusion of peace, and other important affairs.[95] The following section discusses several aspects of these legislative powers and their constitutional limitations, as highlighted by a few leading Constitutional Court interpretations.

A. Legislative Autonomy and Limitations

The power of law making is vested primarily in the Legislative Yuan, now the single parliament, although the Executive Yuan and the Examination Yuan may also propose legislative bills according to the Constitution.[96] As elaborated in chapter 3, the Control Yuan's and the Judicial Yuan's powers to propose legislative bills relating to their respective functions were also confirmed by the Constitutional Court.[97] Since the passage of the Referendum Act in 2004, individual citizens may petition for legislation as well.

---

[94] Art 62 Constitution of the Republic of China (1947).
[95] Art 63 Constitution of the Republic of China (1947).
[96] Arts 58 and 87 Constitution of the Republic of China (1947).
[97] *JY Interpretation No 3* (1952); *JY Interpretation No 175* (1982). For discussion of these, see ch 3.

Ordinarily, the legislature retains the power to manage the detailed rules of the legislative process. However, in 1994, a petition was brought to the Constitutional Court challenging the passage of three organic acts—those creating the National Security Council, the National Security Bureau, and the Bureau of Personnel Administration of the Executive Yuan—due to the contentiousness of the legislative process.[98] Created by the 1966 Temporary Provisions to expand the powers of the President and the administration, these three institutions were not at the time authorised by the Constitution. The 1991 constitutional revision, despite strong opposition, maintained the powers of the President to determine major policies on national security, and stipulated that these three institutions must be formally established by law before 31 December 1993.[99] Unsurprisingly, the opposition parties filibustered, hoping that the three statutes would not be enacted by the deadline, and that the institutions would therefore become illegal. On the evening of 31 December in spite of ongoing—and even physically violent—filibusters, the vote was taken and the Legislative Yuan Speaker suddenly announced that the three statutes had passed. Owing to the chaos, however, the secretariat was unable to count the votes and tally the record.[100] After their announcement, the three statutes were submitted to the President, who executed them before the deadline. Minority legislators immediately petitioned the Constitutional Court, contending that the process by which the three statutes had been passed was illegal, thus rendering them unconstitutional.

The Court in *JY Interpretation No 342* sustained all three statutes by relying on 'the principle of parliamentary autonomy'.[101] According to the Court, the legislative process, which is internal and falls squarely within the jurisdiction of the legislature, is not subject to judicial scrutiny 'unless it is in clear contravention to the Constitution'.[102] In a dispute as to whether a legislative defect will have a grave impact on the enactment of a law, so long as the defect is not evident, the dispute should be resolved by the legislature pursuant to the principle

---

[98] *JY Interpretation No 342* (1994).
[99] Art 9 Additional Articles of the Constitution of the Republic of China (1991). For a further, detailed discussion, see ch 3 section II B.
[100] *JY Interpretation No 342* (1994).
[101] Ibid.
[102] Ibid.

of legislative autonomy.[103] In this ruling, the Court accorded the legislature with great deference over the law-making process. Perhaps aware of the case's contentious nature, the Court in its majority opinion expressly referred to three foreign cases in justification of such deference—a gesture seldom made.[104]

In contrast to the high level of deference given to the legislature as to its law-making process, the Constitutional Court has much more closely scrutinised its constitution-amending process. Although the Court left the procedural details of constitutional revision to the decisions of the National Assembly, it nevertheless emphasised that 'every self-governance decision shall be made in accordance with the principles of the constitutional structure of free democracy'.[105] The Court further demanded that the principle of 'constitutional due process' be applied to the constitution-amending process, which 'must be conducted openly and transparently in order to satisfy the condition of rational communication and, hence, lay the proper foundation for a constitutional state'.[106] With this high standard, the Court struck down the 1999 constitutional revision, in which the National Assembly had unexpectedly altered the status quo from open voting to secret ballots, not only violating principles of openness and transparency but also evading political accountability.[107]

In addition, especially noteworthy are the privileges and immunities invested in the members of the Legislative Yuan that help them to effectively exercise their power. According to the Additional Articles of the ROC Constitution, 'no member of the Legislative Yuan may be arrested or detained without the permission of the Legislative Yuan, when that body is in session, except in case of in flagrante delicto'.[108]

---

[103] Ibid.

[104] As with courts in the civil law tradition, the Constitutional Court has seldom directly referred to foreign cases in majority opinions. However, concurring or dissenting opinions issued by individual justices refer to foreign cases, laws or scholarly works quite often. For further discussion on this issue, see W-C Chang and J-r Yeh, 'Judges as Discursive Agent: The Use of Foreign Precedents by the Constitutional Court of Taiwan' in T Groppi and M-C Ponthoreau (eds), *The Use of Foreign Precedents by Constitutional Judges* (Oxford, Hart Publishing, 2013) 373–92.

[105] *JY Interpretation No 381* (1995).

[106] *JY Interpretation No 499* (2000).

[107] Ibid.

[108] Art 4(8) Additional Articles of the Constitution of the Republic of China (2005).

In addition, Article 73 of the ROC Constitution guarantees that no Legislative Yuan member shall be held responsible outside the Legislative Yuan for opinions expressed or votes cast. The Constitutional Court has held that the immunity conferred by the Constitution 'should be construed as liberally as possible' and accordingly, 'all statements, questioning, motions, voting and directly related conduct made in sessions or committees, such as party negotiations and statements expressed in public hearings, should also be protected'.[109]

Finally, the Court has stated that legislators should not bear any criminal charges, civil liabilities, or administrative responsibilities when they express their opinions or cast their votes in the Legislative Yuan, with the exception that they may be disciplined for the violation of internal parliamentary rules.[110]

B. Financial Control

The power over the purse is critical to the operation of a modern state, and is particularly important when a government has shouldered nearly all the responsibilities of the social and economic lives of its citizens. This has become especially true in recent years, which has seen many nations suffer the fluctuations of global financial crises. The ROC Constitution allocates fiscal power between the Executive Yuan, the Legislative Yuan and the Control Yuan, although this power is primarily associated with the Legislative Yuan.[111] Three months before the end of each fiscal year, the Executive Yuan must present to the Legislative Yuan the budget for the next fiscal year.[112] Within three months after the Executive Yuan's presentation of the final accounting of revenues and expenditures, it is the responsibility of the Auditor General, who is under the Control Yuan but acts independently, to complete an audit and submit its report to the Legislative Yuan.[113]

Notably, Article 70 of the ROC Constitution expressly forbids the Legislative Yuan from making proposals for increases in budgetary

---

[109] *JY Interpretation No 435* (1997).
[110] *JY Interpretation No 401* (1996).
[111] Art 63 Constitution of the Republic of China (1947).
[112] Art 59 Constitution of the Republic of China (1947).
[113] Art 105 Constitution of the Republic of China (1947).

expenditure presented by the Executive Yuan. With this ban, the framers of the Constitution intended to prevent possible pork-barrel politics and spending.[114] When the 2nd Legislative Yuan, Taiwan's first democratically elected legislature, began to exercise the power of the purse, the question was brought to the Constitutional Court as to whether the Legislative Yuan could add, delete or adjust the amount of individual budgetary items, as long as it did not increase the total amount of the general budget.[115] In response, the Court issued *JY Interpretation No 391*, in which it forbade the legislature from making any adjustments to the amounts of budgetary items. In the Court's view, such legislative alteration would qualify as an increase under Article 70. To allow the legislature to increase the budget would undermine the separation of powers between the executive and legislative branches and erode the principle of checks and balances, as it would involve 'the revision and adjustment of the contents of policy implementation and planning, which can easily result in the successes or failures of a policy being unaccounted for, and politics of accountability being difficult to establish'.[116]

Once the general government budget is passed, it is up to the executive to implement it, subject only to the audits by the Auditor-General and the Control Yuan's national audit office.[117] Here, the question may arise as to whether the executive can withhold or suspend particular budgetary items from being implemented. In 2000, although it enjoyed a surprise win in the presidential election, the DPP remained a minority in the legislature. Historically an advocate for policies against nuclear power plants, the DPP government decided to suspend the construction of the fourth nuclear power plant by not executing the plant's budget.[118] Angered, the KMT legislative majority fiercely objected, and threatened to impeach or recall the incumbent DPP President. Eventually, this constitutional controversy found its way to the Constitutional Court.

---

[114] Chang, above n 8, 87–88.
[115] *JY Interpretation No 391* (1995).
[116] Ibid.
[117] See discussion below on the functions of the Control Yuan.
[118] *JY Interpretation No 520* (2001).

The Court distinguished three kinds of circumstances involving the withholding of certain expenditures.[119] First, for 'funds under the statutory budget designated for the maintenance of an agency's normal operations and exercising its legally authorised duties', the withholding of these funds would affect the existence of that agency and thus should be deemed unlawful. Second, if the withholding 'does not involve the adjustment of a critical national policy and meets the conditions under the Budget Act, such as the occurrence of special incidents or managerial changes due to market factors', such a withholding is due to the 'flexibility of budget execution' and should be permitted and deemed as lawful. Third and last, if the withholding 'has the functional effect of changing administrative or critical national policies', it would be deemed unlawful and unconstitutional 'if such withholding does not indeed involve the Legislative Yuan's participation'.[120]

In the Court's view, the Legislative Yuan is vested with the power to participate in the decision-making process regarding critical national policies, as stipulated in Article 63 of the ROC Constitution. While recognising that a popularly elected President may seek to implement his or her campaign promises and accordingly alter critical national policies after inauguration, the Court stressed that 'any change of policy direction or critical policy should nevertheless abide by the check and balance of powers … between the Executive and Legislative Yuan'. In the nuclear power plant case, therefore, the Court mandated a process of dialogue as a final solution.[121]

The Executive Yuan was required to report to the Legislative Yuan, which in turn would decide after hearing the report to oppose it or make other resolutions. Should the two branches continue to disagree with each other, the Legislative Yuan could move for a no-confidence vote and force the premier's resignation. Alternatively, the Legislative Yuan could opt for other solutions such as enacting a law over the construction of nuclear power plants, as long as such law did not fall foul of the Constitution.[122]

---

[119] Ibid.
[120] Ibid, reasoning paras 2 and 3.
[121] Yeh, above n 29, 913.
[122] Reasoning para 6, *JY Interpretation No 520* (2001).

C. Shared Powers and Conflict Resolution

Under the principles of separation of powers and checks and balances, the Executive Yuan and the Legislative Yuan share many powers between them. The relationships between the two political branches are primarily determined by the structure of the government: presidential, parliamentary or semi-presidential. As discussed earlier, however, the government's structure has become a point of dispute after several rounds of constitutional revision.[123] Such disputes have led to judicial resolutions of many political conflicts—especially from 2000 to 2008, when Taiwan had a DPP executive and KMT legislative majority.[124] The following discussion focuses on the other two areas in which the Constitutional Court has dealt with the executive's and legislature's shared powers: foreign policy and personnel appointment.

Regarding foreign relations, the ROC Constitution has given the President the power to conclude treaties, while the President of the Executive Yuan—the premier—and the ministers refer those treaties to the Legislation Yuan for deliberation and ratification.[125] While what was just described is the process in theory, things proceed differently in practice. This is because very few states have formal diplomatic relationships with Taiwan and, as a result, its government seldom enters into treaties with other states. Instead, the government and other states' governments usually reach executive agreements that escape parliamentary oversight. To strengthen parliamentary controls over foreign relations, the Constitutional Court in *JY Interpretation No 329* took a functional approach to treaties.[126] According to the Court, the term 'treaty' may be understood in two ways, each requiring a different form of parliamentary deliberation. The first type of treaty is the typical international agreement, employing the title of 'treaty', 'convention' or 'agreement' and including a clause for ratification. The second type employs no such title and includes no ratification clause but nevertheless: 1) directly involves important national issues such as defence, diplomacy, finance, or the economy; 2) greatly concerns the rights or

---

[123] See chs 1 and 3.
[124] Yeh, above n 29.
[125] Arts 38, 58(2) and 63 Constitution of the Republic of China (1947).
[126] *JY Interpretation No 329* (1993).

duties of individuals; or 3) includes content identical to domestic statutes. An executive agreement with any of the above qualities must be sent for legislative approval unless it is authorised or predetermined by the legislature prior to its conclusion.[127]

JY Interpretation No 329 was concerned with the level of parliamentary control over the agreements reached by authorised agencies between Taiwan and Mainland China. Yet, the Constitutional Court side-stepped this controversial issue by simply stating that existing cross-Strait agreements were not international agreements to which this interpretation referred.[128] Later, in 2003, the Act Governing Relations between the People of the Taiwan Area and the Mainland Area was revised to strengthen legislative oversight. Under this Act, if an agreement requires an amendment to the law or new legislation, the agreement must be submitted to the Legislative Yuan for consideration and approval. Alternatively, if an agreement requires no further statutory actions, it may be submitted to the Executive Yuan for approval and to the Legislative Yuan to be recorded.[129]

Notwithstanding this legislative oversight, agreements with Mainland China still arouse political controversy and stir up much public distrust. On 18 March 2014, as KMT legislators employed tactics to push through the passage of the Service Trade Pact with Mainland China, angry students and other citizens broke into the Legislative Yuan and began a weeks-long occupation of the floor.[130] The unprecedented but peaceful occupation by the 'Sunflower Movement' successfully drew global attention[131] and ultimately pressed the government to rethink the Service Trade Pact and to consider enacting a special law governing the conclusion and approval of cross-Strait agreements.[132]

---

[127] Ibid.

[128] Ibid.

[129] Art 5(2) Act Governing Relations between the People of the Taiwan Area and the Mainland Area, official English translation available at law.moj.gov.tw/Eng/LawClass/LawAll.aspx?PCode=Q0010001.

[130] 'Protesters occupy Taiwan parliament over China trade deal', 19 March 2014, *BBC News*, at www.bbc.com/news/world-asia-26641525.

[131] J Pan, 'Trade Pact Siege: Rallies Held Globe for Sunflower Movement', 1 April 2014 *Taipei Times*, at www.taipeitimes.com/News/taiwan/archives/2014/04/01/2003587023.

[132] C Wang, 'Siege Aftermath: Ker Worked with Speaker to End Student Occupation', 18 April 2014 *Taipei Times*, at www.taipeitimes.com/News/taiwan/archives/2014/04/17/2003588235.

Regarding personnel appointment, the President chooses who will lead independent constitutional institutions, subject to the consent of the Legislative Yuan. This is the case for Constitutional Court justices; the Judicial Yuan President and Vice-President; Control Yuan members, President and Vice-President; and Examination Yuan members, President and Vice-President.[133] The Constitutional Court has called attention to the shared nature of such appointment power over the members of the Control Yuan.[134] In the Court's view, while the President is empowered to initiate decisions regarding appointment, such decisions are subject to the checks and balances of the Legislative Yuan's review.[135]

For appointments to independent commissions that carry out executive functions, however, due regard must be paid to the executive power. The Court determined that the Executive Yuan should retain power over personnel affairs even for members of independent commissions.[136] However, as a check and balance, the Legislative Yuan is not precluded from imposing certain restrictions on the appointment of such members. Yet, there are limits to what the legislature may do. It may not violate an unambiguous constitutional provision. Nor may it either substantially deprive the executive of its power over personnel affairs, or direct a takeover of such power.[137]

If the appointment is to an institution entirely within the power of the executive or the legislature, such appointment should fall squarely into the hands of either respective power. In *JY Interpretation No 645*, the Constitutional Court stated that the executive branch has the power to determine its own personnel, which is 'indispensable for satisfactory performance of the functions of the executive power'.[138] In this case, the Court deemed the National Referendum Review Committee to be organised inside the Executive Yuan as part of the executive branch and, thus, the power of appointment resided primarily with the Executive Yuan.[139] In a similar vein, the appointment to a

---

[133] Arts 5–7 Additional Articles of the Constitution of the Republic of China (2005).
[134] *JY Interpretation No 632* (2007).
[135] Ibid, reasoning para 4.
[136] *JY Interpretation No 613* (2006). See ch 3.
[137] Ibid.
[138] *JY Interpretation No 645* (2008).
[139] Ibid.

parliamentary investigation committee should be solely in the hands of the Legislative Yuan, as illustrated in *JY Interpretation No 585*.[140]

IV. THE CONTROL YUAN AFTER TRANSFORMATION

As discussed earlier, after the 1992 constitutional revision, the Control Yuan was no longer a parliamentary body. According to the Additional Articles of the ROC Constitution, the Control Yuan now has 29 members, including a President and a Vice-President, all of whom serve a six-year term and are appointed by the President with the approval of the Legislative Yuan.[141] All Control Yuan members are intended to be non-partisan and independently exercise the powers in accordance with the Constitution and relevant laws.[142]

Even after its transformation, the Control Yuan's powers are still broadly defined as legislative in nature. The Control Yuan is the highest control body to exercise the powers of impeachment, censure, correction and audit.[143] With respect to audit powers, the Auditor-General has a six-year term, and is appointed by the President with the consent of the Legislative Yuan.[144] The Auditor-General, assisted by the national audit office under the Control Yuan, is tasked with supervising the implementation of government budgets, reviewing revenues and expenditures, and investigating financial misconduct. The Constitutional Court has underscored the independence of the Auditor-General: he or she should not be removed from office for policy reasons or due to changes in the ruling party.[145]

Regarding the powers of censure and correction, the Control Yuan has the power to investigate public and private organisations or individuals. Those investigated by the Control Yuan are obliged to provide detailed responses in due course. If a Control Yuan member

---

[140] *JY Interpretation No 585* (2004).

[141] Art 7(2) Additional Articles of the Constitution of the Republic of China (1992).

[142] Art 7(5) Additional Articles of the Constitution of the Republic of China (1992).

[143] Art 15(1) Additional Articles of the Constitution of the Republic of China (1992).

[144] Art 104 Constitution of the Republic of China (1947).

[145] *JY Interpretation No 357* (1994).

considers a public functionary to be in violation of a law or dereliction of a duty, he or she may submit the case to three or more other members of the Control Yuan for a censure decision.[146] If a case involves criminal violations, the Control Yuan must refer it to a competent judicial authority. Also, the Control Yuan, after investigation, may impose corrective measures on the Executive Yuan and its subordinate bodies.[147] However, deprived of parliamentary status, the Control Yuan's censure decisions or corrective measures have not had any real impact on the Executive Yuan or its subordinate bodies. After all, the Executive Yuan is accountable to the Legislative Yuan but not to the Control Yuan. The investigative powers exercised by the Control Yuan overlap those of the Legislative Yuan and, in criminal cases, those of prosecutors.

If a public functionary's violation of law or other wrongdoings merit more than a censure decision or corrective measure, the Control Yuan may initiate impeachment proceedings. Impeachment proceedings against public functionaries in the central or local governments or against personnel in the Judicial or Examination Yuans are initiated by two or more Control Yuan members and voted upon by a committee of no fewer than nine members.[148] Impeachment decisions are sent to the Public Functionary Disciplinary Sanction Commission, a judicial body, for review and final approval.[149] In other words, the Control Yuan's chief function is to initiate—rather than to finally determine—the impeachment of government officials, including judges and those who exercise independent powers. It should be noted that the Public Functionary Disciplinary Sanction Commission may also receive cases on motions from the executive branch.[150] In addition, the Judge Act of 2011 created a special committee and disciplinary tribunal to determine the disciplinary measures and impeachment of judges.[151] As stated previously, after the 1997 constitutional revision, the Legislative Yuan rather than the Control Yuan now initiates the impeachment

---

[146] Art 19 Control Act (1992).

[147] Art 24 Control Act (1992).

[148] Art 7(3) Additional Articles of the Constitution of the Republic of China (1992).

[149] Art 18 Act on Public Functionary Disciplinary Sanctions (1985).

[150] Art 19 Act on Public Functionary Disciplinary Sanctions (1985).

[151] Arts 4 and 47 Judge Act (2011).

of the President and Vice-President; under the 2005 constitutional revision, the Constitutional Court adjudicates such impeachment proceedings.

The Control Yuan's institutional transformation limited its functions considerably. To summarise what was discussed above, its power to impeach the President and Vice-President devolved to the Legislative Yuan, and the power to impeach judges shifted to a special disciplinary tribunal within the judiciary. The Control Yuan's powers of censure and correction have not been effective, and its power to investigate often overlaps with similar powers exercised by the Legislative Yuan or prosecutors. The Control Yuan's only effective power is its power to audit, which is independently exercised by the Auditor-General rather than Control Yuan members. Since its transformation in 1992, it is no surprise that calls for the Control Yuan's abolition have not ceased.

Notwithstanding the Control Yuan's limited functions, the appointment of its members has still at times become a point of serious political confrontation. At the start of DPP President Chen Shui-bian's second term in 2004, the KMT legislative majority boycotted his nominations of several Control Yuan members. In 2007, the Constitutional Court held this boycott to be unconstitutional and urged that the Legislative Yuan exercise its consent power in a timely manner.[152] Even after this constitutional interpretation, the KMT legislative boycott against the above-mentioned nominees did not end until after the KMT's victory in the 2008 presidential election. In 2008, the newly inaugurated President Ma Ying-jeou appointed the 4th Control Yuan's members, with the consent of the KMT legislative majority. In 2014, the six-year term of the 4th Control Yuan expired and the 5th term saw the nomination of its first female head.[153]

After the Control Yuan's functions had been altered and become more supplementary, proposals for reform and even abolishment were legion.[154] The direction of proposed reforms has varied: toward a body of ombudsmen with the additional power to petition the Constitutional

---

[152] *JY Interpretation No 632* (2007).

[153] C Wang, 'Nominations to Head Yuans Are "Political Rewards": DPP', 8 May 2014 *Taipei Times*, at www.taipeitimes.com/News/front/archives/2014/05/08/2003589824.

[154] Lin et al, above n 51, 210–11, 253–54.

Court over human rights abuses; toward a National Human Rights Commission supervising human rights implementation; or toward an integrity institution primarily responsible for combating corruption and maintaining a clean government.[155] However, none of these reform proposals has been seriously considered.[156] After the 2005 constitutional revision imposed a high threshold for constitutional amendment, the possibility that the Control Yuan would ever reform became quite unlikely.

V. CONCLUSION

In the course of Taiwan's democratisation and constitutional reformation, representative institutions have undergone drastic changes: from three parliaments to one. The Legislative Yuan, now the single parliament, has seen its powers strengthened, having gained additional powers from the two erstwhile parliaments—the National Assembly and the Control Yuan. The transformation of representative institutions has also led to the promulgation of electoral rules that adopted a system of proportional representation and underscored the roles of political parties. But despite successful reforms in representative institutions and the electoral system, the undemocratic operation of political parties and their lack of political accountability remain serious concerns. Thus, to improve transparency and due process of political parties, the enactment of the Political Party Act or other similar statutory schemes must be considered.

The Control Yuan, as it exists after its functional transformation, should be the next target of constitutional reform. Serious and feasible solutions include abolishing it entirely or transforming it into a national human rights commission. However, the office of the Auditor-General, together with the national audit office, should remain intact and continue to function independently without political interference. Although the Control Yuan needs to be reformed, no reforms are likely to be imminent due to the high constitutional revision threshold that has been in effect since 2005.

---

[155] W-C Chang, 'Constitutional Reform of Taiwan in a New Century: On the Abolishment of Control Yuan, Examination Yuan and National Assembly' (2004) 115 *Taiwan Law Review* 209 (in Chinese).
[156] Ibid.

FURTHER READING

Chu, Y-h, 'Democratic Consolidation in the Post-KMT Era: the Challenge of Governance' in M Alagappa (ed), *Taiwan's Presidential Politics: Democratization and Cross-Strait Relations in the Twenty-First Century* (New York, Routledge, 2001) 88–114.

Hsieh, F-s, 'The Origins and Consequences of Electoral Reform in Taiwan' (2009) 45(2) *Issues & Studies* 1–22.

Lin, J-w, 'Vote Buying vs Noise Making: Two Models of Electoral Competition under the Single Non-transferable Vote—Multimember District System' (1998) 30 *Chinese Political Science Review* 93–122.

Yeh, J-r, 'Presidential Politics and the Judicial Facilitation of Dialogue Between Political Actors in New Asian Democracies: Comparing the South Korean and Taiwanese Experiences' (2010) 8 *International Journal of Constitutional Law* 911–49.

Yeh, J-r, 'The Cult of *Fatung*: Representational Manipulation and Reconstruction in Taiwan' in G Hassall and C Saunders (eds), *The People's Representatives: Electoral Systems in the Asia-Pacific Region* (Sydney, Allen & Unwin, 1997) 27–37.

5

Multi-level Governance and Devolution

———••◦◦•———

Central–local Relations in the ROC Constitution – Taiwan as a State versus Taiwan as a Province – Beyond Borderlines: Central–local Relations in Regional and Global Perspectives – Conclusion

T HE ROC CONSTITUTION, as promulgated in China after World War II, stipulated a three-level system in its vertical separation of powers, with Taiwan as a minor and peripheral province that was granted only limited local autonomy in the unitary state. The KMT and the ROC Constitution relocated to Taiwan following the KMT's defeat in the Chinese Civil War in 1949. Despite minor giveaways and concessions at the local level, which were essentially a form of calculated power-sharing by the KMT regime, the KMT governed Taiwan as a peripheral province under martial law rule until the late 1980s.

The application of the overly grand but constrained structure of local autonomy, as stipulated in the Constitution, to the requirements of a dynamic transitional context, has been the focus of central–local relations in Taiwan during its democratic transition.[1] Since the late 1980s, however, democratisation has resulted in a series of constitutional and legislative reforms, which have finally led to substantial

---

[1] For features of transitional constitutionalism, see J-r Yeh and W-C Chang, 'The Changing Landscape of Modern Constitutionalism: Transitional Perspective' (2009) 4 *National Taiwan University Law Review* 145.

changes to central–local relations.[2] The growth of local autonomy during the vibrant transitional period has transformed central–local relations under the Constitution from limited autonomy within a unitary state to a hybrid and dynamic form of transitional federalism. In addition, the realignment of vertical power separation in Taiwan brought about a paradigm shift in central–local relations from 'Taiwan as a province of the Republic of China' to 'Taiwan as a state'.[3] Over time, constitutionally stipulated local autonomy has been deconstructed and rebuilt against the backdrop of cross-Strait relations between China and Taiwan, democratic transition and globalisation.

This chapter begins with a general survey of the ROC Constitution's local autonomy and power allocation in its vertically aligned system of government, and next proceeds to paint a contrasting picture of the realities of that theoretical power allocation in practice. This disparity between constitutional design and reality is typified by the dispute over downsizing the Taiwan Provincial Government, along with two Constitutional Court cases in which the Court sought to resolve the politically contentious dispute between the central government and the Taipei City Government. These disputes, rooted in local autonomy, further reveal the deep-seated power struggle in transitional politics; central–local relations will inevitably continue to play a significant role in the future of Taiwan's democratic transitional politics. Finally, beyond federalism within a sovereign framework, the significance of the development of central–local relations in Taiwan transcends the importance of the establishment of federalism within a sovereign framework. Rather, it should be viewed through the macro lens of the establishment of multi-layer governance and devolution in Asia during a period of unprecedented Asian and global integration.

---

[2] Democratisation has been the major force driving constitutional and regulatory reforms. See J-r Yeh, 'Changing Forces of Constitutional and Regulatory Reform in Taiwan' (1990) 4 *Columbia Journal of Chinese Law* 83; J-r Yeh, 'Democracy-driven Transformation to Regulatory State: The Case of Taiwan' (2008) 3 *National Taiwan University Law Review* 31.

[3] For a complete discussion of Taiwan's struggles as related to its historic entanglement with China, see, eg, PL Hsieh, 'An Unrecognized State in Foreign and International Courts: The Case of the Republic of China on Taiwan' (2007) 28 *Michigan Journal of International Law* 765.

I. CENTRAL–LOCAL RELATIONS IN THE ROC CONSTITUTION

Central–local relations were a controversial issue during the drafting of the ROC Constitution in the 1940s—a time set against the backdrop of the Japanese invasion, Chinese Civil War, and the disintegration of China.[4] In deep conflict with the Communists, the Nationalists were concerned about local separatists and regarded the multi-polar politics that had persisted for decades, since the establishment of the Republic, as the primary threat to national unity. These concerns translated into constitutional codification, which incorporated a heightened level of centralised regulation for central–local relations. The ROC's Constitution allocates the powers of legislation and administration across myriad entities to address a wide range of issues critical to central–local dynamics. In fact, it took two chapters and 22 articles of the Constitution to regulate such central–local relations.

A. Elections and Accountability

The constitution-making process became an extremely difficult task since drafters had to tackle the inherent difficulties in governing a nation with a vast territory, a multiplicity of cultures and ethnic groups, and complex political parties. Though political concerns had driven the KMT Government to pursue a fully centralised nation, reality showed that establishing a Central Government in full control was a virtually impossible feat. Meanwhile, the Constitution also needed to reflect the fruits of the negotiations among the political parties regarding central–local relations. Thus, the 1947 Constitution stipulated a unitary system with three levels of government for China that were characterised by a centralised Central Government and local autonomy to create a limited space for self-governing. According to the Constitution, the government was to be structured vertically, with a rigid hierarchical structure. Elections were established for administrators and legislators at all levels of government.

---

[4] For a more contextual introduction to the drafting and implementation processes of the ROC Constitution see, eg, S Zhao, *Power by Design: Constitution-Making in Nationalist China* (Honolulu, University of Hawaii Press, 1996).

Chapter 10 of the Constitution stipulates the structure of the local government system.[5] Below the Central Government, local autonomous units comprise two levels: province and *hsien* ('counties'). Within the county level, townships or districts further comprise *li* and *lin* ('villages' and 'neighbourhoods', respectively), which are not stipulated in the Constitution, but are created by law. Constitutionally stipulated local governments enjoy basic autonomy and self-government. A province may convoke a provincial assembly to enact regulations as long as they are not in conflict with the Constitution. Citizens of the province elect provincial governors and members of provincial councils (established to exercise provincial legislative power). Likewise, special local entities, which include special municipalities and autonomous regions for national minorities, enjoy equal status with provinces through the Constitution. Special municipalities, megacities such as Beijing and Tianjin and their surrounding areas, were under the Central Government Executive Yuan's direct jurisdiction. The local self-government system of the Mongolian Leagues and Banners was created by law to address minority concerns. Finally, the self-government system of Tibet was constitutionally preserved.

Counties occupy the lowest level of constitutionally stipulated local autonomous government and are the basic units of the ROC Constitution's vertical government system. Counties enjoy basic local autonomy, through the Constitution's assurances that the people of the county shall exercise the rights of initiative and referendum in matters within the sphere of the county's self-government, along with the rights of election and recall of the magistrate and other county self-government officials. Counties also enjoy administrative and legislative powers within their respective regions, but these may only be exercised in accordance with the law and may not be in conflict with the Constitution or with provincial regulations. As the basic unit of the local autonomy system, counties serve a special function because the National Assembly, which is charged with the powers to elect and recall the President and the Vice-President and to amend the Constitution, consists of representatives elected mainly from counties.[6] In the Constitution's vertical government structure—similar to democratic centralism—the

---

[5] Arts 112–136 Constitution of the Republic of China (1947).
[6] Arts 25–34 Constitution of the Republic of China (1947).

National Assembly sits atop the government system where it represents the people and exercises its power to revise the Constitution and to elect the President.

The Constitution's central–local relations constitute a limited form of local autonomy in a unitary state. In 1946, the Republic of China, according to the Constitution, comprised 35 provinces that consisted of more than 3,000 counties, 12 special municipalities, two minority areas (Mongolia and Tibet), and one Special Administrative Region (Hainan). However, this lofty design for governing the territory never panned out in practice. Soon, with the Nationalists' defeat in the Chinese Civil War and the Nationalist Government's relocation to Taiwan, the Constitution encountered a completely different reality.

B. Pre-emption and Regulatory Supremacy

Vertical allocation of powers within the ROC Constitution's government system was defined functionally; though, due to significant overlap among the powers, such textual stipulations are sometimes hard to clarify. Chapter 10 of the Constitution regulates the division of power and responsibility between central and local governments and provides for a mechanism of dispute resolution.[7] Powers are distributed according to four categories: 1) powers vested exclusively in the Central Government; 2) powers vested in the Central Government, the administration of which may be delegated to the provincial and/or county governments; 3) powers vested in the provinces, the administration of which may be delegated to their counties; and 4) powers vested in the counties themselves.

The Constitution further assigns powers within each of the four categories in four separate articles. The first category contains 13 subdivisions in which legislative and administrative powers are assigned to the Central Government exclusively. These powers are primarily sovereign national affairs such as foreign affairs, national defence and the judicial system. Also, the Central Government is granted the most critical powers, including authority over the nation's finances (Article 107). The second category consists of 20 subdivisions,

---

[7] Arts 107–111 Constitution of the Republic of China (1947).

which range from general principles of provincial and county self-government to the division of administrative areas, as well as a wide range of social legislation. These powers predominantly relate to local interests, though nearly all require central reconciliation (Article 108). The third category contains 12 subdivisions, including public health, the industrial sector and communications, and public welfare works (Article 109). Finally, the fourth category covers 11 subdivisions related to fundamental local infrastructure, such as education and public health (Article 110).

Notably, Article 111 stipulates that non-enumerated matters are handled in the following manner: national matters fall within the Central Government's jurisdiction; provincial matters fall within the jurisdiction of their respective provinces, and county matters fall within the purview of the affected county. The Constitution follows a functional approach, tasking the Central Government's Legislative Yuan with dispute resolution. The drafters elected to keep conflict resolution within the scope of the Central Government's authority because allocating power according to the 'nature' of matters while still providing the desired level of flexibility could easily breed ambiguities.

C. Budgetary Control and Devolution

In a unitary state, as prescribed by the Constitution, the power to control the State's finances enables the Central Government to seize substantial control over localities, which traces its roots to the Qin Dynasty which began in 221 BC. Since that time, China has, during most of its history, been a unified empire, with a powerful national government that exercises strict control over its national territory. The national government has always collected taxes and other local revenues both to facilitate top-down reallocation and in response to unrest caused by warlords and local separatists since the establishment of the Republic who have, throughout China's history, exploited local interests and created nations within the nation. These contextual factors pushed the Nationalist Government to create, within the Constitution, a unitary-state structure with, among other things, strong fiscal control.

As a result, Article 107 of the Constitution assigns to the Central Government the powers of finance and national revenues and oversight of state-operated economic enterprises. Article 109 further stipulates that when any province, in overseeing state-operated economic enterprises, finds its funds insufficient, it may, by resolution of the Legislative Yuan, obtain subsidies from the National Treasury. In addition, Article 147 stipulates that 'the Central Government, in order to attain a balanced economic development among the provinces, shall give appropriate aid to poor or unproductive provinces'.[8] These constitutional provisions granted the Central Government the power to distribute funds from the national coffers to provinces on significant matters. Further, the impact of these constitutional revisions should be observed by taking into account the Fundamental National Policies stipulated in Chapter 13 of the Constitution. Article 142 provides that the national economy shall be based on the 'Principle of the People's Livelihood' and shall seek to effect equalisation of land ownership and restriction of private capital to attain balance in national wealth and people's livelihoods. The Constitution's economic system is analogous to that of a socialist economy, in which the Central Government is authorised to concentrate economic resources and dedicate them for public welfare. Fundamental National Policies further provide the Central Government a wide range of national social policies that expand the government's legal capacity to control resources.

The problems inherent in a system of overall budget and finance control, coupled with the dawning of the martial law regime following the KMT's defeat in the Civil War, led to suppression of local autonomy. Given its druthers, the KMT Government would have continued the constitutional structure of central–local relations in Taiwan to mould its governing strategy, which would have preserved the Constitution's unitary structure of central–local relations in Taiwan but for the democratic transition of the late 1980s.

II. TAIWAN AS A STATE VERSUS TAIWAN AS A PROVINCE

As discussed in chapter 2, the Nationalists' retreat to Taiwan upon their defeat on the Mainland has transformed Taiwan, conceived as a peripheral province of China, into the exclusive base of Nationalist

---

[8] Art 147 Constitution of the Republic of China (1947).

governance. In the early years of their rule in Taiwan, the Nationalists maintained a policy of 'striking back', adhering to the framework of the Greater China that was embedded in the Constitution. However, as this policy soon became unsustainable and the Nationalists planned for permanent residence in Taiwan, they amended the Constitution's central–local relations accordingly. Later, followed by the expiry of the martial law decree and the momentum of democratisation, the Constitution underwent fundamental reform, which included drastic changes to central–local relations.

The constitutionally mandated local autonomy and its metamorphosis from textual notion to real-world institution crystallised two models of central–local relations, characterised by two distinct political imaginations. The constitutionally prescribed vertical system is rooted in the concept of a Greater China and stipulates limited autonomy under the highly centralised control of the national government within the framework of a constitutionally safeguarded unitary state. However, the 1990s' democratic transition transformed this model of central–local relations into a more hybrid and dynamic transitional federalism. Through constitutional and legislative revisions, local autonomy has been substantially reformed to usher in a new era of central–local relations. Instead of being positioned at the periphery of China as it was for the drafters of the ROC Constitution, Taiwan is now at the centre of the territorial imagination for constitutional design.

Numerous reforms led to the formation of this new model. First, the rigid and complicated regulations of local governments stipulated in the ROC Constitution were suspended, which provided more leeway for legislative action in the later stages of government readjustment. Second, the excessively grand cascading structure of local government was simplified, transformed and ultimately abolished. Third, the Taiwan Provincial Government downsized and special municipalities gained more autonomy. Fourth, the reins on the highly centralised financial power were loosened and local governments gained control of more resources. Finally, administrative district realignment signified another remarkable step in a new era for central–local relations. The 'Two Capitals' system, wherein the prime areas were subject to the control of Central Government, enabled local political heads to apply enough leverage to break the yoke through challenges to the Central Government. This led to the new system of 'Six Capitals', which provides more balance in regional development and political competition.

A. Constitutional Amendment and Legislative Action

By declaring a state of emergency of sorts during the Chinese Civil War, the KMT compromised the constitutionally stipulated local autonomy as part of its efforts to tighten social control.[9] During the ensuing martial law era, the government did not promulgate the General Principles of Provincial and County Self-Government, a law required by the Constitution to provide a legal basis for local autonomy. Instead, local autonomy was sparingly doled out by the Central Government through a series of ordinances. In 1954, the Executive Yuan promulgated the 'Outline for the Implementation of Local Self-Government in every City and County in Taiwan' (the Outline), which was submitted by the Taiwan Provincial Government and established a foundation for the promotion of local autonomy through executive orders. Since the Outline was only an administrative regulation, the power it allotted local governments had no constitutional guarantee and lacked legal protection. Thus the upper levels of government continually encroached upon the power of the lower levels. In the 1960s, though the Outline was revised to enhance local self-government, local governments continued to lack autonomy, both in terms of their control over constitutionally guaranteed domains and also in areas beyond the scope of their constitutional grant, such as human resources and the budget.[10]

The KMT Government instituted a regime of soft authoritarianism during the martial law era, effectively evading the constitutional requirement of a certain degree of regulated local autonomy. During this time, elections for Central Government positions were suspended in an effort to preserve the legitimacy inherited from the Mainland period. In addition, the Governor of the Taiwan Provincial Government and mayors of special municipalities were subject to the designation of the Central Government. Even as late as 1990, *JY Interpretation No 260* denied the legislative power of the provinces and counties. To avoid falling foul of the Constitution, the Court ruled that according to the constitutionally mandated local government provisions, though

---

[9] For a detailed breakdown of the KMT's policy for governing Taiwan, see PC-m Wang, 'Bastion Created, a Regime Reformed, an Economy Reengineered 1949–1970' in MA Rubinstein (ed), *Taiwan: A New History* (New York, ME Sharpe, 1999).

[10] D Fell, *Government and Politics in Taiwan* (New York, Routledge, 2012) 144.

the Central Government had no authority to enact individual laws for specified provincial assemblies and the organisation of the provincial government, the established provincial representative bodies similarly lacked the requisite legislative power.[11] However, as a result of a politically calculated move by the KMT, specific elections were held at the local level for the purpose of political propaganda to show democracy in contrast with Mainland China's Communist rule.[12] Spurred in large measure by this façade of limited local autonomy, political opponents, many of whom were local Taiwanese elites, emerged from local geopolitics to challenge the KMT in these elections. Opposition forces grew much stronger, finally culminating in the establishment of the first opposition party, the Democratic Progressive Party (DPP).[13] Many dissidents who had started their political careers through elections to local governments later gained high political profile during the subsequent democratic transition.

The 1990s ushered in a period of democratic transition, and with it, the realisation of Taiwan's constitutional change.[14] A series of constitutional revisions, which touched on a multitude of issues, including central–local relations, were initiated in rapid succession.[15] The framework of the ROC's Constitution had proved unsustainable in Taiwan, thus creating the primary goal of political balance at the onset of reform. In response to the long-standing concentration of power in the Central Government, local government heads, regardless of party affiliation, began to lobby for a broader distribution of power. The next problem that plagued reformers was the allocation of resources; with the rapid growth of the population and the expense of urbanisation, local governments called for increased financial liquidity. Finally, administrative

---

[11] *JY Interpretation No 260* (1990).

[12] Regarding *Fatung*, see J-r Yeh, 'The Cult of Fatung, Representative Manipulation and Reconstruction in Taiwan' in Hassall and Saunders (eds), *The People Representatives: Electoral Systems in the Asia-Pacific Region* (Sydney, Allen and Unwin, 1997) 23.

[13] MA Rubinstein, 'Political Taiwanization and Pragmatic Diplomacy: The Eras of Chiang Ching-kuo and Lee Teng-hui, 1971–1994' in Rubinstein (ed), *Taiwan*; and D Roy, *Taiwan: A Political History* (Ithaca, Cornell University Press, 2003) 152.

[14] J-r Yeh and W-C Chang, 'A Decade of Changing Constitutionalism in Taiwan: Transitional and Transnational Perspectives' in AHY Chen (ed), *Constitutionalism in Asia in the Early Twenty-First Century* (Cambridge, Cambridge University Press, 2014) 141.

[15] J-r Yeh, 'Constitutional Reform and Democratization in Taiwan, 1945–2000' in P Chow (ed), *Taiwan's Modernization in Global Perspective* (CT, Praeger, 2002).

efficiency was among the most critical concerns for politicians as well as ordinary citizens; the tri-level structure of the local government, with lower-level local governing groups, quickly became overly complicated and inefficient vehicles for engaging in public administration.

The second constitutional revision, in 1992, effected a remarkable achievement, when local self-government was first constitutionally recognised.[16] Constitutional revisions froze the constitutional requirement that General Principles of Provincial and County Self-Government be promulgated for conducting local legislations, and instead authorised local legislative branches to make self-governing law, thus departing from *JY Interpretation No 260*. This round of constitutional revision also provided for popular election of the provincial governor and municipal mayors. Over time, a series of laws was enacted to institute a new generation of local autonomy. In 1994, the Self-Governance Act for Provinces and Counties and the Self-Governance Act for Special Municipalities were passed by the legislature, thereby providing a legal foundation for local self-government. In December 1994, the first popular elections were held for Taiwan Provincial Governor and the mayors of Taipei and Kaohsiung cities, positions that had previously been government-appointed. Finally, in 1999, the Local Government Act marked the completion of a body of legislation that enshrined local self-government in Taiwan and signalled the abolition of the Outline. This marked the beginning of a new era of central–local relations.

Notably, in the process of renewing the Constitution's central–local relations, two bodies from the original Constitution became obsolete with the changing circumstances. The first was the National Assembly, which was designed under the Constitution as the supreme organ and was bestowed with the highest sovereignty and the symbolism of the Chinese Mainland.[17] Once it had been decided to move from centralism toward democracy by vesting sovereignty directly with the people, and to provide universal suffrage for presidential elections through constitutional mechanisms, the National Assembly became superfluous.

Another notable embarrassment came to the status and function of the Taiwan Provincial Government. Constructed according to the

---

[16] Art 9 Additional Articles to the Constitution of the Republic of China (1992).

[17] The functions and composition of the National Assembly are stipulated in Arts 25–34 Constitution of the Republic of China (1947).

Greater China philosophy, the Taiwan Provincial Government was a single unit of the more than 30 provincial governments. However, after 1949, it became the only province over which the Constitution effectively reigned. The reforms of the 1990s, which included a series of actions designed to simplify the ROC Constitution's government system and implemented universal suffrage for presidential elections, rendered the Taiwan Provincial Government obsolete. Within the small geographic area of Taiwan, the Taiwanese and ROC constituencies overlapped considerably, thus resulting in an overabundance of administrative red tape and inefficient regulation. Above all, to continue to recognise the Taiwan Provincial Government would be akin to clinging to Taiwan's provincial institutions rather than striving to create a new national identity.

B. The Rise and Fall of the Taiwan Provincial Government

From an administrative reform standpoint, downsizing the Taiwan Provincial Government was a direct result of the need for organisational restructuring. The move enhanced administrative efficiency and national competitiveness, both of which required organisational streamlining and simplification of the regulatory process.[18] The provincial government was originally intended to conduct and co-ordinate politics within the counties below. However, the average Chinese province can contain upwards of 100 counties; as a result, provinces became quite important intermediate levels of institutional autonomy. However, since 1949, Taiwan was the only territory under the Central Government's effective control, and by the 1990s, the Provincial Government's existence had outlasted its utility. Preserving the Taiwan Provincial Government was motivated purely by the symbolism it held for the (unattainable) Greater China ideology.

Practically speaking, there was a great deal of overlap between the Taiwan Provincial Government and the Central Government in terms of administrative area and the allocation of power and resources. This has historically led to power struggles between the President and the

---

[18] See J-r Yeh, 'Globalization, Government Reform and the Paradigm Shift of Administrative Law' (2010) 5 *National Taiwan University Law Review* 113.

governor. Particularly following the second constitutional revision, in 1992, which resulted in a direct election for the Taiwan Provincial Governor, constant friction existed between the democratically elected governor and the indirectly elected President, as the direct presidential election did not occur until 1996. Indeed, the popularity of Taiwan Provincial Governor James CY Soong easily surpassed that of President Lee Teng-hui. Under the complex 'Yeltsin effect',[19] their political relationship soon deteriorated. In the eyes of some political observers, the policy of downsizing provincial governments was more an act of political suppression than of genuine constitutional reform. Even so, such political motivations provided legitimacy to the downsizing of the provincial government and also ensured that there was a political impetus behind the government reconstruction of the government at large.

The policy of provincial government downsizing can trace its roots to a consensus reached by the ruling and opposition parties on the need for reform at a 1996 National Development Conference, which occurred shortly after the first direct election of the ROC President. In July 1997, the National Assembly passed a constitutional amendment to effect the change, which included the following key phrases: 'There will be no further elections for the Taiwan Provincial Governor and provincial assemblymen and women as of 21 December 1998,' and 'The restructuring of the functions, business and organisation of the Taiwan Provincial Government will be conducted in accordance with special legal regulations'. To implement the constitutional mandate, the Executive Yuan established a Committee for the Restructuring of the Functions, Business and Organisation of the Taiwan Provincial Government to draft concomitant measures. The Legislative Yuan also passed a series of legislations enabling the downsizing of the Taiwan Provincial Government.[20]

---

[19] 'Yeltsin Effect' is a term used to liken the increasing power of Taiwan's provincial leaders to that of Boris Yeltsin in 1991. 'Concern Grows over "Yeltsin effect"', 30 November 2010 *The China Post*, at www.chinapost.com.tw/taiwan/national/national-news/2010/11/30/281858/Concern-grows.htm.

[20] Legislation includes the Provisional Act for the Restructuring of the Functions, Business and Organisation of the Taiwanese Government and the Local Government Systems Act, and the Revised Act Governing the Allocation of Government Revenues and Expenditures.

The Taiwan Provincial Government now serves only as a symbolic intermediate body between the Central Government and local governments. The term of the first democratically elected Taiwan Provincial Governor ended in 1998, and the Taiwan Provincial Government ceased to be a legal local government entity. The newly downsized Taiwan Provincial Government became a field agency of the Executive Yuan and the democratically elected Taiwan Provincial Assembly was reorganised as the all-appointed Taiwan Provincial Consultative Council, and subsequently stripped of the power to make decisions on matters of local government and the ability to supervise their implementation.

Interestingly, the downsizing of the Taiwan Provincial Government following the constitutional revision in 1997 coincided with the turnover of Hong Kong to the PRC. Both events can be viewed as the promotion of national sovereignty. However, abolishing the Taiwan Provincial Government contrasts with the ROC's continued residence in Taiwan and the PRCs sovereignty claim and, at the same time, refutes institutionally positioning Taiwan as a part of the Greater China. The after-effects of downsizing the Provincial Government were also remarkable from an electoral politics perspective. James CY Soong later split from the KMT and formed the People First Party. Running on an independent ticket for the 2000 presidential election, he split the KMT votes and helped hand the presidency to the DPP candidate Chen Shui-bian, resulting in Taiwan's first regime change.[21] Further, the downsizing of the Provincial Government placed the Central Government at the forefront of daily politics with local governments. Power confrontations between political camps following the transition have tended, more often, to take the form of central versus local governments.

C. Taipei and the Special Municipalities in Transitional Politics

Central–local relations have been one of the most significant issues in Taiwan's transitional politics. With the lifting of martial law and the driving forces of democratisation in full force, the KMT Government

---

[21] Roy, *Taiwan*, above n 13, 227.

took hold of the ruling power and maintained control of the Central Government. Meanwhile, opposition parties still managed to break through and gain a foothold in local elections.[22] Even within the KMT, power struggles between factions of different views towards Taiwanese identity and between mainstream and non-mainstream sections exemplified the struggle between central and local governments. In spite of the downsizing of the Taiwan Provincial Government, the stress of central–local relations continued despite the first regime change in 2000. The disputes between the Taipei City Government and the Central Government underlie the dynamic context of transitional politics behind the transformation of central–local relations in Taiwan.

The period following the first regime change was marked by perhaps the most contentious political disputes in Taiwan's recent history. During the first regime change (2000–2008), President Chen Shui-bian of the DPP did not enjoy a majority in the legislature and faced stiff competition from KMT political star and Taipei City Mayor Ma Ying-jeou. As a result, controversial central–local disputes emerged against heightened political competition. It is interesting to note that, since the first direct presidential election in 1996, all elected Presidents were former Mayors of Taipei City. This demonstrates that the mayor of the capital has certain political advantages against the President in transitional power politics. Further, many disputes between the Central Government and Taipei City occurred during this period and required judicial resolution. The Constitutional Court adjudicated two disputes between the Central Government and Taipei City. Owing to the fact that the downsizing of the Taiwan Provincial Government had eliminated the province's role as an intermediate buffer, the Court sought to initiate dialogue between the parties in both cases and reinforced the concept of local autonomy by providing an interactive solution acceptable to both parties.

The first controversy centred on the financial allocation of the National Health Insurance programme (NHI) between the Taipei City Government and the Central Government. The establishment of the

---

[22] For a discussion of Taiwan's party politics in the 1990s and 2000s see D Fell, *Party Politics in Taiwan: Party Change and the Democratic Evolution of Taiwan, 1991–2004* (London and New York, Routledge, 2005).

NHI programme in 1996 was a great leap forward for social welfare policy in Taiwan. This ambitious national programme has been met with a generally positive reception, but the allocation of the financial burden it created has remained controversial from the beginning. One of the more at-large financial controversies stemmed from the allocation of costs among central and local governments. The municipal governments of Taipei and Kaohsiung constantly lamented about their heavy financial burden while, at the same time, they enjoyed better financial resources due to their classification as 'special municipalities'. The Taipei municipal government even refused to pay the contributions stipulated by law, which resulted in a series of administrative disputes and lawsuits. The tension between the central and local governments was elevated since Mayor of Taipei Ma Ying-jeou and President Chen Shui-bian were the major figures of opposing political parties, which made judicial resolution of the matter all the more politically sensitive. This dispute was finally appealed to the Constitutional Court for adjudication.

In *JY Interpretation No 550*, the Constitutional Court proclaimed that the central and local governments should collectively bear the constitutional duty of supporting an NHI programme. The Court held that the allocation of financial burdens by the National Health Insurance Act to such local governments as Taipei City was constitutional, though the Court did not clearly enumerate how much financial cost could be borne by the local governments. Rather than specify a certain amount or percentage, the Court adopted an approach that favoured negotiation between the parties, under the rationale that since local governments were required to share financial costs, they must be given sufficient opportunities to participate in the course of the policy formulation. Thus, the national government must discuss and consult with local governments when drafting such policies to avoid possibly unreasonable outcomes and must work out sound plans for the fair allocation of associated costs. The Court also demanded that the legislature, in revising relevant laws, allow representatives of local governments to be present as observers and to voice their concerns during relevant legislative sessions.[23] This ruling demonstrated the Court's tendency to be unwilling to intervene in substantive policies, while being more inclined

---

[23] *JY Interpretation No 550* (2002).

to take a rather procedure-centric approach. This case also revealed the disparity of resource allocation among local governments, particularly in favour of special mega-cities such as Taipei City.

Another case in which Taipei City again pitted itself against the Central Government is the Election Postponement Dispute. In order to rearrange the administrative districts (comprised of *li* and *lin*), the Taipei Municipal Government postponed the election of *li* executives. According to the Local Government Act, such an election may be post-poned in light of special circumstances. However, the Central Govern-ment claimed that the rearrangement of the districts of *li* and *lin* could be scheduled while still maintaining the settled election date, and there was no necessity for the postponement, stating that the rearrangement, therefore, did not fall within the 'special circumstances' contemplated by the law. Because Taipei Municipal Government is a protected local self-government entity under Article 118 of the Constitution, and in light of the fact that this petition concerned the delineation of jurisdic-tional boundaries and the dispute resolution mechanism between the local and Central Government, this petition was not merely a dispute involving the interpretation of statutes among different government agencies; rather, it reached the constitutional level of the correlation between the fundamental principles of democratic operation and the jurisdiction of local self-government. Hence, the matter warranted adjudication by the Constitutional Court.[24]

In *JY Interpretation No 553*, the Constitutional Court proclaimed that Taipei City represented a self-governing entity and was thus required to succumb to administrative litigation. The controversy at issue presented a challenge to the legality of the supervisory agency's action, and thus resolving the issue in the administrative litigation was called for by the Court. Incidentally, the Court was aware that, though the Local Government Act provided mechanisms for communication and co-ordination, the local and supervisory governing agencies' failure to implement such mechanisms had directly hampered the functionality of local governments. For the sake of constitutional protection over systematic local self-government, the Court noted that the legisla-ture should strengthen the proper mechanism of local participation in accordance with the meaning and purpose of the Constitution.

---

[24] *JY Interpretation No 553* (2002).

As a result, again, the Court took a more reconciliatory, pro-dialogue approach. Rather than ruling in favour of one side or the other, the Court referred both parties to a dialectical mechanism to resolve the matter.[25]

D. The Rise of Mega Metropolitans and the Changing Geopolitical Landscape

Another development for the new generation of central–local relations is the transformation and function of 'special municipalities'. According to the Constitution, areas are classified as special municipalities to subject strategically important regions to the direct control of the Central Government. Essentially, special municipalities serve as the means by which the Central Government can control geographically important metropolises. The KMT Government imported this unique design from Mainland China to Taiwan in an effort to assert tight control over local politics. In 1967 and 1979, Taipei and Kaohsiung respectively were designated by ordinance as special municipalities. These politically calculated designations were a means of bringing about social regulation. Subjecting the heads of special municipalities to the Central Government's direct oversight, the government was able to utilise local resources to further its goal of centralised control while simultaneously pacifying local elites with lofty official positions. On the other hand, compared with other local governments, special municipalities enjoyed an institutionally higher status and the capacity to direct, or at least influence, the allocation of resources from the Central Government, enabling them to reap more benefits and resources. Further, the heads of special municipalities customarily enjoy high profile and esteem and, like Mayors of Taipei, have always been regarded as presidential hopefuls.

Entering the new millennium, in the trend of re-zoning administrative districts, local governments sought 'upgrades' to special municipality status. Because the differences among municipal cities and counties

---

[25] J-r Yeh, 'Presidential Politics and the Judicial Facilitation of Dialogue Between Political Actors in New Asian Democracies: Comparing the South Korean and Taiwanese Experiences' (2010) 8 *International Journal of Constitutional law* 911; and W-C Chang, 'Strategic Judicial Responses in Politically Charged Cases: East Asian Experiences' (2010) 8 *International Journal of Constitutional Law* 885.

had not been improved by reinventing the Taiwan Provincial Government and because of the increase in the number of metropolitan areas, the counties that failed to upgrade were marginalised even further, in relative terms. Regional disparity became the most potent reason for the call for re-districting. In particular the KMT's previous development-oriented strategy has led to a substantially disproportionate level of development among regions, especially between north and south Taiwan, with the northern region, home to the Central Government, enjoying privilege and abundantly allocated resources.[26]

Proposals to readjust administrative districts had begun as far back as the early 1990s. Following the first regime change in 2000, the redrawing of administrative districts became a hotbed issue upon which both major political parties (the KMT and the DPP) placed much emphasis in efforts to appeal to their respective constituents.

In 2009, to pave the way for the re-districting of administrative districts, the Legislative Yuan revised the Local Government Act. Article 4 of the revised Act stipulates that regions with populations of not less than 1,250,000 that have met special requirements in their political, economic, cultural and metropolitan development may establish special municipalities.[27] Article 7-1 stipulates that where a county/city is to be changed into a special municipality, the county/city government may formulate a plan for such a change for approval by the county/city council, which shall be submitted by the Ministry of the Interior to the Executive Yuan for approval.[28] In 2010, besides Taipei City, which had already been designated a special municipality, Taipei County, Taichung City (merging with Taichung County), Tainan City (merging with Tainan County), and Kaohsiung City (already a special municipality, but further merging with Kaohsiung County) were upgraded to municipal cities under the revised Act, with Taoyuan City next in line for such an upgrade. These special municipalities (including Taoyuan) are referred to as the 'Six Capitals'. This is in fact not settled, as more may be 'upgraded' to special municipality status in the future. The '*X* Capitals' phenomenon, in contrast to the former 'Twin Capitals'

---

[26] See generally MA Rubinstein, 'Taiwan's Socioeconomic Modernization' in Rubinstein (ed), above n 9.

[27] Art 4 Local Government Act (2009).

[28] Art 7-1 Local Government Act (2009).

(Taipei and Kaohsiung), marks a comprehensive change to the geopolitical landscape with profound significance in political competition and resource allocation for different levels of government. The redrawing of administrative districts and the process of upgrading certain regions to the status of special municipality not only revealed the reshuffling of regional local politics, but also drove the change towards local autonomy.

While the special municipality system was designed in China for better national control, as reflected in the Constitution, it evolved in Taiwan to serve the opposite function. It is now anticipated that all of Taiwan's counties will eventually, through strategic mergers among them, be upgraded, over time, to the level of special municipality and, further, that the county government level of administration will be replaced gradually by these special municipalities.

III. BEYOND BORDERLINES: CENTRAL–LOCAL RELATIONS IN REGIONAL AND GLOBAL PERSPECTIVES

Shifting from limited autonomy within the highly centralised national government control that existed in the framework of a unitary state, Taiwan's central–local relations have transformed into a more hybrid and dynamic transitional federalism. In the regional and global context, this transformation is more distinctive and noteworthy when looked at in the light of the trends of regional integration and global governance.

A. Micro Central–local Relations: Taiwan and Her Offshore Islands

Transitioning central–local relations in Taiwan are characterised by a dynamic relativity between the centre and the periphery, and beget the design of an efficient but flexible local autonomy. Having been confined under the Constitution to the structure of Greater China, central–local relations in Taiwan are now liberated from such restrictions, which, in turn, has revealed them to be both more flexible than originally thought and equipped with the capacity to adapt between Taiwan as the centre and Taiwan as the periphery in the context of China.

Nevertheless, following the paradigm transformation of central–local relations, Taiwan has faced challenges from time to time in coping with dynamic politics in lower-level autonomy. Further, flanked by China and Taiwan are affiliated small islands and islets (for example, Kinmen and Matsu) which were once seized and guarded by the KMT as military strongholds in preparation for possible warfare against Communist China. These islands and islets are now open and serve as intermediate transfer stations in cross-Strait exchanges. In the light of their role as transfer stations, these local entities seek interests from both sides of the Taiwan Strait and are prone to attempted exploitation and targeted local patronage from the governments of both sides.

For example, Kinmen is located much closer to China than it is to Taiwan. During the martial law era, Kinmen served as a military field base and relied on a steady supply of goods and materials from Taiwan. However, no longer sought after for its strategic position, Kinmen now depends mainly on income from local arts and tourism. Politically, it has historically been supportive of the KMT, and is much closer to China (in terms of economic ties and geographical position) than most counties. During the DPP regime, local awareness grew stronger, and a sense of more autonomous posturing arose among local elites. It was even proposed that returning to China would better serve Kinmen's interests if the DPP Government's relationship with China continued to deteriorate. Thus, the China–Taiwan–Kinmen triangle characterises Taiwan's role in complex geopolitics and again reveals Taiwan's struggle in its constitutional journey in which it is forced to straddle the divide between the centre and the periphery. Again, the best tactic to confront China and to face the rising self-awareness and surge of local autonomy have no doubt emerged as Taiwan's new challenges for the new millennium.

The resurgence of local autonomy coupled with emerging economic interests has led to a rise in tensions among and within the local development strategies. The Penghu Casino case is one of the best examples of this lesson.[29] Located off the west coast of the Taiwan Strait, only 140 kilometres away from Mainland China, Penghu is the largest amongst Taiwan's offshore archipelagos and consists of 64 small islands and islets. It boasts plentiful natural and cultural resources,

---

[29] For the background and the case see J-r Yeh, 'Changing Faces of Cost-Benefit Analysis: Alternative Institutional Settings and Varied Social and Political Contexts' in MA Livermore and RL Revesz (eds), *The Globalization of Cost-Benefit Analysis in Environmental Policy* (New York, Oxford University Press, 2013).

making tourism a key economic sector. In the 1990s, local elites proposed a casino-development project—a proposal that quickly won the support of the Central Government, despite concerns regarding public morality and environmental degradation. However, since gambling is outlawed in Taiwan, a casino in Penghu required a variance under the current statutes or the enactment of a special law to allow the project to go forward. Campaigns for and against the casino began with great fervour and, following a period of fierce debate within the local community and the Central Government, the Legislative Yuan failed to reach a consensus and the necessary legislation stalled on the legislative floor. This stalemate continued until 2008, when the KMT returned to power in the second regime change and revived the project for economic reasons and to garner local patronage. Owing to public pressure, it was decided through amendment to the Offshore Islands Development Act that a local referendum would be necessary for the casino installation to proceed. In 2009, Penghu's local government organised a public referendum and, much to the government's surprise, the citizens rejected the proposal. For the first time in Taiwan's history, the destiny of a major development project was decided by a local referendum with legal underpinnings.

B. Taiwan in Multi-level Governance

In recent years, global governance has emerged and spread rapidly across the globe. This movement has substantially changed the vertical relations and patterns of operation within regional and global politics. Under globalisation's impact, the traditional modes of international politics, based on the principles of sovereignty and a state-centric approach, have been replaced by a diverse network of regional and global linkages.[30] This drastic change has also cultivated an outgrowth of regional integration. States actively participate in the decision-making process of regional groups and alliances; non-state actors form co-operative institutions that connect relations and engage in policy making within regional spheres. Beyond the classical forms of

---

[30] See, eg, A-M Slaughter, *A New World Order* (Princeton, Princeton University Press, 2004).

sovereignty engagement, two new approaches can be identified in the emerging global and regional networks: 'supra-national entities', such as international and regional organisations, engage in policy making through top-down approaches in an attempt to push sovereign states toward shared goals; 'sub-national actors', such as local governments and NGOs, bridge cross-border connections and thereby seek to influence international policy making.[31]

This trend of global governance, which consists of these and other top-down and bottom-up approaches, provides a chance for Taiwan to engage with the international community. During the martial-law era, ROC Nationalist ideology locked Taiwan into the Greater China complex disregarding the fact that Taiwan had always been dependent on world trade and international activities. This isolation intensified when the ROC was dispelled from the UN and broke off most of its diplomatic ties with the rest of the world. However, the constitutional changes in the 1990s empowered local governments and granted more autonomy for the civil society by cultivating and transforming Taiwan's central–local relations. Though the problem of statehood still haunts Taiwan in terms of its participation in international affairs, non-state entities have filled the gap and comprehensively engaged with Taiwan in global affairs. For example, local governments foster cultural and commercial ties with their counterparts worldwide by establishing such relations as so-called 'sister cities'; NGOs have gathered momentum and grown competent in partaking in international policy making on a wide range of issues, especially humanitarian relief, public health, the environment and climate change.[32]

Recently, China's rise has also led to speculation about a possible 'Asian integration' under China's great economic power.[33] China's influence and its impact on the future of Asia and on global development

---

[31] J-r Yeh, 'Emerging Climate Change Law and Changing Governance' (paper presented to the 8th ASLI Conference, Fukuoka, Japan, May 2011).

[32] See, eg, KA Trisolini, 'All Hands on Deck: Local Governments and the Potential for Bidirectional Climate Change Regulation' (2010) 62 *Stanford Law Review* 669; RR Martella and JW Coleman, 'Ratifying Kyoto via Local Actors: Accomplishments and Limitations of Local Cap-and-Trade programs' (2010) 40 *Environmental Law Reporter News & Analysis* 10780.

[33] See generally G Wang and Y Zheng (eds), *China and the New International Order* (New York, Routledge, 2008).

is likely to stand alone as the preeminent issue for Taiwan in this century, arousing concerns of both economic integration and security.[34] Bearing past experiences in mind and leaning on the support of a new generation of central–local relations, Taiwan is more able than ever to participate and make an impact as an active participant in the open global community. In addition, Taiwan has myriad chances to play a role in the process of Asian integration.[35] The option is vested in the people whether to carry on the struggle between unification with China and Taiwanese independence based upon sovereign ideals, or to transcend this false dichotomy and instead innovate with the dynamic relativity that is developing between the peripherals and the centrals.

IV. CONCLUSION

Against the backdrop of Taiwan's democratic transition, central–local relations have morphed from a limited autonomy within a unitary state into a hybrid and dynamic form of transitional federalism. The ROC Constitution's original concept of local autonomy and power allocation has undergone substantial and numerous rounds of constitutional revision and the subsequent enactment of self-governing laws. Through this process, Taiwan has evolved from a peripheral province of the Republic of China to the epicentre of constitutional design in the region. In the process of reshaping the new model for central–local relations, such examples as the downsizing of the Taiwan Provincial Government and disputes between the Central Government and Taipei City have demonstrated the power struggles inherent in transitional politics. In addition, the trend of redrawing administrative districts led to the upgrade of local governments to the status of special municipalities. However, how best to allocate and utilise administrative resources and co-ordinate the conflicts between special municipalities has become a compelling issue that vexes the central and local governments while

---

[34] See generally J-MF Blanchard and DV Hickey (eds), *New Thinking about the Taiwan Issue: Theoretical Insights into Its Origins, Dynamics, and Prospects* (Abingdon, Routledge, 2012).
[35] See, eg, L-iC Chiu, *Economic and Political Interaction across the Taiwan Strait: Facing the Trend of Economic Integration in East Asia* (Seoul, Korea Institute for International Economic Policy, 2004).

the number of such special municipalities has simultaneously increased. In the context of the meteoric rise of China's economy, regional integration and global governance trends not only change the picture of vertical relations within the government, but also present a chance for Taiwan's citizens to reconsider the diverse relationships in multi-level governance and globalisation.

FURTHER READING

Fell, D, *Government and Politics in Taiwan* (New York, Routledge, 2012).

Slaughter, A-M, *A New World Order* (Princeton, Princeton University Press, 2004).

Yeh, J-r, 'Changing Faces of Cost-Benefit Analysis: Alternative Institutional Settings and Varied Social and Political Contexts' in MA Livermore and RL Revesz (eds), *The Globalization of Cost-Benefit Analysis in Environmental Policy* (New York, Oxford University Press, 2013) 87–103.

Yeh, J-r, 'Globalization, Government Reform and the Paradigm Shift of Administrative Law' (2010) 5 *National Taiwan University Law Review* 113–41.

6

Judicial Review and the Function of the Constitutional Court

Changing Institutions and Process: From the Council to the Court – Functional Transformations: From Rubberstamp to Constitutional Guardianship – Judicial Strategy and Style of Judgment – Conclusion

I N THE CONTEXT of democratic transition, citizen outcry and political negotiation have been the main drivers of political reform under the existing constitutional order. Thus, one may sideline the court in the shaping of the transitional constitutional order, particularly in a new democracy where political factions strive to win a foothold in the elections to get the chance to promote their party's reform agenda. Surprisingly, however, as articulated in the introductory chapter, vibrant reviews and decisions issued by the Constitutional Court and lower courts have contributed tremendously to the democratic transition, beyond the changes ushered in through incremental constitutional revision and the heightened political exchange and civic engagements. Intriguingly, in a new democracy with a thin veil of liberal constitutionalism, how could the judiciary play such an integral role in the flux of democratic transition and constitutional reform? Early constitutional mandates, transitional context, and learned judicial wisdom underpin many of the successes of Taiwan's Constitutional Court. Moreover, the evolution of the Court itself against the flux of political transition may very well explain the integral role the judiciary has played in Taiwan's constitutional development.

Judicial guardianship of constitutional supremacy has been constitutionally guaranteed since the enactment of the ROC Constitution.

Article 171 of the 1947 ROC Constitution states that '[L]aws that are in conflict with the Constitution shall be null and void', and goes on to state that 'if doubts arise as to whether a law is in conflict with the Constitution, interpretation thereon shall be made by the Judicial Yuan'.[1] In addition, the Constitution assigns a number of Grand Justices to be in charge of the power of constitutional interpretation as well as the power to unify the interpretation of laws and ordinances.[2] The Council of Grand Justices—later known as the Constitutional Court—was created in 1948 on Mainland China and subsequently relocated to Taiwan in 1949, with a number of justices reappointed at that time.[3] Taiwan's Constitutional Court has issued more than 700 interpretations since its inception and is Asia's oldest constitutional court (or council).[4]

Throughout its history, the Constitutional Court has undergone dramatic institutional and functional transformations as it has continued to serve the needs of Taiwan's citizenry. The Constitutional Court was tapped to help the formation of a young constitutional democracy, especially during the height of Taiwan's democratisation, during the 1980s and 1990s. The Constitutional Court has continually served as the guardian of constitutional democracy and its landmark decisions have contributed greatly to Taiwan's system of checks and balances, at times reining in the executive and legislative powers.[5] This chapter explores and evaluates the Court's historical developments, its contributions to Taiwan's democratic transitions, and its features and judicial styles that underpin the Court's institutional strength and capacity.

---

[1] Art 171 Constitution of the Republic of China (1947). Article 172 also states that 'ordinances that are in conflict with the Constitution or with laws shall be null and void'.

[2] Arts 78 and 79 Constitution of the Republic of China (1947); Art 5(1) Additional Articles to the Constitution of the Republic of China (2005).

[3] W-C Chang and J-r Yeh, 'Judges as Discursive Agent: The Use of Foreign Precedents by the Constitutional Court of Taiwan' in T Groppi and M-C Ponthoreau (eds), *The Use of Foreign Precedents by Constitutional Judges* (Oxford, Hart Publishing, 2013) 376.

[4] See W-C Chang et al, *Constitutionalism in Asia: Cases and Materials* (Oxford, Hart Publishing, 2014) 312, Table 5.1.

[5] T Ginsburg, *Judicial Review in New Democracies: Constitutional Courts in Asian Cases* (New York, Cambridge University Press, 2003) 125, 144. See also J-r Yeh and W-C Chang, 'The Emergence of East Asian Constitutionalism: Features in Comparison' (2011) 59 *American Journal of Comparative Law* 805, 806.

I. CHANGING INSTITUTIONS AND PROCESSES: FROM THE COUNCIL TO THE COURT

Although the Constitutional Court is recognised as a successful judicial institution, neither the Council of Grand Justices nor the Court was envisaged under the original ROC Constitution, with nods to the 'Judicial Yuan' and 'Grand Justices' as the only references to the judicial branch.[6] The institutional creation and transformation of the Grand Justices was a veritable quagmire through which reformers and the judiciary had to navigate in order to establish the Council of Grand Justices against the backdrop of the legal and political changes of the time. This section further discusses the institutional evolution of the Constitutional Court over the last few decades, including the process of appointment, the Court's powers and jurisdiction and its adjudication procedures. The Court's evolution is distinct from that of its counterparts in the rest of Asia, inter alia the courts in South Korea and Thailand. Most of Asia's constitutional courts were established during the period of democratic transition in the 1980s or later, often with clear authority granted to the court from the outset.[7] By contrast, Taiwan's Constitutional Court's powers were not clearly specified until later in the course of its development. In sum, the key to understanding the power and current status of the Court lies in the evolution of its role over the course of Taiwan's democratic transition.

A. Organisational Evolution

The drafters of the ROC Constitution initially modelled the Judicial Yuan on the US Supreme Court.[8] Under this original plan, the Judicial Yuan would be a final court of appeals, with the Grand Justices exercising

---

[6] Chang and Yeh, 'Judges as Discursive Agent', above n 3, 377.

[7] A Hardin, P Leyland and T Groppi, 'Constitutional Courts: Forms, Functions, and Practice in Comparative Perspective' in A Hardin, P Leyland and T Groppi (eds), *Constitutional Courts: A Comparative Study* (England, Wildy, Simmonds & Hill Publishing, 2009) 12.

[8] Chang and Yeh, above n 3, 377. See C-M Chang, *Ten Lectures on the Democratic Constitution of the Republic of China* (Shanghai, The Commercial Press, 1947) preface (in Chinese).

jurisdiction over civil, criminal and administrative cases, as well as constitutional review on challenged laws that seem to fall foul of the Constitution.[9] However, this original concept was ultimately not executed.

The first Organic Act of the Judicial Yuan was passed in March 1947, following the constitutional mandate, and squarely reflected the model of the US judiciary. Under this Act, nine Grand Justices were to be appointed to the Judicial Yuan to serve as a final court of appeals with petty benches on civil, criminal and administrative cases.[10] Unfortunately, this Act faced fierce opposition from the then-existing judicial institutions including the Supreme Court and the Administrative Court. This resistance probably stemmed, at least in part, from long-standing civil law traditions.[11] In response to the opposition, the Act was swiftly revised, in December 1947.

The revised Organic Act of the Judicial Yuan provided that the Council of Grand Justices would comprise 17 justices who were tasked with interpreting the Constitution and unifying legal interpretations.[12] This was the first time that the term the Council—rather than the Court—of Grand Justices was used. In compromise with the existing institutions, the revised Act held intact the Supreme Court and the Administrative Court, both of which predate the ROC Constitution, and isolated the Council of Grand Justices from these final courts of ordinary jurisdiction. In 1948, upon assuming office, the first Council enacted a general rule on its exercise of powers that limited its jurisdiction to the abstract review of the constitutionality of laws and ordinances upon the requests of competent agencies and the interpretive unification of laws and ordinances.[13] According to this general rule, the Council would not entertain requests for judicial review from ordinary citizens.

The Constitutional Court's autonomous rule was short-lived. It did not take long for the legislature to enact legislation, supplemental to the Organic Act, to regulate the Council's operation. In 1958,

---

[9] Ibid.

[10] Arts 3 and 4 Organic Act of the Judicial Yuan (1947).

[11] Chang and Yeh, above n 3.

[12] Art 3 Organic Act of the Judicial Yuan (1947).

[13] Further information regarding the Rule of the Council of Grand Justices between 1948 and 1958 is available at www.judicial.gov.tw/constitutionalcourt/p01_05.asp.

the Act Regarding the Council of Grand Justices was promulgated to replace the Council's self-enacted rule.[14] The Act maintained the Council's separation from the other courts and affirmed the powers of abstract judicial review and statutory interpretation; however, the 1958 Act permitted petitions from individuals whose constitutional rights were infringed, who had exhausted all other legal remedies, and challenged the constitutionality of the laws or ordinances applied by the 'court of last resort' in its final judgment.[15] The Constitutional Interpretation Procedure Act of 1993 eventually replaced the 1958 Act, following the 1992 constitutional revision that authorised the Grand Justices to adjudicate the dissolution of unconstitutional political parties.[16]

Under the 1993 Act, the Grand Justices remained a separate judicial organ, able to exercise the power of abstract judicial review; however, as part of the Council's additional power to adjudicate the dissolution of unconstitutional political parties, the Act had also implemented court-like trial procedures that the Council also utilised for the purposes of constitutional interpretation.[17] Thus, a brand-new courtroom was built on the top floor of the Judicial Yuan, making the Council appear more like a court and less like an administrative body. Moreover, the Court conducted trials for certain high-profile cases.[18] While the term 'Council' was used within the 1993 Act, the Grand Justices have since begun referring to themselves as 'Justices of the Constitutional Court'.[19] The title of 'Constitutional Court' has replaced 'Council of Grand Justices' as the body's official name in fulfilment of Taiwan's desire for a full and strong judicial authority.

---

[14] The 1958 Act Regarding the Council of Grand Justices, which was subsequently replaced by the 1993 Constitutional Interpretation Procedure Act, can be found at www.judicial.gov.tw/constitutionalcourt/en/p07_2.asp?lawno=73.

[15] Art 5(2) Act regarding the Council of Grand Justices (1958).

[16] Art 5 Additional Articles of the Constitution of the Republic of China (2005).

[17] Art 13 Constitutional Interpretation Procedure Act (1993).

[18] Examples of such interpretations include *JY Interpretation No 392* (1995) regarding whether prosecutors should have the power of detention, *JY Interpretation No 419* (1996) regarding whether the Vice-President may concurrently serve as premier, and *JY Interpretation No 603* regarding whether the government may require citizens to provide fingerprints in applications for an identity card.

[19] The Council's website is located at www.judicial.gov.tw/constitutionalcourt/EN/p01_03.asp.

B. Appointment Process

The ROC Constitution did not specify the number or the tenure of
the Grand Justices. As indicated earlier, the Organic Act of the Judicial Yuan, enacted in March 1947 and borrowing heavily from the
model of the US Supreme Court, stipulated nine Grand Justices, each
with a life tenure guarantee.[20] However, the revised Organic Act of
the Judicial Yuan, enacted in December 1947, altered the number of
Grand Justices from nine to 17 and reduced the Justices' life tenure to
a nine-year renewable term.[21] As a result, from 1948 to 2003, Justices
were appointed six separate times under the revised system, with a few
of the Justices appointed numerous times.[22] The Honourable Justice
Yueh-sheng Weng holds the distinction of being the longest-serving
Justice, having been appointed in 1972, to serve the remaining four
years of the third term of the Justices, and serving until his retirement
in 2007.[23]

The 1997 constitutional revisions further altered the number and
term of the Grand Justices. The number of Justices was decreased to
15, with two Justices serving as the President and Vice-President of
the Judicial Yuan.[24] The Justices' term was amended from a renewable
nine-year term with Justices appointed as a block to a non-renewable
eight-year term with staggered appointments. The new rule of appointment took effect in 2003.[25] That year, eight Justices—including the
two Justices serving as the President and Vice-President of the Judicial
Yuan—were appointed to four-year terms while the remaining seven
Justices were appointed to eight-year terms. Subsequently, Justices were
appointed in 2007, 2008[26] and 2011.

---

[20] Art 3 Organic Act of the Judicial Yuan (1947).

[21] Arts 3 and 4 Organic Act of the Judicial Yuan (1947).

[22] These six terms span the following periods: the first (October 1948–
September 1958), the second (October 1958–September 1967), the third (October
1967–September 1976), the fourth (October 1976–September 1985), the fifth
(October 1985–September 1994), and the sixth (October 1994–September 2003).

[23] The terms of the Constitutional Court and the tenure of each of the Justices
are available at www.judicial.gov.tw/constitutionalcourt/en/p01_04.asp.

[24] Art 5(1) Additional Articles to the Constitution of the Republic of China
(2005).

[25] Art 5(3) Additional Articles to the Constitution of the Republic of China
(2005).

[26] In 2007, several appointments were boycotted due to serious partisan confrontations between the DPP and the KMT. These vacancies were filled in 2008.

The Grand Justices' qualifications were stipulated in the Organic Act of the Judicial Yuan and have remained relatively unchanged. Criteria for selection include the following: a candidate must either: a) have served as a Justice of the Supreme Court for more than 10 years and have a distinguished record of service; b) have served as a member of the Legislative Yuan for more than nine years and made distinguished contributions; c) have been a professor in a major field of law at a university for more than 10 years and have authored publications in a specialised field; d) have served as a Justice of the International Court or have had authoritative works published in the fields of public or comparative law; or e) be a person highly reputed in the field of legal research who has had political experience.[27] Also, the number of Justices qualifying under any one of the above criteria was not to exceed one-third of the total number of Justices.[28] These complex qualification rules were designed to recruit a robust mix of career judges, legislators, legal scholars and persons with a combination of legal and political expertise. In practice, however, the vast majority of the Grand Justices appointed were law professors with distinguished records or career judges of the highest courts within the various jurisdictions.[29] Prior to the 1990s, career judges represented the bulk of the appointments. Since then, however, law professors have comprised roughly half of the Constitutional Court.[30]

Unlike career judges, who are chosen by national exams, Taiwan's Grand Justices have been appointed predominantly by Taiwan's political branches through the power-sharing mechanism. The ROC Constitution initially assigned the Control Yuan to provide consent to presidential appointments of Grand Justices. However, the 1992 constitutional revision transferred such power of consent to the National Assembly, which power was subsequently bestowed on the Legislative Yuan through the 2000 constitutional revision, thus reflecting the institutional shift from three parliaments to one, as discussed in chapter 4. Presently, all Justices appointed by the President must be subsequently confirmed by the Legislative Yuan.[31]

---

[27] Art 4 Organic Act of the Judicial Yuan (1947).
[28] Art 4 Organic Act of the Judicial Yuan (1947).
[29] Chang and Yeh, above n 3, 376.
[30] W-C Chang, 'The Role of Judicial Review in Consolidating Democracy: The Case of Taiwan' (2005) 2 *Asia Law Review* 73.
[31] Art 5(1) Additional Articles to the Constitution of the Republic of China (2005).

Interestingly, Taiwan's Constitutional Court is the only constitutional court in Asia to adopt a co-operation model, which involves co-ordination between two political branches when appointing Justices. Conversely, most Asian constitutional courts adopted a representational model whereby the executive, legislative and judicial branches each enjoy an equal share of the power of appointment.[32] In practice, the co-operation model has been vulnerable to political manipulation, demonstrating a tendency to politicise Asia's constitutional courts. Particularly in a semi-presidential system, where the president may not enjoy the majority in the legislature, bitter disputes between presidential nomination and legislative consent over the appointment of Grand Justices have occurred. Such a conflict occurred in Taiwan during the period of the DPP's control over the Executive Yuan and the KMT's control over the Legislative Yuan. In 2007, due to serious partisan confrontations between the DPP and the KMT, the KMT legislative majority boycotted four of the eight nominees. These boycotts were due to the nominees' previous service to the DPP government or association with volunteer organisations that possessed a slant towards independence. In early 2008, Ma Ying-jeou of the KMT achieved victory in the presidential election. Further, in the early months of his presidency, President Ma appointed another four candidates who were swiftly confirmed by the KMT legislative majority. As evidenced, this method of presidential appointment with legislative confirmation may invite unwelcome political intervention that could eventually undermine the judiciary's independence.

C. Powers and Jurisdictions

The Constitutional Court's two primary powers, which were vested by the ROC Constitution, are the power to interpret the Constitution and the power to unify legal interpretations.[33] Before the 1980s, the majority of interpretations rendered by the Constitutional Court involved unifying statutory interpretations. However, since the late 1980s, constitutional interpretations have dominated the Constitutional Court's docket.

---

[32] Chang et al, *Constitutionalism in Asia*, above n 4, 369–71.
[33] Art 78 Constitution of the Republic of China (1947).

The Court's power of constitutional interpretation encompasses the following four principal types of jurisdiction, which are similar to those of constitutional courts based on the European style: abstract review, concrete review, individual complaint and competence dispute.[34] A constitutional organ or one of the central or local government agencies may request abstract review whenever doubts arise over the constitutionality of relevant laws or ordinances.[35] Further, since the Constitutional Interpretation Procedure Act of 1993, members of the Legislative Yuan may petition the Constitutional Court requesting interpretation of constitutional provisions or a ruling on the constitutionality of laws, if that petition is supported by at least one third of the total legislators.[36] Although this appellate channel allows even a legislative minority to levy a constitutional challenge to the final enactment of laws, the Constitutional Court has indicated that the legislators should nevertheless endeavour to revise the impugned laws prior to petitioning the Constitutional Court.[37]

Concrete review was not granted the Court either by the Constitution or by statute. Rather, the Constitution Court itself created the authority through *JY Interpretation No 371*.[38] This interpretation addressed whether the Court had the exclusive power of judicial review or if ordinary courts had concurrent jurisdiction to review the constitutionality of statutes while adjudicating concrete legal disputes. In response, the Constitutional Court asserted its exclusive power of judicial review, while reserving for the ordinary courts a referral power in cases in which the constitutionality of laws or regulations may be at issue.[39] According to the Constitutional Court, '[I]n trying a case where a judge, with reasonable assurance, has suspected that the statute applicable to the case is unconstitutional, the judge may suspend the pending procedure on the grounds that the constitutionality of the statute is a prerequisite issue and petition to the Constitutional Court for interpretation.'[40]

---

[34] Chang et al, above n 4, 328–35.
[35] Art 5 Constitutional Interpretation Procedure Act (1993).
[36] Art 5(1)(3) Constitutional Interpretation Procedure Act (1993).
[37] See, eg, *JY Interpretation No 603* (2005).
[38] *JY Interpretation No 371* (1995).
[39] Ibid.
[40] Ibid.

As stated earlier, the 1958 Act granted the Council of Grand Justices jurisdiction over individual complaints. Since then, any individual, legal entity or political party may file constitutional petitions with the Constitutional Court if they believe their constitutional rights have been infringed, all other remedies provided by law for such infringement have been exhausted, and they have doubts about the constitutionality of laws or regulations applied in the final judgment by the court of last resort. Remedies for such infraction available through the Constitutional Court are limited to the review of constitutionality of the challenged laws and regulations. The Constitutional Court cannot resolve the case or provide any direct remedies. Yet, if the Constitutional Court invalidates the impugned statutes or ordinances, the petitioner will then be entitled to a retrial or an extraordinary appeal to the ordinary courts in accordance with such decision.[41]

The Constitutional Court's final area of jurisdiction is the resolution of disputes over the respective competence of official bodies. According to the Constitutional Interpretation Procedure Act, government organs or central–local governments may petition the Constitutional Court for competence resolution should they have doubts about respective jurisdictions or encounter conflict with other organs or governments.[42] Throughout the period of Taiwan's democratic transition, the Constitutional Court has played a pivotal role in resolving competence disputes between the executive and legislative branches and among the different levels of government.[43]

In addition to the above primary powers, the Constitutional Court enjoys such ancillary powers as the adjudication of impeachment proceedings, dissolution of unconstitutional political parties and the resolution of electoral disputes.[44] Taiwan's constitutional revision of 2005 conferred on the Constitutional Court the power to adjudicate the impeachment of the President and Vice-President should the

---

[41] *JY Interpretation No 185* (1984).

[42] Art 5 Constitutional Interpretation Procedure Act (1993).

[43] J-r Yeh, 'Presidential Politics and the Judicial Facilitation of Dialogue between Political Actors in New Asian Democracies: Comparing the South Korean and Taiwanese Experiences' (2010) 8 *International Journal of Constitutional Law* 911.

[44] T Ginsburg, 'Ancillary Powers of Constitutional Courts' in T Ginsburg and RA Kagan (eds), *Institutions and Public Law: Comparative Perspectives* (New York, Peter Lang Publishing, 2004) 225.

Legislative Yuan approve the motion of impeachment.[45] The constitutional revision of 1992 established the Constitutional Court's power to dissolve political parties whose 'goals or activities endanger the existence of the Republic of China or the nation's free and democratic constitutional order'.[46] To date, neither presidential impeachment nor dissolution of unconstitutional political parties has been presented to the Constitutional Court.

The avenues to gain access to the Constitutional Court have increased incrementally through laws and judicial interpretations. Unlike the US Supreme Court, which exercises judicial authority over cases or controversies arising below and enjoys original jurisdiction in only limited, constitutionally enumerated types of matter, the breadth of the Constitutional Court's jurisdiction has served an important role in Taiwan's democratic transition. All in all, the Court has gained diverse opportunities to play a role in a number of high-profile cases involving citizens' rights and political matters, and has helped steer the process of democratisation.

D. Adjudication Procedure

Procedurally, the Constitutional Court's rules for rendering interpretations and issuing opinions are provided by the Constitutional Interpretation Procedure Act of 1993, which replaced the Council Act of 1958. As indicated earlier, among other changes, the 1993 Act established more trial-like procedures for the Constitutional Court. Before 1993, the Constitutional Court adjudicated cases without hearing oral arguments. Rather, it relied solely on written submissions from petitioners and government agencies. Following the 1993 Act, however, the Court has the discretion to hold an oral hearing.[47] Upon the request of petitioners or the Justices, the Constitutional Court may order the petitioners, relevant parties, or government agencies to submit briefs and other relevant documents. Occasionally the Court may also convene

---

[45] Art 2 Additional Articles to the Constitution of the Republic of China (2005).
[46] Art 5(5) Additional Articles to the Constitution of the Republic of China (2005).
[47] Art 13 Constitutional Interpretation Procedure Act (1993).

informal sessions in which legal scholars or other experts are invited to provide relevant legal or policy analyses, particularly for comparative understandings.[48]

A panel of three Grand Justices carries out a preliminary review to determine whether admit or dismiss the petition. The panel's draft decision is then submitted to the Constitutional Court for deliberation.[49] To render interpretations, the definition of a quorum depends on the nature of the interpretation at issue. To render an interpretation or rule on the constitutionality of statutes, a quorum is defined as two thirds of the Grand Justices currently in office, and two thirds of those present are required for consent. For matters regarding the constitutionality of administrative rules, a quorum is similarly defined as two thirds of the incumbent Grand Justices, but votes of only half of those present are necessary for consent. For matters regarding a unified interpretation of laws or administrative rules, the number of Grand Justices required to constitute a quorum is reduced to half of the incumbents, and half of those present are required for consent. The most stringent requirements govern the dissolution of an unconstitutional political party. For such matters, a quorum is comprised of at least three quarters of the incumbent Grand Justices, and two thirds of those present are required for consent.

Notably, the rules concerning quorums required for interpretations by the Constitutional Court have undergone significant changes. During the first decade, the first-term Council relied on its self-enacted rule for rendering interpretation. During this period, interpretations required only a simple majority for passage. The 1958 Council Act altered this simple-majority rule by requiring the presence of three quarters of the sitting Grand Justices to constitute a quorum and three quarters of those present to pass a constitutional interpretation. This high threshold was a reprisal enacted in an effort to paralyse the Constitutional Court as a result of Legislative Yuan's discontentment over *JY Interpretation No 76*, which held that the National Assembly, the Legislative Yuan, and the Control Yuan all stood on an equal footing with Parliament.[50]

---

[48] DS Law and W-C Chang, 'The Limits of Global Judicial Dialogue' (2010) 86 *Washington Law Review* 523, 563.

[49] Arts 10 and 11, Constitutional Interpretation Procedure Act (1993).

[50] J-r Yeh, 'The Cult of *Fatung*: Representational Manipulation and Reconstruction in Taiwan' in G Hassall and C Saunders (eds), *The People's Representatives: Electoral Systems in the Asia-Pacific Region* (Sydney, Allen & Unwin, 1997).

After the Constitutional Court passes draft interpretations, concurring or dissenting Justices may provide their own separate opinions within five days. The Constitutional Court's majority interpretations, as well as concurring and dissenting opinions, are then released to the public.[51] As Table 6.2 in section II shows, the issuance of concurring and dissenting opinions has risen sharply since the late 1980s.[52] Especially in recent years, it has not been uncommon for one interpretation to be accompanied by six to seven individual concurring or dissenting opinions.[53]

As mentioned, Taiwan's Constitutional Court has undergone many changes since its inception. These changes were designed mostly to accommodate political fluctuations. It is therefore reasonable that these changes have not followed a highly consistent trajectory. For instance, the Constitutional Court's impeachment power and scope of authority have evolved over time. Until recently, individuals' complaints were eligible only for abstract review. In spite of the changes and reforms that have taken place, the exact effects of JY Interpretations remain ambiguous.

Previous elaboration has shown that some of the Constitutional Court's powers were expanded over time by the Court itself through various interpretations it issued. Though perhaps restricted at least somewhat by legislative constraints, the Court has performed an incredible operational transformation, which is discussed in the following section.

II. FUNCTIONAL TRANSFORMATIONS: FROM RUBBER STAMP TO CONSTITUTIONAL GUARDIANSHIP

The launch of the Council of Grand Justices coincided with the constitutional crisis that resulted from the ROC government's retreat to Taiwan. The first-term Council was called upon to resolve these crises and to act, to some extent, as a legal advisor to the government.[54] With

---

[51] Art 17 Constitutional Interpretation Procedure Act (1993).

[52] Chang and Yeh, above n 3, 382–84.

[53] See www.judicial.gov.tw/constitutionalcourt/p05.asp.

[54] See ch 4. See also Y-s Weng, 'Interpretations of the Constitutional Court and the Developments of Rule of Law and Democratic Constitutionalism in Taiwan' in D Ehlers, H Glaser and K Prokati (eds), *Constitutionalism and Good Governance: Eastern and Western Perspectives* (Baden-Baden, Nomos, 2014).

the Temporary Provisions' imposition that expanded the President's extra-constitutional powers, coupled with the Martial Law Decree that substantially restricted individual rights, authoritarian governance under the KMT took hold. Understandably, the Council did not become an effective judicial institution until the Martial Law Decree was lifted in 1987 and the subsequent political liberalisation and democratic transition began.[55] During the 1990s era of Taiwan's democratic transition, the Constitutional Court was able to steer the transitional agenda, help resolve political and constitutional hurdles, and safeguard fundamental rights and freedoms. From 2000 to 2008, in which the DPP held the presidency and the KMT held a legislative majority, the Court was embroiled in an overabundance of political confrontations and power struggles.

Over the course of Taiwan's democratisation, the Constitutional Court has proved itself an indispensable institution. Subsection A provides an overview—mostly statistical—of the Constitutional Court's activity since its inception, followed by subsection B, which recapitulates the Court's functional transformation from rubber stamp to constitutional guardian.

A. Overall Performance

The impact of the Constitutional Court's functional transformations is exhibited best by examining the number of petitions it has received over the course of its existence. According to the Judicial Yuan's statistics, the number of petitions to the Court has risen sharply, as follows: 658 petitions in the first term (1948–1958), down to 355 in the second (1958–1967), rising to 446 in the third (1967–1976), dramatically increasing to 1,145 in the fourth (1976–1985), roughly doubling to 2,702 in the fifth (1985–1994), and falling slightly to 2,334 in the sixth (1994–2003).[56] In the sixth term, the Constitutional Court received a

---

[55] Chang, above n 30; T Ginsburg, 'Confucian Constitutionalism? The Emergence of Constitutional Review in Korea and Taiwan' (2002) 27 *Law & Social Inquiry* 763.
[56] See www.judicial.gov.tw/constitutionalcourt/p05.asp.

yearly average of nearly 250 petitions. Since 2003, this yearly figure has more than doubled to an average of 520 petitions.[57]

In addition, among the petitions submitted to the Constitutional Court, the majority have originated from individuals concerned about infringement by impugned laws or regulations of their constitutionally protected rights. According to the Judicial Yuan, altogether, there were 7,640 petitions made from the Court's first to its sixth terms (1948–2003). Of these, 6,825 (89.33 per cent) were from individuals and 815 (10.67 per cent) were from government agencies.[58] Following its first and second terms, the Court has consistently received at or above 90 per cent of its petitions from individuals over the course of its subsequent terms—a trend that supports the view that one of the Constitutional Court's paramount functions is to safeguard the fundamental rights and freedoms of individuals.[59]

Table 6.1 shows the sharp rise in the number of interpretations issued by the Constitutional Court from 1948 to 2013.[60] The fact that the Court issued a majority of its interpretations in the years since the 1980s tends to support the theory that increased political liberation and democratisation have dramatically increased the efficiency of the Court.

The Constitutional Court's functional transformation is further reflected in the number of uniform or constitutional interpretations. As Table 6.1 indicates, during its first three terms, the Court dealt mostly with the uniform interpretation of statutes or ordinances in the context of the Temporary Provisions and the imposition of martial law. During this period, the Court could act only as a legal advisor to resolve technical legal issues for the authoritarian government.[61] In its fourth term, the Court broke away from this limited role, with the number of

---

[57] According to the Judicial Yuan, the Constitutional Court received 459 petitions in 2003, 465 petitions in 2004, 524 petitions in 2005, 500 petitions in 2006, 549 petitions in 2007, and 624 petitions in 2007. The information is available at www.judicial.gov.tw/constitutionalcourt/p05.asp.

[58] See www.judicial.gov.tw/constitutionalcourt/p05.asp.

[59] In the first term, 65.65% of the petitions were from government agencies while 34.35% from individuals. In the second term, 19.44% of the petitions were from government agencies while 80.56% from individuals. See www.judicial.gov.tw/constitutionalcourt/p05.asp.

[60] See www.judicial.gov.tw/constitutionalcourt/p05.asp.

[61] Y-s Weng, 'Interpretations of the Constitutional Court' 321–60.

Table 6.1: The number and type of interpretations by the
Constitutional Court (1948–2013)

	First term 1948–1958	Second term 1958–1967	Third term 1967–1976	Fourth term 1976–1985	Fifth term 1985–1994	Sixth term 1994–2003	2003–Feb 2013
Number of Interpretations	79	43	24	53	167	200	150
Uniform/ Constitutional Interpretation	54/25	35/8	22/2	21/32	18/149	9/191	15/135
Unconstitutional findings	0	1	0	4	37	72	67
Admonitory Decisions	0	0	0	0	19	37	9

Source: Data compiled by author.

its constitutional interpretations surpassing the number of uniform interpretations. In addition, since its fifth term, the Court has delivered far more constitutional interpretations than any others. In fact, the constitutional interpretations have since represented over 90 per cent of the interpretations rendered by the Court. Thus, this shift has signalled the Council of Grand Justices' transformation into a genuine and effectively functional constitutional court.

The final indicator of the transformative Constitutional Court is the number of interpretations in which the impugned statutes or ordinances were deemed unconstitutional. As illustrated in Table 6.1, the Constitutional Court's first three terms produced only one interpretation with an unconstitutional declaration. The fourth term had only four such findings of unconstitutionality. The number of unconstitutional findings rose dramatically in the Court's fifth term: with a finding of unconstitutional in 37 out of 149 total constitutional interpretations (24.8 per cent). The ratio of unconstitutional findings climbed again in the Court's sixth term (72 out of 191 constitutional interpretations, or 37.7 per cent), and again to a record high (67 interpretations out of 135 constitutional interpretations, 49.6 per cent) in the period from 2003 to 2013. The Constitutional Court unequivocally has become a powerful constitutional institution, signalled by the fact that the Court has struck down nearly half of the challenged statutes and regulations that have come before it.

At times, the Constitutional Court may issue admonitory interpretations in which impugned statutes or regulations are held constitutional but with warnings.[62] The issuance of such judicial warnings began in the fifth term of the Constitutional Court and rose to a record high in the sixth term. However, recently, the number of admonitory decisions has been in decline. With the record high number of unconstitutional findings in the last decade, this may suggest that the Court has become even more uninhibited in its final decision-making authority.

B. Changing Functions in Response to Changing Contexts

Before the 1980s, the Constitutional Court's impacts were limited due to the effects of authoritarian governance. For the most part, the Court served as a legal advisor, rendering decisions that unified interpretations of statutes or ordinances. However, in a few cases, the Court was called upon to resolve constitutional crises that resulted from the ROC government's retreat from the Mainland to Taiwan.

JY Interpretation No 31, rendered in 1954, was one of the Constitutional Court's first notorious decisions, occurring at a time when the KMT was determined to 'take back the Mainland' and assert its legitimacy to govern as the only government over the whole of China.[63] When the first-term legislative representatives' tenure expired in 1954 and no election could be held on the Mainland, a constitutional solution was required. The Court extended the representatives' terms, ruling that 'the nation was under crisis and the country could not hold the election of the second term legally'.[64] Because of the Court's ruling, as discussed in earlier chapters, those first-term representatives continued to serve for the next four decades, resulting in representative distortions.[65] Following the deaths of most of those representatives, the Temporary Provisions and relevant statutes were revised to

---

[62] For a comparative discussion of such judicial warnings, see Chang et al, above n 4, 456–59.

[63] Yeh, 'The Cult of *Fatung*', above n 50, 23.

[64] *JY Interpretation No 31* (1954).

[65] See ch 4.

fill vacancies by holding supplementary elections or adding more seats to elect representatives locally. Occasionally, the Constitutional Court was called upon to provide legitimacy for these politically expedient solutions. For instance, in *JY Interpretation No 85*, the Constitutional Court ruled that the calculation of the total number of members of the National Assembly should be based on those who were able to convene.[66] Likewise, in *JY Interpretation Nos 117* and *150*, the Constitutional Court affirmed the constitutionality of adding extra posts to both the Legislative Yuan and the National Assembly via legislative enactments.[67]

As previously mentioned, during its first three terms, the Constitutional Court rarely asserted itself as the guardian of democratic constitutionalism. On rare occasions, however, the Court nevertheless risked undermining its own institutional authority by standing in opposition to the other branches of government. In *JY Interpretation No 86*, which was decided in 1960, the Court held that the law that allowed the Ministry of Justice to supervise the lower courts was inconsistent with the Constitution and subsequently required all courts to be placed under the Judicial Yuan.[68] However, this decision was ignored by the other branches of government, and the impugned law was not revised until 1980, two decades following the original decision.

Tom Ginsburg and Tamir Moustafa have argued that courts in an authoritarian context may still provide such social-control functions as controlling administrative agents, legitimising controversial policies, and providing credible commitments in the economic sphere.[69] Prior to the 1980s, the Constitutional Court had indeed performed such functions.[70] For example, when it faced disputes arising over controversial issues such as land reform and redistributive measures, the Court was often required to simultaneously deal with technical and interpretive aspects

---

[66] *JY Interpretation No 85* (1960).

[67] *JY Interpretation No 117* (1966); *JY Interpretation No 150* (1977).

[68] *JY Interpretation No 86* (1960).

[69] See T Moustafa and T Ginsburg, 'Introduction: The Functions of Courts in Authoritarian Politics' in T Moustafa and T Ginsburg (eds), *Rule by Law: The Politics of Courts in Authoritarian Regimes* (Cambridge, Cambridge University Press, 2008).

[70] For further discussion of the Court's efforts, see W-C Chang, 'The Governing Functions of the Constitutional Court and Administrative Courts of ROC' in J-Y Huang (ed), *The Legacy and Sustainability of Rule of Law* (Taipei, Sharing, 2013) (in Chinese).

of issues concurrently, in order to lend a sense of legitimacy to the disputed policy.[71]

Aside from legitimating social and political policies, the Constitutional Court also began to bolster its own institutional authority, particularly in the early 1980s, when the fourth-term Court rendered several decisions that reinforced the legal standing of its own interpretations. For instance, in *JY Interpretation No 177*, the Court stressed that 'an Interpretation given by this Yuan in response to a petition shall also be applicable with respect to the legal action of the petitioner, for which the original petition was made'.[72] Further, in *JY Interpretation No 185*, the Court made it clear that its interpretations 'shall be binding upon every institution and person in the country, and each institution shall abide by the meaning of these interpretations in handling relevant matters' and that any 'prior precedents which are contrary to these interpretations shall automatically be nullified'.[73] More important, the Court fashioned a remedy that had previously been unavailable to successful petitioners. The Court stated in *JY Interpretation No 185* that 'in the case of a final and irrevocable judgment where the statute or ordinance or the interpretation of such a statute or ordinance applied in rendering such judgment is deemed contrary to the Constitution … the party against whom such final and irrevocable judgment is entered shall be entitled to file for a retrial or an extraordinary appeal on the basis of said interpretation'.[74] As expected, individual petitions to the Constitutional Court rose sharply after this interpretation.

Political liberalisation and democratisation in the late 1980s and early 1990s placed the Constitutional Court at the centre of transitional politics. Perhaps the most prominent case was *JY Interpretation No 261*, in which the Constitutional Court ordered 'those first-term national representatives who have not been re-elected on a periodical basis to cease the exercise of their powers no later than December 31, 1991'.[75] The Court went even further, requiring the government 'to hold, in due course, a nationwide second-term election of the national

---

[71] The Court dealt with such issues in various interpretations, such as *JY Interpretation Nos 78* (1957), *124* (1968) and *125* (1968).
[72] *JY Interpretation No 177* (1982).
[73] *JY Interpretation No 185* (1984).
[74] Ibid.
[75] *JY Interpretation No 261* (1990).

representatives including a certain number of representatives-at-large ... so that the constitutional system will function properly'.[76] *JY Interpretation No 261*, with other reform measures, made possible the unprecedented political and constitutional reforms that stemmed from the 1990s and early 2000s. Political disputes and controversies that have arisen from these reforms, however, continue to demand judicial resolution. The pinnacle of the Constitutional Court's institutional power and strength was reflected in its rendering of *JY Interpretation No 499*, in which the Court invalidated in its entirety the constitutional revision of 1999.[77]

The Constitutional Court's institutional prominence grew during the 1990s, transforming it into an even more indispensable judicial authority entering the new millennium. From 2000 to 2008, with the DPP-controlled presidency and Executive Yuan and the KMT's legislative majority, serious political confrontations required judicial resolution. Because of the prudent and skilful way the Court has handled these cases, it has become the primary mediator of highly charged political disputes.[78] At the same time, the Constitutional Court has been equally vigilant in safeguarding individual rights and freedoms, as evidenced by the record-high number of individual petitions and findings of unconstitutionality, discussed above. The Court's judicial strategy and style of judgment as employed in representative landmark interpretations are discussed below, in Section III.

III. JUDICIAL STRATEGY AND STYLE OF JUDGMENT

To negotiate democratic transition and to mediate high-profile political disputes, the Constitutional Court has had to develop innovative judicial skills and strategies while preserving its own institutional authority. Some of the strategies the Court has developed help to avoid further controversies while others free the Court of the burden of making

---

[76] Ibid.

[77] *JY Interpretation No 499* (2000). For further discussion on this interpretation, see ch 2.

[78] Yeh, above n 43, 920, 932; W-C Chang, 'Strategic Judicial Responses in Politically Charged Cases: East Asian Experiences' (2010) 8 *International Journal of Constitutional Law* 885.

difficult decisions. Examples of these strategies include using a pro-dialogue approach, providing various constitutional declarations, and carrying out a proportionality review. The Court employs other strategies to strengthen the institution itself, and others to further its own capacity for reasoning, including referring to foreign jurisprudence and bodies of international law, as well as ensuring that a unified court is presented when confronting socially divisive issues. Each of these strategies will be discussed in the following subsections.

A. Pro-dialogue Approach

The Constitutional Court's pro-dialogue approach refers to the Court's ability to skilfully avoid direct confrontation with political organs and to facilitate dialogue between competing government branches.[79] As opposed to exhibiting weakness or indecisiveness on the part of the Court, this approach demonstrates that the Court does not take an autocratic approach, ignoring the positions and interests of Taiwan's other political organs.[80]

The Constitutional Court often resorts to its pro-dialogue approach when called upon to deal with major disputes of profound political importance and in cases that involve significant conflicts of rights. In such cases, the Court might apply the 'statutory delegation' and 'statutory reservation' doctrines, and leave the disputed provisions intact, to be revised, replaced or authorised through future legislative measures. All in all, this type of decision making requires extensive inter-branch and inter-party collaboration.[81]

One example of such cases of high political import is the nuclear-installation case discussed in chapter 3.[82] In this case, while the legislative and executive branches debated the constitutionality of unilateral cancellation of the nuclear power plant installation project by the Executive Yuan, the Constitutional Court deferred issuing a definitive ruling, opting instead to set forth all possible alternatives for political

---

[79] Yeh, above n 43, 931.
[80] Ibid.
[81] Ibid, 948.
[82] *JY Interpretation No 520* (2001).

resolution and call for further meaningful political engagement between the premier and the legislature. The Court applied a similar strategy in the case concerning the NHI system, as discussed in chapter 5.[83] Recall that this case involved a dispute between the central and local governments on the constitutionality of the local governments' contributions to the insurance programme subsidy. In deciding this case, rather than adjudicating a final resolution, the Court ordered the competent authorities to discuss and consult with local governments to form the necessary regulations. Likewise, the legislature, when revising relevant laws, is judicially mandated to allow representatives of local governments to be present and observe the legislative process and to express their opinions.[84]

'Statutory delegation' is a judicial doctrine, developed by the Constitutional Court, which requires administrative regulations to take effect under the law. Before the late 1980s, administrative agencies' commonly enjoyed blanket authorisation to enact secondary ordinances or regulations. Without legislative authorisation, these secondary regulations would otherwise infringe individuals' constitutionally protected rights and freedoms.[85] The Constitutional Court ultimately remedied this overextension of authority in *JY Interpretation No 247*, decided in 1989. In this interpretation, the Court held that an explicit statutory delegation is necessary for the making of secondary administrative regulations.[86] In other cases, the Court held that rules that exceeded statutory authorisation were unconstitutional.[87] Further, in *JY Interpretation Nos 313* and *367*, the Court required that statutory authorisations be clear and specific, and deemed unconstitutional those that lacked such characteristics.[88] By applying this doctrine, the Court has in fact urged the legislature to weigh the utility of providing the requisite delegation to the bodies promulgating these disputed regulations, thereby facilitating dialogue between the executive and the legislative branches. In some cases, the legislature may have already provided the necessary

---

[83] *JY Interpretation No 550* (2002).
[84] Ibid.
[85] See, eg, *JY Interpretation No 151* (1977).
[86] *JY Interpretation No 247* (1989).
[87] See, eg, *JY Interpretation No 210* (1986); *JY Interpretation No 217* (1987); *JY Interpretation No 268* (1990).
[88] *JY Interpretation No 313* (1993); *JY Interpretation No 367* (1994).

delegation. Such occasions were unaltered by the Court's ruling. Nevertheless, this holding provided far more legitimacy to otherwise disputed and controversial administrative regulations.

Another doctrine often applied by the Constitutional Court is the doctrine of 'statutory reservation'. This doctrine requires any regulation involving the restriction of rights and freedoms to be reserved by law. Although this concept is not expressly written in the ROC Constitution, it finds its basis in Article 23 of the Constitution, which stipulates that none of the constitutionally enumerated rights and freedoms shall be restricted by law, except as may be necessary under certain extenuating circumstances.

This doctrine of 'statutory reservation' is well established by the Constitutional Court, as demonstrated in *JY Interpretation No 443*, in which the issue involved the right of a draftee to apply for an exit permit to go abroad. Here, the Court applied the doctrine of 'statutory reservation', to develop a 'Multi-Level Reservation Structure', finding that certain rights and freedoms, such as the physical freedom of the people, as stipulated in Article 8 of the Constitution, shall not be limited, even by the legislature. The limitation of the impediment to such rights is reserved in the Constitution, whereas freedoms and rights under Articles 7, 9–18, 21 and 22 may be limited by law upon the satisfaction of certain conditions, as stipulated in Article 23 of the Constitution. In cases in which such statutory delegation exists, that delegation should be specific and precise. Further, the determination of which freedom or right shall be regulated by law or by administrative regulations authorised by law shall depend on the intensity of such regulations. Under this structure, the freedom to move freely is stipulated in Article 10, upon which, according to Article 23 of the Constitution, any limitation shall be made only by law and only where such limitation is necessary.[89] The Court adopted approaches for disputes concerning taxation. Where, as Article 19 of the Constitution provides, the people shall have the duty of paying taxes in accordance with the law, the Court has adopted the principle of 'taxation by law'. With these and other such rulings, political resolutions must be made in prospective legislation that facilitates political dialogue between regulatory authorities and the legislature.

---

[89] *JY Interpretation No 443* (1997).

Both doctrines elaborated above could serve as effective catalysts to spur negotiation between the legislative and executive branches. The Constitutional Court has often refrained from intervening in the political process between the two branches of government, citing these doctrines as the reasoning behind its decision. Rather than inserting itself between the branches, this laissez-faire approach gives way to political dialogues and affords both branches with the opportunity to develop political, amiable solutions. In so doing, the Court plays a vital role in stabilising existing regimes and minimising the effects of political upheavals.[90]

B. The Variety of Constitutional Declarations versus the Politics of Unconstitutionality

According to Articles 171 and 172 of the ROC Constitution, laws and ordinances in conflict with the Constitution are null and void. Notwithstanding this mandate, however, the Constitutional Court has developed a variety of declarations to deal with impugned statutes or ordinances, including unconstitutional declaration, admonitory declaration, limited constitutionality declaration, limited unconstitutionality declaration, prospective declaration, and unconstitutional declaration with imposed deadlines for invalidation.[91]

The Constitutional Court first issued an unconstitutional declaration without invalidation of impugned provisions in *JY Interpretation No 86*. In this interpretation, although the Court found the law permitting the Ministry of Justice to supervise lower courts unconstitutional, it fell short of directly invalidating it.[92] Owing to the suppressive political atmosphere at that time, the Court may have found itself with no alternative other than to issue such a declaration. Unsurprisingly, the KMT government ignored this interpretation for roughly two decades.

Interestingly, however, even after the 1980s, when judicial decisions were largely respected, the Constitutional Court still issued declarations

---

[90] Yeh, above n 43, 948.
[91] For further discussions on these various types of declaration in a comparative perspective, see Chang et al, above n 4, 443–61.
[92] *JY Interpretation No 86* (1960).

of unconstitutionality without accompanying direct invalidations. In *JY Interpretation No 483*, for example, the Court found that the relevant provisions in the Public Functionaries Appointment Act and the Public Functionaries Remuneration Act, which permitted transfers of civil servants to lower rank positions, were inconsistent with constitutional protection of the right to hold public office.[93] However, having considered that an overhaul of the system may require a comprehensive change that the Court was, at the time, unwilling to set in motion, the Court instead issued an unconstitutional declaration and urged the competent authority to promptly review and amend the impugned provisions.[94] In addition, unconstitutional declarations without invalidation are sometimes necessary when dealing with unconstitutional government inaction. In *JY Interpretation No 632*, the Court found it unconstitutional for the Legislative Yuan not to exercise its consent power over the appointment of the Control Yuan members.[95] As there was no action to be invalidated, an unconstitutional declaration of such inaction became a plausible substitute.

Second, the Constitutional Court may make admonitory declarations by maintaining the constitutionality of impugned provisions while providing warnings for lawmakers to take measures for improvement. A shown in Table 6.1, the fifth-term Constitutional Court began the practice of issuing admonitory declarations. The number of such declarations reached a peak in the sixth term but has sharply declined over the past decade. Also noteworthy is that the Court may initially sustain the challenged statute with a warning, only to subsequently invalidate it if no improvement efforts have been undertaken. For example, in *JY Interpretation No 211*, the Court sustained the impugned provision of the Customs Smuggling Control Act, which imposed a penalty without judicial remedy, yet it nevertheless expressed concerns and urged the lawmakers to consider revision.[96] A decade later, in *JY Interpretation No 439*, the same provision was challenged again before the Court.[97] This time, and without hesitation, the Constitutional Court invalidated the provision.

---

[93] *JY Interpretation No 483* (1999).
[94] Ibid.
[95] *JY Interpretation No 632* (2007). For the discussion of this controversy, see ch 4.
[96] *JY Interpretation No 211* (1986).
[97] *JY Interpretation No 439* (1997).

The third kind of alternative declaration is the declaration of limited constitutionality or unconstitutionality. Often, such a declaration entails the Constitutional Court's efforts to sustain legislative enactments to the fullest extent possible. For example, in *JY Interpretation No 509*, the Constitutional Court construed the provision of criminal defamation to exclude those who failed to demonstrate the truth of the defamatory statement but nevertheless had reasonable grounds to believe that the statement was the truth. With this interpretation, the provision was found to not infringe upon the constitutionally protected freedom of speech.[98]

The Court issued a declaration of limited unconstitutionality in *JY Interpretation No 585*. As discussed in previous chapters, this case concerned a special commission created by the KMT legislative majority for the investigation of a gun-shooting incident before the 2004 presidential election.[99] The Constitutional Court ruled only that a portion of the provisions concerning the special commission were unconstitutional.[100] It was the KMT legislative majority's intention for the commission to fully investigate the incident, with its findings substituting for judicial decisions. These provisions were found to be unconstitutional because parliamentary investigations should not transcend either the separation of powers or the system of checks and balances. The Court's skilful construction met with its share of criticism, even from within the Court's own ranks. The dissenting opinion argued that the majority distorted not only the legislature's intent when it created such a commission but also the intent of the constitutional framers who gave no such investigative power to the legislature.[101] Perhaps the most telling criticism levied against this opinion is the fact that the majority's carefully crafted interpretation was not well received by either the KMT or the DPP, though the primary reason for their disdain is likely that neither of the parties was entirely vindicated by the decision. The KMT legislative majority exacted its revenge on the Constitutional Court by cutting back the remuneration of the Justices—which, unsurprisingly, the Court later found unconstitutional in *JY Interpretation No 601*.[102]

---

[98] *JY Interpretation No 509* (2000).

[99] For further discussion of this case, see Yeh, above n 43, 920, 932.

[100] *JY Interpretation No 585* (2004).

[101] See, eg, the dissenting opinion by Justice Tzong-Li Hsu, in *JY Interpretation No 585* (2004).

[102] *JY Interpretation No 601* (2005). For further discussions, see Yeh, above n 43 920, 932.

The last, but most commonly used, declaration is the prospective declaration or unconstitutional declaration with imposed deadlines for invalidation. In such a declaration, while the Court finds that an impugned provision is unconstitutional, it nevertheless sustains its validity for an express period of time, or until the completion of necessary revisions. In other words, the Court—due to a variety of considerations—may decide not to invalidate the law immediately, but rather to prospectively invalidate it.[103] The politics of unconstitutionality are vividly revealed in this type of declaration, which enables the judiciary to mitigate practical consequences and political impacts of judicial rulings. This type of judicial ruling has been tested in quite a number of jurisdictions around the world, including Taiwan.[104]

The first time the Constitutional Court experimented with prospective ruling was *JY Interpretation No 218*, which the Court issued in 1987. In this decision, the Constitutional Court found a tax regulation 'inconsistent with the meaning … as contemplated by the Income Tax Act and must cease to be operative within six months from the date of issue of this interpretation'.[105] The tax regulation was subsequently revised, in compliance with the Court-imposed six-month deadline. The Constitutional Court issued a prospective ruling for only the second time with *JY Interpretation No 251* in 1990. The Court found the police-ordered system of detention and forced labour under the Act Governing the Punishment of Police Offences unconstitutional, but sustained its validity until 1 July 1991, by which date it stipulated that all relevant laws must be revised.[106] This case is particularly noteworthy since, only a decade prior, the Court had already issued an unconstitutional declaration against a similar such exercise of police power, though the parties did not comply with the provisions of this earlier ruling.[107] The second time around, riding the wave of political and democratic reforms that had only recently taken hold, the Court's decision in *JY Interpretation No 251* and the deadline it imposed were satisfied.[108]

---

[103] Chang et al, above n 4.
[104] Ibid.
[105] *JY Interpretation No 218* (1987).
[106] *JY Interpretation No 251* (1990).
[107] *JY Interpretation No 166* (1980).
[108] See also Chang et al, above n 4, 454–55.

The Court again imposed yet another deadline for action in *JY Interpretation No 261*, which involved a high-profile constitutional crisis regarding the continuation of the first-term national representatives who had not stood for election since 1948. The Court ultimately held that those representatives must cease to exercise their powers follow-ing 31 December 1991.[109] At the time, with so many legal and political efforts geared towards facilitating Taiwan's democratisation, though this deadline was unprecedented, the parties complied so as to not derail the progress made so far. Since then, the Court has continued to experiment with prospective declarations and has imposed several deadlines by which certain bodies must reform or repeal the challenged provisions.

The frequency of prospective rulings with imposed judicial dead-lines has risen over time. In the fifth-term Constitutional Court, among the Court's 37 unconstitutional rulings, nine (24.3 per cent) were rendered with judicial deadlines. Of the sixth-term Court's 72 unconstitutional rulings, 20 (27.8 per cent) included judicial deadlines. Between October 2003 and December 2012, the Court imposed 34 judicial deadlines among the 66 unconstitutional rulings, the ratio of which was 51.5 per cent. Altogether, by the end of 2012, the Court imposed deadlines in 36 per cent of the unconstitutional declarations it has issued.[110]

Prospective rulings with imposed deadlines have been utilised both in unconstitutional findings against organic acts and those that centre on controversial policies. In *JY Interpretation No 613*, the Constitu-tional Court found the appointment method for the members of the National Communication Commission (an independent regulatory commission) unconstitutional. Yet, the Court decided to uphold the impugned act's validity for another two and a half years. In addition, temporal validity may also be given to impugned controversial poli-cies where deliberation and revision may be quite time-intensive. For example, in *JY Interpretation No 666*, the Court struck down a law that penalised prostitutes but did not penalise those engaging in sexual

[109] *JY Interpretation No 261* (1990).
[110] Updated from J-r Yeh, 'The Politics of Unconstitutionality: An Empirical Analysis of Judicial Deadlines and Political Compliance in Taiwan' (paper presented to the International Conference on Empirical Studies of Judicial Systems, Academia Sinica, Taipei, June 2011) Tables 1 and 2.

transactions with the prostitutes, on the grounds that the law violated the equality principle. Having considered that it may take some time for further policy deliberation, the Court provided a two-year period for temporary validity of the impugned law.[111]

The Court's practice of prospective rulings and judicial deadlines has been met with a fair share of suspicion.[112] In sustaining the temporal validity of impugned provisions, the Constitutional Court, and more broadly, courts in general, may be seen as ineffective guardians of the Constitution. Owing to the temporary nature of the validity of an impugned statute following such a ruling by the Court, certain remedies may be unavailable to individuals who have suffered or otherwise been harmed under the statute. Worse still, courts may risk undermining institutional authority if the respective parties do not comply with the agreed-upon deadlines. Political branches may not take the necessary care to revise impugned provisions and observe the Court's deadlines. However, such prospective rulings may still provide for better (and more frequent) interaction between the political and judicial branches of government.[113] Especially at a time of such profound democratic transition, it may be necessary and desirable for constitutional rulings to embody at least a certain degree of flexibility and, at times, rather than acting merely as arbiters in formalistically distinguishing illegality from legality, courts may be expected to act as efficient managers and key mediators in resolving conflicting agendas during the course of complex reforms.[114] The flexibility that courts provide for political branches may induce better compliance, which in turn may encourage courts to increase the usage of such declarations. This seems to be the case of prospective rulings and judicial deadlines in Taiwan, which have increased in frequency during the last several decades and, on average, have been substantially complied with.[115]

---

[111] *JY Interpretation No 666* (2009).

[112] For further discussions on pros and cons of this practice, see Chang et al, above n 4, 447–56.

[113] J-r Yeh, 'An Analysis of JY Interpretations with Judicial Deadlines' (1996) 6 *National Science Council Research Journal: Humanity and Social Science* 1, 12–15 (in Chinese).

[114] Ibid.

[115] Yeh, 'The Politics of Unconstitutionality'.

C. The Principle of Proportionality

The principle of proportionality has been widely used in many jurisdictions—one of them Taiwan's Constitutional Court, where the principle has been employed as one of the Court's key tools.

The principle of proportionality is not expressly written into the Constitution. However, Article 23, which serves as the basis for the doctrines of statutory delegation and reservation, requires that the government establish 'necessity', prior to infringing upon rights guaranteed under the Constitution. While the term 'necessary', as it is used in Article 23, seems to imply a certain degree of proportionality, such a requirement was not a recognised principle until the Court first mentioned the principle of proportionality in *JY Interpretation No 414* (issued in 1996), which required that the legislature consider proportionality when revising laws.[116] Since this interpretation, the Court has made extensive use of the principle, primarily weighing different interests of the individuals and the public without delving any deeper into the principle's substance.[117] However, in *JY Interpretation No. 476*, in 1999, the Court formulated a four-pronged test for applying the principle when it was called upon to rule on the constitutionality of the death penalty and life sentences for the crimes of manufacturing, transporting and selling narcotics.[118] The Court directly adopted a three-pronged test, which it borrowed from German constitutional jurisprudence: 'reasonableness', 'necessity' and 'not causing excessive restrictions'. The Court held that the sentences satisfied all three prongs. The Court went a step further, examining the legislative purpose of the disputed provisions, which was later adopted as the fourth prong of the test. This inquiry into the legislative purpose serves to determine whether the legislature's purpose is 'legitimate' and whether the means adopted are in accordance with the legislative intent.[119] The Court has since begun employing this four-pronged test in subsequent interpretations.

Notwithstanding the fact that the Court applied the principle of proportionality, *JY Interpretation No 476* is a controversial interpretation,

---

[116] *JY Interpretation No 414* (1996).
[117] For instance, *JY Interpretation No 428* (1997).
[118] *JY Interpretation No 476* (1999).
[119] Ibid.

since the Court upheld sentences up to and including death for drug smuggling as being consistent with the principle of proportionality. Many similarly disagreed with the Court in its later interpretation, *JY Interpretation No 554*, in which the Court declared the criminal punishment for adultery consistent with the principle of proportionality.[120] This decision was controversial, and primarily struck a discord with activists for women's rights, who doubted the Court's holding that there is no less severe means other than criminal punishment to satisfy the legislative purpose.

The application of the principle of proportionality in the above cases invited debate and criticism from scholars and NGOs regarding the principle's effectiveness, leading some to describe it as a 'toothless tiger', since the Constitutional Court could always manipulate the tests to find leniency in the disputed provisions. In any event, critics argued, the legislators could always argue that there are no other means that cause less harm at their disposal. The Court addressed these criticisms in *JY Interpretation No 584*, in 2004, when it established different standards of review for applying the principle of proportionality. In cases in which the legislators intend to regulate the subjective eligibility of individuals in selecting their occupations, such as setting standards regarding knowledge, competency, age, physical conditions and moral standards, the Court held that such restrictions must be narrowly tailored and balanced against safeguarding other matters of the public interest. In other scenarios, where the legislators intend to restrict the exercise of the freedom of occupation by restricting the method, time or place of such occupations or demonstrations, the legislature is granted greater leeway, and the broadly stated purpose of safeguarding public interests may be sufficient. Despite the development of these different standards, the Court still held, in its interpretation, that precluding individuals convicted of offences such as manslaughter and snatching from applying for employment as taxi drivers is constitutional.[121]

The principle of proportionality's 'teeth' gradually developed in subsequent cases. In *JY Interpretation No 603* in 2005, for example, the Constitutional Court declared the provisions of the Household Registration Act, which required the applicant's fingerprints for the issuance

---

[120] *JY Interpretation No 554* (2002).
[121] *JY Interpretation No 584* (2004).

of a state identity card, unconstitutional. The Court's reasoning was that compulsory fingerprinting for the purpose of record keeping is inconsistent with the constitutional intent to protect individuals' right to information privacy. Also, this measure failed to achieve balance between cost and benefit and should, therefore, be considered an excessively unnecessary means to achieve a government end.[122]

These cases show that the discussion of the principle of proportionality has been vibrant before the bench and among the Justices of the Constitutional Court. In some cases, the Court used the principle of proportionality to declare disputed provisions unconstitutional, while in many others the Court upheld the constitutionality of the disputed provisions. In any event, this principle has been an important tool of the Court's, and its application has provided the Court with a great foundation and the necessary flexibility for evaluating legislative restrictions. Also, the principle of proportionality has allowed the Court to go further than just providing procedural solutions, which is the key difference between the principle of proportionality and the pro-dialogue approach. By using the principle of proportionality, the Court could determine, in examining the merits of legislative action, whether to defer to the legislature's intent or to mandate a different approach.

D. Judicial Reference to Foreign Law and the Incorporation of International Law

Judicial reference to foreign and international law has always been a key strategy for Taiwan's Constitutional Court. Although in most cases, the Court's majority opinions do not refer directly to foreign legal authorities, their influence is quite obvious. For instance, the principle of proportionality, as mentioned above, was derived from the reading of German constitutional jurisprudence. In contrast, foreign and international legal sources have always been visible in separate (concurring or dissenting) opinions of individual justices, particularly since the late 1980s.[123]

The first time the Constitutional Court directly cited foreign jurisprudence in its majority opinion was in *JY Interpretation No 165*. In citing

---

[122] *JY Interpretation No 603* (2005).
[123] Chang and Yeh, above n 3, 374.

a Japanese Supreme Court case, the Constitutional Court supported its decision to extend less immunity to local councillors relative to their national counterparts.[124] Regarding the incorporation of international law, the Constitutional Court first adopted its monistic attitude towards international treaties in *JY Interpretation No 329*, in 1993, and requested the government's respect for its international treaty obligations. Through this interpretation, the Court granted treaties the same effect as domestic laws.

Judicial reference to foreign and international law is useful in strengthening the Constitutional Court's reasoning. As one of the Court's key strategies, this approach has three important functions: to enrich the substantial content of human rights, to provide a benchmark for future legislative change, and to promote judicial engagement with and understanding of foreign and international laws.[125]

For the first function, to enrich the substantial content of human rights, the constitutional revisions over the last two decades did not focus on expanding the list of rights, which therefore makes more prominent the judiciary's function of adding new rights and new contents of rights to the existing list.[126] By referring to foreign and international law, the Constitutional Court can either create new rights or refine understandings of existing rights.[127] For instance, in *JY Interpretation No 582*, a criminal defendant's right to cross-examine witnesses was affirmed not only from the text of the Constitution, but also from the body of foreign and international law.[128] The Court held in reasoning that an accused's right to examine a witness is universally provided, whether in a civil or common law jurisdiction, and referred to the constitutions and criminal codes of the United States, Japan and Germany. The Court referred to Article 14(3)(v) of the International Covenant on Civil and Political Rights (ICCPR) to prove such a right.[129] Recently, the Court referred in *JY Interpretation No 709* to the right of adequate

---

[124] *JY Interpretation No 165* (1980).

[125] Chang et al, above n 4, 441.

[126] W-C Chang, 'The Convergence of Constitutions and International Human Rights: Taiwan and South Korea in Comparison' (2011) 36 *North Carolina Journal of International Law and Commercial Regulations* 117.

[127] Chang et al, above n 4, 432.

[128] Ibid, 433.

[129] *JY Interpretation No 582* (2004).

housing enshrined in the International Covenant on Economic, Social and Cultural Rights (ICESCR) when dealing with the constitutionality of the Urban Renewal Act. In *JY Interpretation No 710*, the Constitutional Court referred to the ICCPR's protection of personal freedoms and due process guarantees.

For the second function, to provide a benchmark for future legislative change, both *JY Interpretation Nos 549* and *578* are appropriate case studies. In both cases, the Constitutional Court examined the Labour Insurance Act and the Labour Standards Act and advised the government to overhaul the entire statutory regime with relevant international labour conventions.[130] In this vein, the Court relied on international law to provide guidance for future legislation revisions.

Lastly, the Court's function of channelling dialogues on the understanding of domestic and international norms is found in *JY Interpretation No 392*.[131] In this case, an active debate between the majority and dissenting opinion is evident. The dissenting opinion defended the prosecutor's power to detain a criminal defendant by referring to the conservative readings of relevant provisions in the ICCPR and the European Convention on Human Rights. In contrast, the majority opinion disagreed with such a view, referring to a decision by the European Court of Human Rights in disallowing prosecutorial detention.[132] Such vibrant debate between the majority and separate opinions of individual Justices may create the possibility for Justices holding different positions to find a new common ground in the understanding of international human rights.[133]

Also noteworthy, there is an apparent linkage between the Justices' foreign educational backgrounds and their jurisdictional preference for seeking foreign precedents. In this vein, Justices could rely on foreign sources with which they are more familiar, to level up the content of the judicial reasoning, and to provide more authority and legitimacy to the ruling. This is particularly helpful when Taiwan's Constitutional Court has to make some ambiguous statement in reasoning. In addition, this

---

[130] Chang, 'The Convergence of Constitutions and International Human Rights', above n 126, 122.
[131] Ibid, 124.
[132] *JY Interpretation No 392* (1995).
[133] Chang, above n 126, 126.

trend is significant to the Court's process of internationalisation. When Taiwan's position in the international community is taken into account, the judicial engagement by the Constitutional Court of foreign and international bodies of law is even more noteworthy.

E. A United Court versus a Divided Society

One of the key strategies for the courts in confronting highly contested issues is to try to unite the Justices' diverse opinions and to provide a single judicial voice for dispute resolution.[134] Often with the evolution of the courts, concurring or dissenting opinions—if they are permitted at all[135]—typically become increasingly frequent. In turn, this phenomenon is often reflected in a diversity of opinions and styles of reasoning.[136]

In Taiwan, separate opinions were not permitted prior to the 1958 Council Act. At the time, the Act allowed only 'dissenting opinions' including dissents with the result or with the reasoning, which should have been categorised as concurring opinions, in concurrence with the judgment but for different reasons.[137] As Table 6.2 shows, no separate opinion was issued in the first-term Constitutional Court, steadily increasing in subsequent terms, most notably in the decade from 2003 to 2013, where the Court issued 452 total opinions (more than double the previous term), with concurring opinions greatly outnumbering dissenting opinions (261 to 137)—a reverse of the patterns exhibited by all previous Courts. It should be noted that the 1958 Council Act did

---

[134] Chang, above n 79, 885–910.

[135] It has been a tradition in the common law system that justices issue their separate concurring or dissenting opinions. In contrast, however, courts in a civil law system usually do not permit or have the custom to have justices issue separate opinions. Yet, in recent decades, more civil law systems have begun permitting the issuance of separate opinions, particularly for the top courts and constitutional courts. For example, the German Constitutional Court began the issuance of separate opinions in 1971. For further discussion on judicial opinion writing and legal systems, see T Groppi and M-C Ponthoreau (eds), *The Use of Foreign Precedents by Constitutional Judges* (Oxford, Hart Publishing, 2013).

[136] Ibid.

[137] Art 17 1958 Council Act. In 1987, the Enforcement Rules were revised to distinguish dissents with the reasoning from dissents with the result. Yet, as the 1958 Council Act was not yet changed, these separate opinions were still called 'dissenting opinions'.

Table 6.2: The number of individual opinions issued (1948–2013)

	First term 1948– 1958	Second term 1958– 1967	Third term 1967– 1976	Fourth term 1976– 1985	Fifth term 1985– 1994	Sixth term 1994– 2003	2003– 2013
Concurring opinion	0	0	0	0	7	74	261
Dissenting opinion	0	36	38	56	103	115	137
Concurring in part and dissenting in part	0	0	0	0	0	4	54
Total	0	36	38	56	110	193	452

Source: Data compiled by author.

not require the release of the names of the Justices who issued separate opinions. Such release was allowed but not required until the 1977 revision of the Enforcement Rules of the 1958 Council Act.[138] Eventually, the Constitutional Interpretation Procedure Act of 1993 institutionalised the issuance of concurring and dissenting opinions.[139] The first two concurring opinions were issued in *JY Interpretation No 315*, which coincided with the end of the fifth-term Court.[140]

The proliferation in the issuance of separate opinions has strengthened the quality of judicial decisions. Concurring opinions usually cement and provide further details to back up the majority. And, as challenging and critical as they are, dissenting opinions help the majority to further defend its position and to better articulate the reasoning behind its decision. However, at the same time, with the justices' diverse opinions, it is sometimes challenging for the courts to come together on a single, unified majority opinion, especially when the courts are faced with highly charged political or social controversies. When such

---

[138] In 2002, owing to the Government Archive Act, all of the names of Justices who issued separate opinions prior to 1977 were made public.

[139] Art 17 Constitutional Interpretation Procedure Act (1993).

[140] *JY Interpretation No 315* (1993).

situations arise, justices often take a unified stance in espousing an opinion or split according to their respective views, largely mirroring the societal divisions regarding the same issues. Thus, chief justices often play a pivotal role in trying to unite the courts.[141]

Perhaps Taiwan's most politically divisive period was between 2000 and 2008, when the DPP controlled the executive branch and the KMT held a legislative majority. In that era, the Constitutional Court was frequently called upon to resolve high-profile political disputes. As Table 6.2 shows, separate opinions were more prevalent during this period than any other in the Court's history. Very few interpretations—especially highly contested ones—during those eight years were rendered without separate opinions.[142] It is clear that considerable difficulty existed in the efforts—if any were undertaken—to bring accord to the Justices' diverse stances with a view to unite the Court. There were, however, exceptions to this general rule. In *JY Interpretation No 627*, the sitting DPP President was charged with scandalous embezzlement and the Court issued the interpretation with a single and unified voice to provide the guidance in balancing presidential immunity with the need for prompt criminal investigation.[143]

IV. CONCLUSION

Judicial review has become a common phenomenon in recent global democratic transitions, and as this chapter has shown, Taiwan is no exception. It is unequivocal that the Constitutional Court has become *a* powerful, if not *the most* powerful, institution in Taiwan's constitutional development.

The rise of Taiwan's Constitutional Court has not been without hurdles. During the process of democratic transition in the 1990s and the period of divided government in the 2000s, the Court was often called upon to resolve highly contested disputes and politically charged cases. To survive these political confrontations, the Constitutional

---

[141] J-r Yeh, 'Divided Society and Consolidated Court' in J-r Yeh (ed), *Professor Yueh-Shen Weng's Public Law World* (Taipei, Angle, 2009) (in Chinese).

[142] See also the list of concurring and dissenting opinions since October 2003 by the Judicial Yuan, available at www.judicial.gov.tw/constitutionalcourt/p05.asp.

[143] For further discussion of this case, see Chang, above n 79.

Court has shown its resolve as an evolving court. Despite the fact that some restraints remain, the Court has evolved from a rubber stamp to a real guardian of the Constitution. The Court's guardianship may not be powerful, but the Court has shown itself to be a cautious, highly sophisticated, and strategic body. These qualifications have proved to be essential in the context of Taiwan's profound transition.

Taiwan's Constitutional Court has developed various judicial strategies to deal with the myriad challenges that have arisen. These strategies include the pro-dialogue approach, the variety of constitutional declarations, the principle of proportionality, judicial reference to foreign and international legal sources, and the strategy of presenting a united court. Through its employment of these strategies—which demonstrate both transitional and transnational characteristics—the Court has managed to control its agenda and concurrently preserve itself as an institution capable of maintaining its integrity.

FURTHER READING

Chang, W-C, 'Strategic Judicial Responses in Politically Charged Cases: East Asian Experiences' 8 *International Journal of Constitutional Law* 885–910.

Chang, W-C, 'The Role of Judicial Review in Consolidating Democracy: the Case of Taiwan' (2005) 2 *Asia Law Review* 73–88.

Chang, W-C and Yeh, J-r., 'Judges as Discursive Agent: The Use of Foreign Precedents by the Constitutional Court of Taiwan' in T Groppi and M-C Ponthoreau (eds), *The Use of Foreign Precedents by Constitutional Judges* (Oxford, Hart Publishing, 2013) 373–92.

Ginsburg, T, *Judicial Review in New Democracies: Constitutional Courts in Asian Cases* (New York, Cambridge University Press, 2003).

Weng, Y-s, 'Interpretations of the Constitutional Court and the Developments of Rule of Law and Democratic Constitutionalism in Taiwan' in D Ehlers, H Glaser and K Prokati (eds), *Constitutionalism and Good Governance: Eastern and Western Perspectives* (Baden-Baden, Nomos, 2014) 321–60.

Yeh, J-r, 'Presidential Politics and the Judicial Facilitation of Dialogue between Political Actors in New Asian Democracies: Comparing the South Korean and Taiwanese Experiences' (2010) 8 *International Journal of Constitutional Law* 911–49.

7

Rights and Freedoms

Rights Discourse in a Transformative Society – Civil and
Political Rights – Socio-economic Rights – Indigenous Peoples
and Collective Rights – The Incorporation of International
Human Rights – Conclusion

S
IMILAR TO OTHER constitutions, the 1947 ROC Constitution
includes a list of fundamental rights and freedoms.[1] However,
that list is not as extensive as those in constitutions drafted more
recently. Not included are human dignity, the right to know, privacy
rights, the right of marriage, etc. Regrettably, constitutional reforms in
the 1990s and 2000s placed the focus on the reform of the system of
government and made no further incorporation of fundamental rights
and freedoms. This has led the judiciary—especially the Constitutional
Court—to assume an expansive role in the elaboration of these rights
and freedoms. However, judicial incorporation of fundamental rights
and freedoms beyond the constitutional text has been responsive to
social and political demands amid profound transformation.[2] Thus, civil
engagement in rights discourse has underpinned the judicial recognition
and articulation of human rights in many ground-breaking judicial decisions. At the same time, international convergence of human rights has

---

[1] Arts 7–22, Constitution of the Republic of China (1947).
[2] J-r Yeh and W-C Chang, 'The Emergence of East Asian Constitutionalism:
Features in Comparison' (2010) 59 *American Journal of Comparative Law* 805, 832–33.

also played a significant part.[3] The above developments have occurred in the realm of civil and political rights, as well as in the realm of social and economic rights. However, the intensity and pattern of recognition of these rights are varied and reflective of changing social, economic and political dynamics.

The first part of this chapter offers an analysis of the discourse and politics of rights in the wake of rapid social and political transitions. In it, a central focus is placed on the role of civil society and non-governmental organiations in championing the rights discourse. The next two parts of the chapter discuss exemplary cases on the articulation and implementation of rights. The rights to political representation, referendum and free speech are underscored among civil and political rights, whereas the right to health, the right to work, and the equality clause receive the focus of social-economic rights. Most of these rights are developed through judicial decisions, some of which are heavily influenced by international human rights regimes. The fourth part of the chapter highlights the rights of Taiwan's indigenous peoples, exemplifying the evolutionary development of collective rights in the transitional and transnational contexts. The chapter ends by examining the incorporation of international human rights in a dialectical context, taking the issue of the death penalty as an example.

I. RIGHTS DISCOURSE IN A TRANSFORMATIVE SOCIETY

The list of the fundamental rights and freedoms guaranteed by the 1947 ROC Constitution encompasses comprehensive protection, although it is not perfect by contemporary standards. It must be remembered that, in the era of martial law, the authoritarian KMT government severely curtailed the Constitution's human rights protections by enforcing special laws authorising strict social control: the Publication Act, the Civil Association Act, the Public Gathering Act and so forth. A sizable gap therefore existed between the Constitution's text and stark realities.

---

[3] J-r Yeh and W-C Chang, 'The Emergence of Transnational Constitutionalism: Its Features, Challenges and Solutions' (2008) 27 *Penn State International Law Review* 89; W-C Chang, 'The Convergence of Constitutions and International Human Rights: Taiwan and South Korea in Comparison' (2011) 36 *North Carolina Journal of International Law and Commercial Regulations* 593.

Significant changes came only after July 1987, when martial law was lifted. Human rights protection since then has witnessed a significant evolution—even a transformation. At that time, legislation was introduced to remedy those human rights violations that had occurred during the martial law period. Additionally, human rights as enumerated in the Constitution were confirmed, secured and upheld through civil advocacy and a series of judicial interpretations. As the process of democratic transformation took hold, the means of progressive governmental policies, legislative action and landmark judicial decisions achieved the end of further deliberating and expanding many constitutionally stipulated rights.

The evolution of the protection of human rights did not occur in a vacuum. Instead, the significant drivers of this process included the context of democratisation, the burgeoning of civil society, the momentum for reform and the judicial incorporation of human rights. An emergent civil society pushed the government to repeal suppressive laws, enact quasi-constitutional statutes[4] and embrace the international human rights conventions.[5] Another way for these non-governmental organisations to advance human rights was to seek judicial recognition by the Constitutional Court.[6] The following discusses the rights discourses these social groups have advanced in the wake of constitutional reform or through constitutional litigation.

A. Rights Discourse in the Wake of an Emergent Civil Society

The end of martial law and the close of the Temporary Provisions era were brought about in the hope that the constitutional order would begin functioning as originally intended. Upon the 1987 repeal of the

---

[4] J-r Yeh and W-C Chang, 'A Decade of Changing Constitutionalism in Taiwan: Transitional and Transnational Perspectives' in AHY Chen (ed), *Constitutionalism in Asia in the Early Twenty-first Century* (Cambridge, Cambridge University Press, 2014) 150–52; J-r Yeh and W-C Chang, 'The Changing Landscape of Modern Constitutionalism: Transitional Perspective' (2009) 4 *National Taiwan University Law Review* 145, 156–57.

[5] Chang, 'The Convergence of Constitutions and International Human Rights', above n 3.

[6] W-C Chang, 'Public Interest Litigation in Taiwan: Strategy for Law and Policy Changes in the Course of Democratization' in PJ Yap and H Lau (eds), *Public Interest Litigation in Asia* (New York, Routledge, 2011).

Martial Law Decree, bans on organising political parties, newspapers, voluntary associations and public gatherings were lifted one after another. The final abandonment of these special laws would not have been possible without the efforts of adamant political dissidents—organising into a growing opposition party—along with a rising civil society. In return, the repeal of these suppressive laws further empowered civic engagement for reform in the public square.

The interaction between civil society and the regime has been a primary factor contributing to the formation of rights discourse in Taiwan, especially as non-governmental organisations have proliferated. Taiwan has seen two major waves of non-governmental organisation establishment: one in the early 1980s and the other in the late 1980s.[7]

The first wave occurred largely from 1980 to 1986. A contamination of rice oil in 1979 led to the creation of the first voluntary consumer group in 1980. Following this, the Awakening Foundation, a group of women lawyers, was formed in 1982. The Taiwan Association for Human Rights, composed of human rights lawyers, was subsequently founded in 1984. Eventually, in 1986, the first opposition political party, the DPP, was established.[8]

The second wave in the growth of non-governmental groups essentially started in July 1987, upon the lifting of the Martial Law Decree. The Taiwan Environmental Protection Union and the Humanistic Education Foundation were both formed in that year, followed by the Homemaker's Union and Foundation, a women's and environmentalist group. Thereafter, the 1990s democratisation heralded a thriving of social groups for the advocacy of rights, social justice and political reform. Exemplary groups included the Judicial Reform Foundation, created by a group of human rights lawyers; the Gender/Sexuality Rights Association, advocating for gay rights; and the Wild at Heart Legal Defence Association, the first group of environmental lawyers.[9]

In addition to forming non-governmental organisations, civil society supported increased human rights protection by holding demonstrations demanding statutory revisions. In this regard, May 1991 witnessed a watershed event. During that month, agents of the Ministry of

---

[7] Ibid, 138–39.
[8] Ibid.
[9] Ibid, 139.

Justice's Bureau of Investigation stormed National Tsing-Hua University's campus to arrest a group of students thought to be affiliated with the 'Independent Taiwan Association'. In support of the student detainees, other students from across Taiwan refused to attend classes and orchestrated sit-ins. At the same time, academics from 15 universities and research institutions established the 'Academic Alliance Against Political Persecution', which demanded the repeal of the Anti-Sedition Law and the release without punishment of the detainees. These demands attracted widespread support via public demonstrations joined by citizens' associations of farmers, teachers, students, labourers, environmentalists and indigenous peoples—all chanting for the repeals of the Anti-Sedition Law and of the Criminal Code's Article 100. Legislators from both sides of the aisle were forced to respond, but they ultimately only repealed the Anti-Sedition Law; they made no commitment to repeal Article 100.

On 21 September 1991, two prominent academics—Lee Chen-yuan and Lin Shan-tien—formed the 'Article 100 Action Alliance' to demand the abolition of Article 100. On 8 October, the Alliance held a sit-in in front of the Presidential Office, only to be dispersed by the military police. In other sit-ins across Taiwan, the police forcibly removed many teachers and students. As a result, even greater protests ensued. On 29 February 1992, the Executive Yuan decided that the provision should be revised and not abolished. The 'Article 100 Action Alliance' petitioned the provisional meeting of the National Assembly, and families of victims under Article 100 initiated a hunger strike. On 19 April the DPP organised a demonstration that became a prolonged protest, in which demonstrators called for direct presidential elections, the cancellation of plans for the fourth nuclear power plant, and the abolition of Article 100. The police ended the demonstration by forcibly dispersing those involved. Under mounting pressure, the KMT government passed a resolution on 29 April calling for the revision of Article 100. Less than a month later, on 16 May, the revision was enacted by the Legislative Yuan.

B. Rights Discourse in the Wake of Constitutional Reform

The ROC Constitution, and specifically Articles 7 to 22, includes a brief list of rights and duties. Its coverage of rights and freedoms includes the right to equality (Article 7); the right to personal freedom and due

process (Article 8); the right not to be placed under military trial—
except as to soldiers (Article 9); the rights of residence and movement
(Article 10); the right to free speech (Article 11); the right to privacy
of correspondence (Article 12); the freedom of religion (Article 13);
the rights of assembly and free association (Article 14); the rights to
exist, work and hold property (Article 15); the rights to sue and lodge
complaints (Article 16); the rights of election, recall, initiative and referendum (Article 17); and the rights to take public examinations and hold
public offices (Article 18). Aside from these rights, three duties are also
listed, including the duty to pay taxes (Article 19), the duty to perform
military service (Article 20), and the duty—as well as the right—to
receive a national basic education (Article 21).

Compared to other constitutions written in more recent decades, the
ROC Constitution's coverage of rights is in no way expansive or elaborative. It does not, for example, guarantee human dignity in general or
include specific rights, such as the right to know, the right to reputation,
the right to privacy, the right of marriage, the right to health, the right to
social security, or the right to a clean environment. Nor does it expressly
guarantee the rights of indigenous peoples or provide explicit protections to the disabled or other disadvantaged groups. While Article 22
states that all other freedoms or rights shall be guaranteed under the
Constitution—as long as they are not detrimental to the social order or
to public welfare—these unenumerated rights await judicial interpretation by the Constitutional Court.[10] It is thus little wonder that human
rights groups and activists have attempted to add to the enumerated list
in the wake of constitutional reforms.

In the early 1990s, the advent of reform ignited a serious discussion about the future of the ROC Constitution, encompassing its
possible revision and even its complete overhaul. That such changes
were thinkable speaks to that era's ever-evolving political and social circumstances. In the end, it was decided that the Constitution would be
revised.[11] Before the first constitutional revision in 1991, several drafts
of a new constitution were proposed, each significantly expanding the

---

[10] For a discussion of how the Constitutional Court has elaborated these unenumerated rights, see subsection I.C.
[11] For the historical context, see chs 1 and 2.

coverage of fundamental rights and freedoms.[12] For example, these drafts included the guarantee of human dignity; the rights to life and restrictions on the imposition of the death penalty; further elaboration of personal freedoms; habeas corpus and due process; as well as specific rights such as the right to know, the right to reputation, the right of privacy, the right of marriage, the right to health, the right to social security, the right to a clean environment, and comprehensive labour rights. Also provided for were the protection of indigenous people's rights and those of other disadvantaged groups. It was evident that the citizenry strongly demanded expansive coverage of new rights.

Unfortunately, owing to strict partisanship on both sides of the aisle, the revision agenda concentrated on the reforms of government structures instead of on the expansion of rights and freedoms. Yet human-rights-oriented groups and citizens had not given up their advocacy in these rounds of revision. Eventually, these groups were successful in writing policy directives that obliged the government to either formulate or prioritise policies that would emphasise fundamental rights and freedoms. These policy directives generated more than a dozen provisions that ultimately found their way into Article 10 of the Additional Articles of the ROC Constitution.

For example, environmentalist groups secured a statement that 'environmental and ecological protection shall be given equal consideration with economic and technological development'.[13] Similarly, women's groups were reassured that 'the state shall protect the dignity of women, safeguard their personal safety, eliminate sexual discrimination, and further substantive gender equality'.[14] For the disabled, there were promises that 'the state shall guarantee insurance, medical care, obstacle-free environments, education and training, vocational guidance, and support and assistance in everyday life for physically and mentally handicapped persons, and shall also assist them to attain independence and

---

[12] These drafts included those proposed by Mr Koh, Se-kai in 1988, by Mr Jen, Nan-rung in 1989, by Mr Lin, Yi-hsiung in 1989, and by the DPP-led Peoples' Constituent Assembly in 1991, among others.

[13] Art 10(2) Additional Articles of the Constitution of the Republic of China (2005).

[14] Art 10(6) Additional Articles of the Constitution of the Republic of China (2005).

to develop'.[15] For the indigenous peoples, constitutional recognition of cultural pluralism was provided,[16] along with state guarantees to 'actively preserve and foster the development of aboriginal languages and cultures', to 'safeguard the[ir] status and political participation' and to 'provide assistance and encouragement for aboriginal education, culture, transportation, water conservation, health and medical care, economic activity, land and social welfare'.[17]

Also extensively guaranteed in the policy directives were economic, social and cultural rights. For example, regarding the right to health, it was demanded that the state should promote universal health insurance and promote the research and development of both modern and traditional medicines.[18] Moreover, the state was obliged to provide for social assistance, welfare services, social insurance, medical and health care, as well as employment for all citizens.[19] While the rights and duties to receive education were guaranteed, educational, scientific and cultural priorities were still expressly written in.[20] Even small and medium-sized business groups were able to obtain a promise that the state would assist and protect their survival and development.[21]

These policy directives were intended to function as expressions of constitutional concerns that would garner appropriate government action. There is, however, no judicial mechanism to enforce the directives if the government fails to act.[22] Often, the directives are regarded as merely declarative, or even as so much window dressing. Nevertheless, the Constitutional Court has—perhaps surprisingly—found a way to

---

[15] Art 10(7) Additional Articles of the Constitution of the Republic of China (2005).

[16] Art 10(11) Additional Articles of the Constitution of the Republic of China (2005).

[17] Art 10(11) and (12) Additional Articles of the Constitution of the Republic of China (2005).

[18] Art 10(5) Additional Articles of the Constitution of the Republic of China (2005).

[19] Art 10(8) Additional Articles of the Constitution of the Republic of China (2005).

[20] Art 10(10) Additional Articles of the Constitution of the Republic of China (2005).

[21] Art 10(3) Additional Articles of the Constitution of the Republic of China (2005).

[22] W-C Chang et al, *Constitutionalism in Asia: Cases and Materials* (Oxford, Hart Publishing, 2014) 961–68.

give meaning to these policy directives in the course of its constitutional interpretations. In *JY Interpretation No 578*, the Court found constitutional (albeit with a warning) a law that penalised employers who failed to contribute—by a fixed percentage—to employee pension funds.[23] In the Court's view, though the law aimed to provide social security for employees, it might have been too restrictive for small- to medium-sized employers, groups the protection of which was demanded by the policy directives.[24] When examining the constitutionality of laws or regulations, the Court may presume their constitutionality if they implement the policy directives or, conversely, presume their unconstitutionality if they contravene those directives. In sum, the Court often assesses the implementation of policy directives by way of proportionality review, wherein the adoption of directives via government action is judged with a view to the balancing of rights and interests.

Notwithstanding the progress made in the inclusion and interpretation of policy directives, human rights and social groups remain discontented with the Constitution's enumeration of fundamental rights and freedoms. Efforts by civil society to either piece together a new comprehensive list of rights or to enact a new constitution have not ceased, even after the constitutional revision of 2005 increased the threshold requirement for future revisions, thereby rendering them nearly impossible to effectuate. In April 2006, the Constitutional Reform Alliance—consisting of dozens of human rights organisations and social groups—published a new constitutional draft after several months of heated debate and deliberation.[25] Entitled 'A Love Letter to Our Country', this new draft contained more than 50 provisions on the protection of fundamental rights, including a very detailed list of civil, political, economic, social and cultural rights. Special protections were afforded to underprivileged members of society, such as the disabled, and elaborative provisions covered the development of indigenous peoples. Most noteworthy was the list's international emphasis: restrictions to or interpretations of fundamental rights should parallel international human rights.[26]

---

[23] *JY Interpretation No 578* (2004).

[24] Ibid.

[25] Constitutional Reform Alliance, *Taiwan's New Constitution*, 28–31.

[26] Draft Arts 48 and 52, New Constitutional Draft by the Constitutional Reform Alliance (2006).

C. Rights Discourse and Incorporation by the Judiciary

When human rights and social groups have sought to further rights discourse in the courts, they have focused primarily on the Constitutional Court. This is reflected in two types of litigation. First, constitutional petitions may be used to challenge statutes that have encroached upon fundamental rights and freedoms already existing in the Constitution.[27] This tactic was popular at the beginning of the movement towards democratisation in the late 1980s and early 1990s. Second, constitutional petitions may request the Court to construe new rights that are not written into the Constitution, particularly through Article 22, which affords constitutional protection to 'all other freedoms and rights that are not detrimental to social order or public welfare'.[28] Occasionally, as discussed in chapter 6, the judicial construction of new rights and freedoms has been channelled via reference to international human rights and comparative constitutional laws.[29]

The petitions brought before the Constitutional Court at the beginning of the democratic transition entailed a wide array of rights. One of the first petitions challenged the constitutionality of a mandatory death penalty imposed on three young men involved in a well-known kidnapping case. The Taiwan Association for Human Rights was the first human rights organisation to criticise the mandatory death penalty publicly. Although the Court in *JY Interpretation No 263* upheld the constitutionality of the penalty, it nevertheless urged judicial caution in imposing it.[30] The petition, though it failed, helped to at least raise public awareness of the importance of the right to life and the problems with the mandatory death penalty.

The next—and successful—line of constitutional petitions began with female lawyers and women's groups such as the Awakening Foundation (founded in 1982), who challenged statutes infringing sex and gender equality.[31] In 1990, several women's groups initiated a three-year

---

[27] Chang, 'Public Interest Litigation in Taiwan', above n 6.

[28] Art 22 Constitution of the Republic of China (1947).

[29] W-C Chang and J-r Yeh, 'Judges as Discursive Agent: The Use of Foreign Precedents by the Constitutional Court of Taiwan' in T Groppi and M-C Ponthoreau (eds), *The Use of Foreign Precedents by Constitutional Judges* (Oxford, Hart Publishing, 2013); Chang, above n 3.

[30] *JY Interpretation No 263* (1990).

[31] Chang, above n 6.

project, centred on the equality of women in the family, to revise the Civil Code. That same year, these groups not only tried a test case in court, but also lobbied the newly elected Legislative Yuan to overhaul the Civil Code. Joined by legislators, women's groups petitioned the Constitutional Court to review the constitutionality of a Civil Code provision that privileged fathers in cases where parents disagreed over child custody.[32] In *JY Interpretation No 365*, the Court found that the provision violated the Constitution, and required it to be amended within two years or else be made null and void.[33] This victory was followed by even more successful petitions. For example, *JY Interpretation Nos 410* and *452* found unconstitutional provisions of the Civil Code that were disadvantageous to women.[34]

The success of constitutional litigation by women's groups opened the door to even more litigation by other human rights and social groups. Such groups began to see constitutional litigation as an effective way to advance their respective rights agendas. To illustrate, after scholarly associations asserted their freedom of association, *JY Interpretation No 479* held that restrictions on naming associations were unconstitutional.[35] For the gay and lesbian community, the right to free speech was dealt with in *JY Interpretation No 617*.[36]

Constitutional litigation has also been used to further recognise unenumerated rights. In *JY Interpretation No 242*, the Constitutional Court, in resolving legal disputes regarding second marriages in Taiwan, extended constitutional protection to marriage rights. When the KMT government relocated from Mainland China to Taiwan, many couples suffered inevitable separation. Thus, myriad individuals remained legally married to their spouses across the Taiwan Strait.[37] In *JY Interpretation No 399*, the Court recognised the right of an individual to select his or her own name as part of the right to personality. There, the Court invalidated an interpretive rule by the Ministry of the Interior that had restricted such a right beyond the legislative mandate.[38] In *JY Interpretation No 293*, the Court recognised privacy rights in striking

---

[32] Ibid.
[33] *JY Interpretation No 365* (1994).
[34] *JY Interpretation No 410* (1996); *JY Interpretation No 452* (1998).
[35] *JY Interpretation No 479* (1999).
[36] *JY Interpretation No 617* (2006)
[37] *JY Interpretation No 242* (1989).
[38] *JY Interpretation No 399* (1996).

a balance between the legislative supervision of state-owned banks over information disclosure and the right of privacy held by individual customers.[39] Privacy rights have since been frequently relied upon during constitutional review. This can be observed in *JY Interpretation No 535*, in which the Court considered randomised street police checks,[40] and *JY Interpretation No 603*, which dealt with collecting fingerprints when issuing national identity cards.[41]

In *JY Interpretation No 554*, sexual freedom was afforded constitutional protection, but was nevertheless compromised when it was held constitutional to criminalise adultery in order to protect marriage.[42] The Constitutional Court has also affirmed a constitutional right to reputation as necessary to realise human dignity, which is intimately linked with the maintainence and protection of individual sovereignty and moral integrity. As a result, in *JY Interpretation No 656* a court-imposed public apology was found constitutional as a way to restore a damaged reputation.[43] Most noteworthy is the Court's reference to international human rights documents in its construction of new rights. For example, in *JY Interpretation No 587*, the Court referred to the United Nations Convention on the Rights of the Child, to which Taiwan is not a party, in order to establish a child's right to identify his or her blood parents.[44] In *JY Interpretation No 623*, the Court again referenced the Convention when it affirmed a child's right to be free from sexual exploitation over the right to free speech.[45]

The variety of rights agendas advanced by social groups or concerned individuals has substantially enriched the docket of the Constitutional Court. Judicial construction of fundamental rights and freedoms has not been merely a reflection of judicial preference. Rather, this construction is perhaps better characterised as a reflection of societal responses to the ongoing social and political demands that have accompanied society's profound transformations.[46]

---

[39] *JY Interpretation No 293* (1992).
[40] *JY Interpretation No 535* (2001).
[41] *JY Interpretation No 603* (2005).
[42] *JY Interpretation No 554* (2002).
[43] *JY Interpretation No 656* (2009).
[44] *JY Interpretation No 587* (2004).
[45] *JY Interpretation No 623* (2007).
[46] Yeh and Chang, 'The Emergence of East Asian Constitutionalism', above n 2.

II. CIVIL AND POLITICAL RIGHTS

The list of fundamental rights and freedoms enshrined in the Constitution encompasses primarily civil and political rights. Included are due process; the right to sue; the freedom of speech; the freedom of religion; the right to assembly and association; the rights of election, recall, initiative and referendum; and the right to hold public office. Unfortunately, until the late 1980s, these rights were severely curtailed in the shadow of martial law and authoritarian rule. However, after that time, which saw the beginning of democratisation, these rights have served as pillars of a civil democratic polity. This evolution is underscored in the discussion below. As the following sections demonstrate, the now-extensive protection of the rights to political participation and free speech developed against the backdrop of profound democratic transition.

A. Right of Political Participation

The incremental and piecemeal introduction of elections—in local levels of government during authoritarian rule and, more profoundly, at the national level during the early 1990s—is considered to have been an integral institutional foundation for the peaceful transition to Taiwan's constitutional democracy. The constitutional guarantee to the right of political participation, in elections and in other methods of public participation, not only helped peaceful democratic transition but also entrenched democratic constitutionalism.

The right of political participation guranteed by Article 17 of the Constitution entails the rights of election, recall, initiative and referendum. Although the right of election was substantially enhanced by the renowned judicial order *JY Interpretation No 261*[47]—which considered the comprehensive re-election of national representation—as well as follow-up constitutional revisions in the early 1990s, the right of political participation has evolved in tandem with Taiwan's democratic transition. Aside from the legislative agenda and public debates on constitutional reform, the Constitutional Court has played a pivotal role in the shaping and reshaping of these rights.

---

[47] *JY Interpretation No 261* (1990). For detailed discussions of this interpretation, see chs 2 and 4.

With *JY Interpretation No 261* and the 1991 constitutional revision, constitutional grounds for a comprehensive electoral overhaul existed during the infancy of Taiwan's era of democratisation. As part of the reform package, a system of proportional representation was introduced. This new system altered the weight of each individual vote, a change which entailed some controversy. For example, the system of proportional representation was challenged on the question of whether the right to recall representatives would be compromised in the case of party-list representatives.[48] The Constitutional Court in *JY Interpretation No 331* unequivocally affirmed the new electoral system and clarified that party-list representatives would be deprived of their seats should they lose their membership in the political parties from which they were elected.[49]

Besides the right of recall, the major focus of the right of political participation remains the right of election, which includes the right to vote and the right to stand for election. With the successful introduction of general suffrage by various constitutional revisions, these rights have encountered little constitutional controversy. However, in the most recent constitutional revision, in 2005, the right of election became an issue, as the Legislative Yuan's electoral design contained voting disparties.[50] In its recent *JY Interpretation No 721*, the Court validated the disparity on the grounds that it accommodated the residents of remote areas and smaller districts.[51] On the other hand, the right to stand for election may be abridged by law. When elections were made possible after the constitutional revision of 1991, many leaders of social and political groups became interested in running. Potential candidates included Xia Liu, a disabled woman renowned for her leadership in disability rights advocacy. However, Liu was ineligible to run for election since she failed to the meet the minimum educational qualifications set by the Public Service Election and Recall Law. Her failure to meet these qualifications stemmed from the serious nature of her disabilities, which had limited her opportunity to obtain a sufficient education. In response to her challenge to the educational requirement, the Constitutional Court held in *JY Interpretation No 290* that while

---

[48] *JY Interpretation No 331* (1993).
[49] Ibid.
[50] For a discussion on the voting disparities in the election for the Legislative Yuan, which arose as a result of the 2005 constitutional revision, see ch 4.
[51] *JY Interpretation No 721* (2014).

the legislature could constitutionally impose such restrictions, special attention must be paid to 'the circumstances of those who have difficulty completing compulsory education, for example, those with physical or other disabilities who have difficulties completing a normal education, and appropriate rules should be stipulated accordingly by reasonable discretion of the legislature'.[52]

The right of political participation also includes the rights of initiative and referendum. Although explicitly guaranteed by the Constitution, these rights were never practised during the period of martial law, and therefore the debate over this right began only after the lifting of the Martial Law Decree. While many believe the well-educated citizens of Taiwan are entitled to referenda on major policies, including those implicating Taiwan's future, the ruling KMT government has long regarded referenda as something threatening to its governing legitimacy. Historically, the KMT has been critical of and thus suppressive of any referenda. In 2003, after more than a decade of public campaigning and strong civic advocacy, a compromise was reached in the Referendum Act. Regrettably, in the Act's final form, the KMT legislative majority included a procedure for proposing referenda that is so complex as to render their use virtually impossible. To underscore the Act's sheer impracticality, in order for a national referendum to pass, half of Taiwan's eligible voters must cast a ballot. Finally, half of those who cast a ballot must vote for the referendum's passage.[53] Thus, the remarkably high threshold set by the legislature has become a most significant barrier to the exercise of the right of referendum.

Still, national referenda have been held twice, during the presidential elections in 2004 and 2008, respectively. In 2004, in addition to the presidential election, President Chen Shui-bian initiated a pair of national referendum proposals that would strengthen Taiwan's national defence, as well as open negotiations with China as an equal. However, both proposals failed to meet the required threshold. In 2008, the DPP as the ruling party and the opposition KMT each initiated referendum proposals as the culmination of a political confrontation on the eve of the presidential election. Owing to low voter turnout, these proposals failed to meet the legal requirements.

---

[52] *JY Interpretation No 290* (1992).
[53] Art 30 Public Referendum Act (2009).

In March 2013, the ruling KMT government ironically called for a public referendum. This call came amid mounting public backlash against the possible construction of Taiwan's fourth nuclear power plant—a backlash stirred by the 2011 tragedy in Fukushima, Japan, in which an earthquake, tsunami, and consequent epic nuclear meltdown brought catastrophic losses of life and irreversible environmental damage. Taiwan's political observors have argued that, without a lowering of the referendum threshold, the incumbent government's call for a public referendum amounted to a political stunt. As of this writing, the government still refuses to revisit the controversial referendum threshold. The construction of Taiwan's fourth nuclear power plant is a matter yet to be settled.

Another special right related to the right of political participation is the right to hold public office. Guaranteed by the Constitution, particularly in Article 18, the right to hold public office reflects an historical Chinese tradition. As mentioned in previous chapters, each public-office holder must have successfully taken a state-held public examination. The current manifestation of this constitutionally guaranteed right has much to do with the new wave of immigrants from Mainland China. Owing to cross-Strait hostility, special restrictions have been imposed on recent immigrants from Mainland China affecting their right to public service. For example, the Act Governing Relations between the People of the Taiwan Area and Mainland Area required a 10-year waiting period before those from the mainland who had obtained a household registration could serve as public functionaries. This provision was challenged in the Constitutional Court by a woman who had been married to a Taiwanese man for some time and had passed the competitive exam for public functionaries. The Court in *JY Interpretation No 618* upheld the special restriction because it was within the legislature's proportional discretion in light of the different cross-Strait political systems.[54]

B. Free Speech and Social/Political Transition

If the rights of election and participation have provided a general infrastructure for Taiwan's democratic transformation, then perhaps the constitutionally enshrined right of free speech has served as the catalyst

---

[54] *JY Interpretation No 618* (2006).

of that transformation. The ROC Constitution explicitly guarantees the freedom of expression, including the freedoms of speech, teaching, writing and publication. One of the normative foundations on which the guarantee of free speech has been built is the principle of popular sovereignty. According to the Constitutional Court, 'as sovereignty lies with the people, the people shall enjoy the right to freely discuss and fully express their opinions so that facts will be sought after and the truth will be discovered, and that the public will shall be formed by means of the democratic process to propose policies and enact laws'.[55] Additionally, the protection of free speech exists to preserve and cultivate a diverse civil society in which 'the dignity of each individual's independent existence and his or her autonomy to freely engage in activities' ought to be respected fully.[56]

During the era of martial law, however, freedom of speech had been substantially restricted. A system of prior restraints and censorship was imposed on the press and individual publications. In this era, as demonstrated by *JY Interpretation No 105*, the Constitutional Court rubber-stamped such infringments. The Court there held that, as long as judicial remedies were available to those whose publications had been restricted or even confiscated, the system of prior restraints remained constitutional.[57] With political suppression rampant during the era of martial law, *JY Interpretation No 105* clearly underscored the Court's institutional constraints at that time. When Taiwan eventually experienced democratisation, the notorious Publication Act was abolished entirely. Hence, prior restraints were no longer imposed on the press or individual publications.

Before the late 1980s, notwithstanding the ban on outdoor assemblies and parades, street protests were frequently staged. Protestors were fined or even sentenced to jail. Upon the lifting of the Martial Law Decree in 1987, outdoor assemblies and parades were permitted but prior approvals were still required, entailing a number of substantive and procedural restraints. It took a series of civic campaigns and constitutional adjudications to moderate this excessive control. In *JY Interpretation No 445*, involving an illegal environmental protest in which

---

[55] *JY Interpretation No 445* (1998), reasoning para 8.
[56] Ibid.
[57] *JY Interpretation No 105* (1964).

the leaders were sentenced to jail, the Constitutional Court invalidated several provisions of the Assembly and Parade Act.[58] According to the Court, 'the freedom of assembly is a form of freedom of speech exercised by the people through action' and 'for the general public who do not have easy access to the media,' it is 'an important means to express their opinions openly.' In reviewing the Assembly and Parade Act, the Court, influenced by the United States' free speech jurisprudence, distinguished between content-based and content-neutral restrictions.[59] The Court justified the system of prior approvals for outdoor assemblies or parades as long as the competent authority could only impose procedural requirements such as time, place, or manner restrictions but could not consider the purposes or contents of the public gatherings.[60]

Consequently, the Court held null and void a provision under which the competent authority could deny an application for an outdoor assembly if it 'advocates communism or secession of territory', as it would have allowed government censorship of the contents of a political speech prior to the approval of an assembly or parade.[61] The Court also invalidated two provisions according to which the competent authority could deny the application for an outdoor assembly, on the grounds that these provisions were neither specific nor clear enough.[62] In the view of the Court, the competent authority could deny an application only upon 'a factual showing of clear and present danger' but not the 'future possibility of such occurrence'.[63]

The Court reasoned that the freedom of assembly should at least entail the right to hold a spontaneous assembly or parade. Aside from those mentioned above, other provisions containing procedural restraints were upheld as constitutional, including Article 29 of the Assembly and Parade Act, which imposed criminal sanctions for holding an authorised outdoor assembly or parade that did not disperse when ordered to do so. Although the Court advised the competent

---

[58] *JY Interpretation No 445* (1998).
[59] GR Stone et al, *Constitutional Law*, 7th edn (New York, Aspen, 2013).
[60] *JY Interpretation No 445* (1998), holding para 1.
[61] Ibid, para 2.
[62] These restrictions were allowed when '[t]here are facts showing the likelihood that national security, social order or public welfare will be jeopardized,' (subparagraph 2) and '[t]here is the likelihood that public safety or freedom will be jeopardized, or there will be serious damage to property' (subparagraph 3).
[63] *JY Interpretation No 445* (1998), holding para 2.

authority to exercise caution when issuing dispersal orders, it nevertheless held that imposing criminal sanctions was within the range of legislative discretion.[64]

Since the release of *JY Interpretation No 445*, criticism against the system of prior approvals and criminal sanctions has raged on. In 2008, the debate over the abolition of prior approvals reached an apex when a mainland Chinese envoy came to Taiwan for an unprecedented official visit that garnered heated public protests which were brutally suppressed by the Taiwanese government.[65] Petitions once more made their way to the Constitutional Court. In March 2014, the Court issued *JY Interpretation No 718*, resuming its consideration of the constitutionality of the Assembly and Parade Act.[66] This time, the Court invalidated the requirement for obtaining an approval 24 hours prior to the holding of an outdoor assembly or parade, arguing that it was unnecessary and disproportionate, in light of the spontaneous nature of many outdoor assemblies and parades. Regrettably, however, the Court did not rerule on the constitutionality of criminal sanctions.[67]

The approach of distinguishing between content-based and content-neutral restrictions has become quite entrenched in the Constitutional Court's freedom of expression jurisprudence. In *JY Interpretation No 644*, the Court invalidated a provision in the Civic Organisation Act prohibiting the creation of civic organisations whose purpose or activities would advocate for communism or the partition of national territory.[68] At the same time, however, the Court held constitutional the penalisation of unapproved uses of radio frequencies, and even the confiscation of equipment, on the grounds that these measures were merely restrictions on property rights, not speech content.[69] As difficult as it may be to accomplish, a more delicate balance must be struck between the regulation of radio frequencies and the right of fair access to media, as illustrated in *JY Interpretation No 364*, one of the Court's earlier interpretations.[70]

---

[64] Ibid.
[65] A student movement called 'Wild Strawberries Movement' was triggered. Further information is available at en.wikipedia.org/wiki/Wild_Strawberries_Movement.
[66] *JY Interpretation No 718* (2014).
[67] Ibid.
[68] *JY Interpretation No 644* (2008).
[69] *JY Interpretation No 678* (2010).
[70] *JY Interpretation No 364* (1994).

Notably, the Court has written a series of interpretations which guarantee the freedom of expression but balance it against other fundamental rights and freedoms. For example, on the balance between free speech and the right of reputation, the Court in *JY Interpretation No 509* narrowly construed criminal defamation to exclude the criminalisation of defamatory statements where the speaker has reasonable grounds to believe that the statement was true when disseminated, and has evidence to support that belief.[71] The Court also stressed, in relation to the same provision, that prosecutors should carry the burden of proof to show that the accused had the requisite *mens rea*.[72]

In *JY Interpretation No 656*, the Court affirmed the restriction on the right not to speak by a court-ordered public apology, as long as the apology does not include self-humiliation or the degradation of one's humanity.[73] In the Court's view, 'the right to reputation, necessary in the realisation of human dignity, aims to maintain and protect the individual sovereignty and moral integrity' and, at the same time, 'freedom of speech under Article 11 of the Constitution protects not only the active freedom of expression, but also the passive freedom to withhold expression'. Thus, in order to comply with the principle of proportionality, court-ordered apologies must strike a proper balance between these two ideals.[74]

The Court has deemed commercial speech, such as that in pharmaceutical advertisements and tobacco labels, to be within the scope of protected speech.[75] In the Court's view, commercial activities 'involve protection of property rights and possess the characteristics of commercial speech'[76] but, as the commercials at issue are closely related to public health, they should be strictly regulated. In order to advance substantial public interests, the government may adopt more restrictive means through legislation requiring disclosure of specific product information, thereby restricting the right not to speak.

---

[71] *JY Interpretation No 509* (2000).
[72] Ibid, reasoning para 3.
[73] *JY Interpretation No 656* (2009).
[74] Ibid, reasoning para 2.
[75] *JY Interpretation No 414* (1996) (regarding the constitutionality of regulatory restrictions on pharmaceutical advertisements); *JY Interpretation No 577* (2004) (regarding the constitutionality of tobacco labels).
[76] *JY Interpretation No 414* (1996), holding.

The Court also included obscene speech within the scope of protected speech, although it permitted a greater extent of restriction in this regard.[77] According to *JY Interpretation No 617*, the guarantee of free speech exists to provide individuals the opportunity to acquire sufficient information and to attain self-fulfilment; consequently, the expression of sexually explicit language and the circulation of sexually explicit material—for profit or not—should be subject to constitutional protection.[78] However, in order to maintain sexual morality and social decency, due respect should be paid to lawmakers as they make judgments with respect to the common values held by the majority of society, while still taking into account the minority's sense of sexual morality and its cognition of social decency.[79] Relying on a similar construction, the Court also held a criminal provision of the Child and Juvenile Sexual Transaction Prevention Act to have limited constitutionality. The Court wrote that 'a person's conduct will not be subject to the said provision if the information distributed by him or her neither contains child or juvenile sexual transactions nor is intended to induce children or juveniles to engage in sexual transactions and necessary precautionary measures have been taken to limit the recipients of such information to those who are 18 years of age or older'.[80]

Taiwan's development of free speech, as articulated within the Court and outside it, has demonstrated a liberal reading of rights. Compared to the stereotypical Asian construction that emphasises community harmony over individual freedom, Taiwan's experience has been unique. As a new democracy without a liberal tradition, Taiwan's culture of freedom of expression has been influenced by deep reflections on its historical authoritarian suppression and by its vision of a liberal democratic community. Though its government and its people both embody the overriding imperative of economic prosperity, Taiwan has nevertheless been able to articulate freedoms of speech and expression sufficient to safeguard its society's innovative spirit. Amazingly, the Constitutional Court has paid as much attention to these freedoms as it has to other economic and social rights.[81]

---

[77] *JY Interpretation No 407* (1996); *JY Interpretation No 617* (2006); *JY Interpretation No 623* (2007).

[78] *JY Interpretation No 617* (2006), reasoning para 1.

[79] Ibid, reasoning para 2.

[80] *JY Interpretation No 623* (2007).

[81] Yeh and Chang, above n 2, 832–33.

III. SOCIO-ECONOMIC RIGHTS

The list of fundamental rights and freedoms guaranteed by the ROC Constitution is centred on the civil and political rights of classical liberalism.[82] This liberal inclination is partly the result of the constitution-making process itself. In 1946, as the Communist Party boycotted the Constituent Assembly, the KMT and its political allies with their pro-bourgeoisie political ideology dominated the proceedings. As a result, the ROC Constitution expressly guarantees civil and political rights, while relegating social and economic rights that demand further government action to the chapter on policy directives. Accordingly, Chapter 13 of the Constitution includes four sections on the following fundamental national policies: national defence; foreign policy; the national economy, social security, education, and culture; and frontier regions. The majority of these sections is concerned with the state's duty to provide for the realisation of social, economic and cultural rights.[83] As stated earlier, these policies—although they are not directly enforceable—carry some weight when courts balance them against other competing interests or values.

Taiwan's realisation of socio-economic rights has occurred primarily through statutes, policies and supplementary judicial interpretations. These statutes were the result of competitive electoral politicking during democratic transitions that reflected the concerns of a burgeoning civil society. The following illustrates this path of development by focusing on three areas: health insurance and the right to work; gender equality and the changing family structure; and, finally, the waves of immigration and equality.

A. Health Insurance and the Right to Work

Before the 1990s, there were separate systems of public insurance for soldiers, civil servants, teachers, labourers and farmers, each with a considerably different framework of premiums and benefits. Under the KMT's governing ideology of state corporatism, such highly differentiated systems were utilised—and even manipulated—as a way to exert

---

[82] See Dissenting Opinion of Justice Geng Wu, *JY Interpretation No 472* (1999).
[83] Arts 137–69 Constitution of the Republic of China (1947).

social and political control over different classes of citizens. Criticism against the system's distortions was expressed openly during the transition to democracy, culminating in the inclusion of a one-policy directive in the 1992 constitutional revision that required the government to promote universal health insurance.[84]

Under the strong leadership of President Lee Teng-hui, who succeeded to the presidency upon Chiang Ching-kuo's death in 1988 and was subsequently elected by the National Assembly in 1990, measures were undertaken to implement these policy directives. The National Health Insurance Act, which created a system of universal health care for everyone, was passed in 1994 and became effective in 1995. Taiwan's National Health Insurance programme (NHI) is a single-payer compulsory social insurance plan, adminstered by the Executive Yuan's Ministry of Health and Welfare, which centralises the disbursement of health-care funds. This system provides universal and equal access to health care and covers nearly 99 per cent of the nation's citizens and residents. Notably, the social equality implicit in the system of universal health care—along with the political equality reflected by national elections, and especially the direct presidential elections that have occurred since 1996—has substantially contributed to a political and social cohesion distinctive of Taiwan.

Such praise notwithstanding, the NHI has still encountered its share of controversy, particularly around its mandate of compulsory subscription. Arguing that the NHI imposed a late charge on individuals beyond what was constitutionally permitted, a few legislators challenged the constitutionality of the NHI before the Constitutional Court. In response, the Court unequivocally affirmed the compulsory programme in *JY Interpretation No 472*.[85] Importantly, the Court defended the NHI not in terms of the direct protection of social rights but on the grounds that such social policy was entirely at the discretion of the government and should be held constitutional as long as it did not disproportionately encroach upon the rights of individuals.[86] In the view of the Court, compulsory subscription was a reasonable measure for realising a system of national health insurance.[87] Moreover, for

---

[84] Art 18 Additional Articles of the Constitution of the Republic of China (1992).
[85] *JY Interpretation No 472* (1999).
[86] Ibid, reasoning para 2.
[87] Ibid.

those without the ability to pay premiums, the government should give appropriate assistance and relief and should not refuse to pay benefits, thereby fulfilling the constitutional demand to promote national health insurance for the underprivileged, as prescribed by the Additional Articles of the Constitution.[88]

The other area of socio-economic rights that has caught judicial attention in recent years is the right to work. Article 15 of the Constitution guarantees this right, along with the right of existence and the right of property.[89] Whether the right to work guaranteed by Article 15 should only be understood negatively or entails both negative and positive freedoms has been the subject of debate. Despite minority opinions that have insisted on the guarantees of both,[90] a majority of the Constitutional Court has understood Article 15 as a classical liberty, guaranteeing negative freedoms, while the government may at the same time implicate positive aspects by legislation or programmes responsive to the demands of policy directives. Accordingly, the Court stringently reviews cases of government abridgement of the negative right to work while deferring to legislative or executive programmes that fulfill the positive right to work.

In *JY Interpretation No 584*, the Court stated that the right to work includes within its meaning the freedom to choose an occupation, which may nevertheless be limited by law in service of the public welfare, by the qualifications needed for any particular career, and by other requirements for engaging in specific occupations.[91] Influenced by German jurisprudence on the question of occupational freedom, the Court has exercised varying degrees of judicial scrutiny depending on the nature of the restriction.[92] For the Court, 'the legislators are not prevented from imposing appropriate restraints as may be necessary for the public interest, on the exercise of the freedom of occupation in respect of the method, time or place where an occupation may be undertaken or the persons who may engage in an occupation or the

---

[88] Ibid.

[89] Art 15 Constitution of the Republic of China (1947).

[90] See Dissenting Opinion of Justice Yueh-chin Hwang, *JY Interpretation No 514* (2000).

[91] *JY Interpretation No 584* (2004), reasoning, para 1.

[92] W-C Chang and J-r Yeh, 'Internationalization of Constitutional Law' in M Rosenfeld and A Sajó (eds), *The Oxford Handbook of Comparative Constitutional Law Comparative Constitutionalism* (New York, Oxford University Press, 2012).

activities that may be carried out. Where the legislature intends to regulate the subjective eligibility of the people in the choice of their occupation, such as knowledge and competency, age, physical conditions, and moral standards, there must exist concerns of more important public interest than the mere imposition of restraints on the exercise of the freedom of occupation, and such restraints may be imposed only if and when it is necessary to do so.'[93]

JY Interpretation No 584 involved the constitutionality of the Act Governing the Punishment for Violation of Road Traffic Regulations, which disqualified those convicted of certain offences from obtaining work as taxi drivers. The disputed provision was enacted after an incident in which an outspoken women's rights activist was killed and possibly raped by a taxi driver after leaving a policy conference; the woman's body was never found. Horrified, the general public reacted by demanding stricter regulations over taxi drivers. In *JY Interpretation No 584*, finding a difficult balance between the freedom of occupation and concern for the social order, the Court held constitutional the disputed provision but cautioned the legislature that restraints ought to be reviewed and modified from time to time.[94]

In 2008, the Court in *JY Interpretation No 649* declared unconstitutional a provision in the Physically and Mentally Disabled Citizens Protection Act that allowed only vision-impaired individuals to enter the massage business. The Act was designed to specially protect the right to work of the physically and mentally disabled. Yet, the Court found that the Act's restriction on the occupational freedom of others—namely those who were not visually impaired—violated equal protection and the principle of proportionality. In the view of the Court, the disputed provision failed to deliver that which its drafters had intended: 'after nearly 30 years since the statute's enactment, and despite the availabilities of multiple occupations, the socio-economic condition of the vision-impaired has yet to see any significant improvement.'[95] The Court exercised a similarly stringent review in *JY Interpretation No 711*.[96] In this case, a challenge was brought against a provision in the Pharmacists Act that constrained pharmacists to practising at a single location

---

[93] *JY Interpretation No 584* (2004), reasoning para 1.
[94] *JY Interpretation No 584* (2004).
[95] *JY Interpretation No 649* (2008).
[96] *JY Interpretation No 711* (2013).

only. Also challenged was an interpretation by the relevant agency that a pharmacist who was also a qualified nurse could only practise these qualifications at the same institution. Relying on the above-mentioned framework it had developed after *JY Interpretation No 584*, the Court unequivocally found the provisions at issue unconstitutional.

In contrast to the stringent review the Court has reserved for restrictions to occupational freedom, the Court has accorded deference to legislative and government actions that support the positive right to work. For example, *JY Interpretation No 549* concerned the constitutionality of a provision of the Labour Insurance Act which refused insurance payments to a child adopted by an insured who died before the adopted child had been recorded in the household registry for more than six months. Although it held the disputed provision constitutional, the Court advised further revisions to be undertaken with 'an overall examination and arrangement regarding the survivor allowance, insurance benefits and other relevant matters', and 'in accordance with the principles of this Interpretation, international labour conventions and the pension plan of the social security system'.[97] Finally, in *JY Interpretation No 578*, the Court struck a balance between the positive right of labourers to work and the property rights of employers, holding constitutional a provision in the Labour Standards Act that obliged employers to pay for workers' retirement pensions.[98]

B. Gender Equality and the Changing Family Structure

In Taiwan, the traditional family structure began to change in the 1960s along with the fast-growing economy. Women were released from domestic life to join the workforce, and the traditional extended family was gradually reduced to a nuclear family in which one or both parents worked to support it.[99] Such a fundamental social transformation—coupled with the profound political changes that have occurred since the late 1980s—has given rise to a burgeoning civil society in which women's rights groups and activists are empowered to advocate law and

---

[97] *JY Interpretation No 549* (2002).

[98] *JY Interpretation No 578* (2004).

[99] A Thornton and TE Fricke, 'Social Change and Family: Comparative Perspectives from the West, China and South Asia' (1987) 2 *Sociological Forum* 746.

policy changes for gender equality and beyond.[100] Constitutional petitions, together with legislative lobbying, have become effective strategies for these women's rights groups and activists.[101] The advancement of gender equality and the relationship between parents and children are the two areas which have seen the most success.[102]

Beginning in the early 1990s, women's rights groups and activists were working on a proposed revision of the Civil Code that would give equal rights to women in families. In 1993, these groups proposed the first draft of the amended Civil Code, and held numerous news conferences to generate public support. They also lobbied new legislators, who had just been elected in 1992's first national legislative election.[103] At the same time, a petition was brought in the Constitutional Court challenging Article 1089 of the Civil Code, which privileged the decision of the father in cases of parental disagreement over how to exercise parental rights over a child. The Court responded in *JY Interpretation No 365* that the provision at issue was incompatible with the equality of both sexes under the law.[104] According to the Court, a parental dispute 'should be resolved based on the premises of the principle of gender equality and the best interest of the child; in the event that such a disagreement arises, the nearest relative or a conference of relatives, or the family court decision shall have the right of final decision, unless there are extraordinary circumstances in which steps other than the normal course of action should be considered.'[105] The Constitutional Court gave the legislature two years to revise Article 1089 in accordance with its decision.[106] Following this ruling, the Ministry of Justice quickly drafted a revised Article 1089, together with other similar provisions, and sent the bill to the Legislative Yuan for discussion. The revised provisions came into force in September 1996, just before the deadline set by the Constitutional Court.

JY Interpretation No 410 was another great success. In 1995, a female lawyer affiliated with a women's rights group petitioned the Court,

---

[100] Yeh and Chang, above n 2; Chang, above n 6.

[101] Chang, above n 6.

[102] Yeh and Chang, above n 2.

[103] Chang, above n 6.

[104] *JY Interpretation No 365* (1994).

[105] Ibid.

[106] Ibid.

challenging Article 1 of the Enforcement Act of the Part on the Family of the Civil Code. The provision at issue prohibited the application of the Civil Code ex post facto, which affected the property and inheritance a married woman had acquired before marriage. While the Court did not strike down the disputed provision, it issued a clear warning urging the legislature to undertake revision; the Legislative Yuan quickly responded to this warning and completed a revision as prescribed by the Court in less than two months.[107] *JY Interpretation No 452*, petitioned by another woman lawyer, involved the former Article 1002 of the Civil Code, which required wives to take the residence of their husbands. The Court unequivocally held Article 1002 inconsistent with sex and gender equality. In the view of the Court, the law failed to consider that 'the other party of the marriage also has the right to choose the residence and does not cover specific circumstances, which is in violation of the principle of equality and proportionality of the Constitution'.[108] Apart from the success of constitutional litigation, women's efforts in lobbying for new legislation also reaped rewards. The Act of Gender Equality in Employment of 2002 and the Gender Equity Education Act of 2004 exemplified these significant achievements.

In contrast with the liberal attitude the Constitutional Court has exhibited in advancing sex and gender equality in the family sphere, the Court's attitude toward ensuring women's sexual freedom and reproductive rights has been rather conservative. In *JY Interpretation No 554*, the Court held constitutional the criminal punishment of adultery, as a way of supporting marriage and the family.[109] In one line of cases, the Court has accorded constitutional protection to the institutions of marriage and the family that trumps sexual freedom.[110] As in most Asian states, Taiwan adopted a rather lax abortion policy. Although abortion is prohibited by criminal sanction, exceptions are made for a wide range of reasons—from genetic concerns to the physical and mental health of the mother.[111] Behind this lax abortion policy lies,

---

[107] *JY Interpretation No 410* (1996).

[108] *JY Interpretation No 452* (1998).

[109] *JY Interpretation No 554* (2002).

[110] *JY Interpretation No 242* (1989); *JY Interpretation No 362* (1994); *JY Interpretation No 552* (2002); *JY Interpretation No 554* (2002).

[111] Art 9 Genetic Health Act (2009).

however, not the recognition of women's sexual or reproductive freedom but rather the state's interests in overseeing public health and exercising population control.[112]

Last but not least is political equality between men and women. Women's equal right to vote is expressly granted in the ROC Constitution. Particularly noteworthy is the gender quota. Article 134 of the Constitution stipulates that in certain kinds of elections, the number of women to be elected shall be fixed by law.[113] Since the 1950s, women have represented more than 20 per cent of the members of local legislatures.[114] The constitutional revision of 2005 changed the electoral method of the Legislative Yuan, and demanded that the number of elected female members on each party's list must not be less than half of the total.[115] In the election of 2012, for the first time, women made up more than 33 per cent of the Legislative Yuan.[116]

The relative early and easy acceptance of a gender quota under the Constitution may be explained in the contexts of nation building and political developments. In many new states or transitional democracies, political mobilisation is called for in the pursuit of independence or in the making of a new constitution. Men and women alike become mobilised for the greater political cause. As called upon to participate in a national movement, women are granted the equal right to political representation. Indeed, not only women, but also ethnic and other minorities who were long marginalised in the old power structure may take advantage of this great moment to become enfranchised. It is thus of no surprise that, as exemplified in quite a few Asian constitutions, many nationalist constitutions enacted after World War II emphasise special political representation for women and other minorities.[117]

---

[112] R Rubio-Marin and W-C Chang, 'Sites of Constitutional Struggle for Women's Equality' in M Tushnet, T Fleiner and C Saunders (eds), *Routledge Handbook Of Constitutional Law* (New York, Routledge, 2013).

[113] Art 134 Constitution of the Republic of China (1947).

[114] Rubio-Marin and Chang, 'Sites of Constitutional Struggle for Women's Equality', above n 112.

[115] Art 4(2) Additional Articles of the Constitution of the Republic of China (2005).

[116] Rubio-Marin and Chang, above n 113.

[117] Ibid.

C. Waves of Immigrants and Equality

A society of immigrants, Taiwan's residents hail from the Pacific islands, the Chinese mainland, Southeast Asia, and beyond. The waves of immigration that have surged onto Taiwan's shores include the arrival of the first generation from China in the seventeenth century, the relocation of the KMT government after 1949 and, most recently, the immigration of foreign spouses and workers, primarily from the Chinese mainland and Southeast Asia, since the 1990s. These waves have catalysed several constitutional issues in their respective assertions of equality and citizenship.

Cross-Strait hositilities have also had an influence on Taiwan's international presence. In 1979, when the United States broke ties with Taiwan in order to establish a formal diplomatic relationship with the PRC, President Chiang Ching-kuo responded by declaring a 'three-nos policy'—no contact, no compromise, and no negotiation—with respect to the PRC. Cross-Strait links were broken and were not re-established until 1987, when the ban on cross-Strait visits was lifted and the Martial Law Decree was suspended. The constitutional revision of 1991 provided a constitutional basis for laws dealing with the special rights and obligations of those in China who technically remained citizens of the ROC.[118] Accordingly, the Act Governing Relations Between the People of the Taiwan Area and the Mainland Area was enacted in 1992. These re-established links have since brought all kinds of cross-Strait exchange negotations and agreements—especially after 2008, now that the KMT government has lifted most prohibitions and increased Taiwan's ability to trade with China. The ever-increasing cross-Strait exchange, however, has brought with it increased political controversies and national security concerns.

To date, more than 300,000 cross-Strait couples have married, and about 10,000 mainland spouses move to Taiwan each year.[119] As expected, concerns have arisen over the rights of Chinese mainlanders—'mainland spouses'—who married Taiwanese partners. According to the law, while

---

[118] The Additional Articles of the ROC Constitution provide that 'Rights and obligations between the people of the Chinese mainland area and those of the free area, and the disposition of other related affairs may be specified by law'.

[119] See   www2.mac.gov.tw/mac/RuleView.aspx?RuleID=3&TypeID=1   (in Chinese).

mainland spouses enjoy rights virtually equivalent to those Taiwanese people enjoy, certain limits have been imposed due to national security concerns. One such limit, for example, restricts mainland spouses' right to hold public office. As discussed earlier, the Constitutional Court in *JY Interpretation No 618* held such a special restriction to be within the legislature's discretion, in light of the different political systems across the Strait.[120] In 2013, a challenge was brought against a provision in the Act Governing Relations Between People of the Taiwan Area and Mainland Area that allowed mainlanders to be deported without due process of law. The Court in *JY Interpretation No 710* held that the provision violated the guarantees of physical freedom and due process enshrined by Article 8 of the Constitution.[121]

The rights of foreign workers are also a constitutional concern. There are now more than 450,000 foreign workers in Taiwan, most of whom immigrated from Southeast Asian countries such as the Philippines, Vietnam, Thailand and Indonesia.[122] These foreign workers usually come from lower-income classes, and are driven overseas by domestic economic depression and the need to make a living. In 2005, a group of Thai workers rioted at the Kaohsiung subway construction site, an unprecedented event that lasted for 17 hours. This incident resulted partly from harsh labour conditions,[123] as well as from the constitutional concerns implicated by Taiwan's willingness to deport foreigners without due process of law.[124] In 2013, the Court released *JY Interpretation No 708*, in which it held the deportation provisions unconstitutional. Remarkably, the Court accorded to foreigners the

---

[120] *JY Interpretation No 618* (2006).

[121] *JY Interpretation No 710* (2013).

[122] For statistics on foreign workers in Taiwan, see Workforce Development Agency, statdb.mol.gov.tw/html/mon/c12030.pdf.

[123] For relevant news, see news.ltn.com.tw/news/focus/paper/50820 (in Chinese).

[124] In 2010, the National Immigration Agency arrested and detained a Thai national, on the grounds that he did not physically leave Taiwan after receiving a deportation order in 2008 for having provided false information on her immigration documents. In the same year, the Agency again arrested and detained an Indonesian national, on the grounds that she was dismissed by her employer after having fled from her place of employment. Under detention, these foreigners' petitions for habeas corpus were both rejected because they had not been arrested and detained as criminal suspects.

guarantees of physical freedom and due process.[125] In the view of the Court, 'physical freedom is a fundamental human right and the foundation of all freedoms and rights of humankind. Protecting the physical freedom of each individual, regardless of his nationality, is a common principle upheld by all modern rule-of-law states. Thus, the guarantee of physical freedom under Article 8 of the Constitution extends to foreign nationals, and they shall receive the same protection as domestic nationals.'[126]

IV. INDIGENOUS PEOPLES AND COLLECTIVE RIGHTS

Before the large-scale arrivals of the Han ethnic group, Taiwan was long home to the Austronesian language family. Presently known as 'indigenous peoples', Austronesians are considered to be the original inhabitants of the island. They can be divided into tribes, and have maintained integral territories, distinct peoples, cultures, political institutions, social structures and economic patterns.[127]

Since the sixteenth century, the valuable inheritance of the indigenous peoples' ancestors has continued to be challenged by the governing powers. The oppression of this people group lasted through the 1980s; only upon democratisation did the indigenous movement find success, via methods ranging from constitutional revision to the incorporation of international human rights. In an attempt to detail the rights of indigenous peoples comprehensively, this section first discusses their historical discrimination before proceeding to the indigenous movement and their eventual success in obtaining equal rights.

A. Historical Discrimination

At present, indigenous peoples make up around 2 per cent of Taiwan's population (around 530,000). According to the official statistics, the ROC government recognises 16 tribes: the Amis, Atayal, Paiwan,

---

[125] *JY Interpretation No 708* (2013).

[126] Ibid, holding para 1.

[127] C-L Lee and S-Y Lin, 'The Rights of Indigenous Peoples and Taiwan's New Constitution' (paper presented to the International Conference on Constitutional Reengineering in New Democracies: Taiwan and the World, Taipei, October 2005) 209.

Bunun, Tsou, Rukai, Puyuma, Saisiyat, Yami, Thao, Kavalan, Truku, Sakizaya, Sediq, Hla'alua and Kanakanavu.[128] In these tribes, community members still speak native languages. In addition, ceremonies and traditions, such as hunting, are still maintained as part of the community life. Yet, it must be noted that the number of tribes the government recognises is still far from accurate. Owing to international assimilation efforts by previous colonial states, many indigenous people in Taiwan have lost their identities, and are impossible to trace.

Indigenous peoples first encountered state power when their territories were taken over by the Dutch East India Company from 1624 to 1662. In order to grow commodities such as sugar, the Dutch colonial power brought in a large number of Chinese settlers.[129] Of all the indigenous tribes—spreading from hill to plain—those living on the plains became the first exposed, due to their easy accessibility, to the colonial power and the Han ethnic group. Nevertheless, at that time the customs and legal norms of the indigenous peoples were—mostly—encountered with respect.

The Cheng family, which ended Dutch governance in Taiwan, brought in more Chinese settlers of Han descent.[130] Because the Cheng family represented the Han ethnic group, under their governance the differentiation of the indigenous tribes and the Han was highlighted for the first time in history. Indigenous peoples who had accepted the assimilation of the Han culture were considered to be more civilised and privileged than those who had not. This trend continued even after the island's leadership passed to the Qing Dynasty.

The Qing Dynasty, adopting the ruling style of the Cheng family, divided the tribes into two groups. The first group was called *shou-fan* ('cooked' barbarians), referring to the tribes who had been influenced by Han culture—generally those living on the plains. The other group was called *sheng-fan* ('raw' barbarians), referring to the indigenous tribes, widely considered to be uncivilised, who lived in mountains and remained largely inaccessible to the government.[131] As assimilation

---

[128] General information regarding Taiwan's indigenous peoples is available at http://www.apc.gov.tw/portal/docList.html?CID=6726E5B80C8822F9.

[129] S Simon, 'Paths to Autonomy: Aboriginality and the Nation in Taiwan' in C Storm and M Harrison (eds), *The Margins of Becoming: Identity and Culture in Taiwan* (Wiesbaden, Harrassowitz, 2007) 223.

[130] Ibid, 223.

[131] Ibid, 224.

continued via marriages and trades, the *shou-fan* slowly lost their identity while the *sheng-fan* were able to maintain their culture and customs.[132]

The mountain tribes were exposed to state administrative control only upon Taiwan's occupation by the Japanese, who were the first to conduct comprehensive land and population surveys in indigenous areas.[133] The Japanese colonial government divided the Taiwanese people into two groups: on one side were the Han and the assimilated tribes, and on the other were the unassimilated tribes. The former group was subjected to Japanese laws and regulations, whereas the latter was subjected to the control of the 'indigenous police', who decided all disputes on a case-by-case basis.[134] In order to subdue the indigenous communities, the colonial government often resorted to the violent use of state power.[135]

The Japanese colonial government's segregation policy was later inherited by the KMT government, which challenged the culture and customs of the indigenous peoples thoroughly in attempts to strengthen the country's Chinese identity.[136] To some extent, these actions reflected the ideals of statesmen who had long regarded the indigenous peoples as an uncivilised, backward population whose distinctiveness ought to be eliminated.[137]

As this backdrop suggests, although assimilation had long manifested itself between some of the indigenous tribes and the Han ethnic groups, discrimination was still rampant during the Japanese colonial era and the period of early KMT governance. The prime examples of this historical discrimination are the land and name controversies.

With respect to the land controversies, during the period of colonial governance, the Japanese forcibly moved many indigenous communities down the mountains and into the plains in efforts to extract forest products. The KMT government carried on this tradition in order to facilitate effective police control.[138] In addition, the KMT government

---

[132] T-S Wang, 'Taking Note of Indigenous Peoples' Laws in Legal Science and State Law' (2013) 134 *Chengchi Law Review* 12–13 (in Chinese).

[133] Simon, 'Paths to Autonomy', above n 129, 224.

[134] Wang, 'Taking Note of Indigenous Peoples' Laws', above n 132, 18–19.

[135] Simon, above n 129, 224.

[136] Wang, above n 132, 21.

[137] Lee and Lin, 'The Rights of Indigenous Peoples', above n 127, 209.

[138] Simon, above n 129, 224.

nationalised the mountain regions and implemented the 'reserve land' system. According to this system, indigenous peoples could register to gain land rights, but if they did not cultivate the land, it could be returned to the government. Moreover, although non-indigenous peoples are barred from buying indigenous peoples' land, in practice expropriation by the government and corporate developers in sectors such as travel and mining can still plunder the land from indigenous peoples.[139]

Of equal concern are the name disputes. As mentioned above, the KMT government invested much effort in forced assimilation in order to emphasise the country's Chinese identity. These efforts included requiring indigenous peoples to adopt Chinese names and to learn Mandarin.[140] In addition to this policy, a marriage between an indigenous woman and a Chinese man meant the loss of the wife's indigenous identity, whereas, if the situation were reversed (that is, if an indigenous man married a Chinese woman), the Chinese woman could retain her identity.

B. The Indigenous Movement

Historical discrimination drove the indigenous groups to protest even before the launch of democratisation. Since 1983, the indigenous movement paralleled the democratisation process of the 1990s. Publications promoted indigenous autonomy and indigenous organisations were formed.[141] Among these developments was the formation of the Alliance of Taiwan Indigenous Peoples in 1984, which co-ordinated protests and demonstrations on behalf of the indigenous communities.[142] An important result of the indigenous movement was that the issue of indigenous rights reached the constitutional level at a time of constitutional reform. In order to adequately address this issue, four rounds of constitutional revisions were necessary: in 1991, 1992, 1994, and 1997.

---

[139] C-L Lee, 'The Constitutional Rights of Indigenous People: Few Preliminary Thoughts' in C-L Lee (ed), *The Inheritance and Change of Human Rights Thinking* (Taipei, New Sharing, 2010) 351 (in Chinese).

[140] Simon, above n 129, 225.

[141] Lee, 'The Constitutional Rights of Indigenous People', above n 139.

[142] I Neary, *Human Rights in Japan, South Korea and Taiwan* (London, Routledge, 2002) 107–08.

An initial success of the indigenous movement was seen in the first revision of the Constitution, in 1991, in which the indigenous peoples' representation in the Legislature received a firm constitutional guarantee. At the same time, the terms the Constitution employed were controversial. For example, the Additional Articles used *shan-bao* (mountain people) to refer to indigenous groups. Further, the *shan-bao* was divided into two main categories: 'plains tribes' and 'hill tribes'. These terms were discriminatory and represented the labels the government forcefully attached to indigenous peoples.

The Constitution's controversial terms powered another wave of protests that demanded a renaming. Activists also strongly advocated for the passage of an 'indigenous clause' in the Constitution. The basic concept of the indigenous clause originated in the idea of human rights and therefore was intended as a way to include indigenous rights (that is, collective and individual rights) in the Constitution's chapter on rights. The demand of indigenous activists was partly answered: the 'indigenous clause' was indeed added to the Constitution in the 1992 revision, guaranteeing the identity, political participation and social welfare of indigenous peoples. However, the clause was added to the policy directives instead of to the chapter on rights,[143] and the discriminatory *shan-bao* term was retained. Fortunately, the rename movement bore fruit in the revision of 1994. Since then, the more generalised 'indigenous people' has been used as the constitutional term of choice[144]—any reference otherwise in laws, regulations or policy directives must be restyled as 'indigenous people'.

By the time of the fourth round of constitutional revision in 1997, the realisation was achieved that one of the indigenous peoples' defining characteristics is their collective nature. The word 'indigenous people' in the policy directives was replaced with 'indigenous peoples'.[145] This word change reflects the government's recognition of the unique status of indigenous peoples—that not only do they share a collective nature, they are also composed of multiple tribes.

---

[143] Art 18(6) Additional Articles of the Constitution of the Republic of China (1992).

[144] Art 9(7) Additional Articles of the Constitution of the Republic of China (1994).

[145] Art 10(10) Additional Articles of the Constitution of the Republic of China (1997).

Finally, new paragraphs were added to the policy directives requiring the state to actively protect indigenous languages and cultures.[146]

C. Gradual Progress and the Implementation of Indigenous Rights

As the Constitution now recognises the collective nature of indigenous peoples, their rights must be implemented by statutes in all respects. In 1996, the Council of Indigenous Peoples was organised to administer issues relevant to indigenous peoples.[147] The discussion of indigenous autonomy became more vibrant after the regime change in 2000, when the newly elected DPP government decided to recognise the 'partnership' between the state and indigenous groups.[148] In 2005, The Indigenous Peoples Basic Law was passed in order to reaffirm the collective rights of indigenous peoples. More recently, in 2009, the incorporation of the ICCPR and the ICESCR into domestic law ensured that the domestic legal system remained committed to the indigenous rights protected by these two covenants.

The rights of indigenous peoples can be divided into collective rights and individual rights. Regarding collective rights, Article 1 of both the ICCPR and the ICESCR guarantees indigenous peoples the right of self-determination—in particular, the right to determining their political status and to pursue economic, social and cultural development. Regarding individual rights, all rights guaranteed by the ICCPR and the ICESCR, such as the rights of religion, housing, are equally applicable to indigenous peoples. Article 27 of the ICCPR further emphasises the right of the members of ethnic, religious and linguistic minorities to enjoy their own cultures and use their own languages. Incorporating these rights into domestic law and policy, Taiwan has shown gradual progress towards full protection of indigenous rights.

As for the right of indigenous peoples to use their own languages, indigenous peoples had previously been forced to use Chinese names.

---

[146] Art 10(9) Additional Articles of the Constitution of the Republic of China (1997).

[147] Neary, *Human Rights in Japan, South Korea and Taiwan*, above n 142, 108.

[148] Wang, above n 132, 26.

To correct this historical rights infringement, the Name Act was revised in 1995 to permit the use of native names on official documents, albeit written in Chinese. However, the compulsory use of Chinese characters was abolished by the Name Act's revision in 2001. Since then, the native names of indigenous peoples have been accepted in Roman characters.

With respect to the right of culture, the 2001 revision of the Act Controlling Guns, Ammunition and Knives marked a significant step towards the protection of indigenous cultures. Previously, it had been a criminal offence for indigenous peoples to manufacture and possess hunting guns without proper registration. In accordance with the revision, however, these actions ceased to be criminal. Instead, a mere administrative penalty would be assessed in those cases where indigenous peoples failed to register their guns.[149] Regrettably, even after the revision, the right of culture has not been fully realised in practice. Although the possession of hunting guns by indigenous peoples has been decriminalised, most prosecutors tend to prosecute indigenous peoples anyway by applying the prohibition to the general public. Fortunately, courts have become increasingly willing both to consult the customs of indigenous peoples and refer to international human rights law. In so doing, defendants in these cases are found not guilty most of the time.[150]

As has been previously mentioned, aside from culture and language, issues related to the land have become major points of controversy between indigenous peoples and the government. Land is vitally important to indigenous peoples, as its possession often leads to the manifestation of the rights to pursue economic, social, and cultural development; moreover, land is especially important to the collective right of self-determination.

For indigenous peoples, many land disputes remain unresolved. However, they secured at least one victory in the Asia Cement case. In 1973, the Asia Cement Company rented the farming land of the Truku

---

[149] Art 20 Act Controlling Guns, Ammunition, and Knives (2001).

[150] Judgments of this type can be found primarily in the Taitung District Court; for instance, Taitung District Court Judgment (27 November 2012), 101-Su-218; Taitung District Court Judgment (3 September 2012), 101-Su-152. Some judgments even refer to relevant articles in the ICCPR; for instance, Taitung District Court Judgment (7 January 2013), 101-Zhongsu-5.

tribe in Hualien, under agreement that the land would be returned after 25 years. Yet when the leases expired, Asia Cement refused to return the land and, with the help of the township government, falsified documents showing that the Truku had relinquished their rights to the land. Indigenous peoples launched a 'Return Our Land' campaign and took the matter to court. In 2000, although a court ruled in favour of the Truku tribe, the township government refused to register the land under the tribe's name.[151] It was not until 2012, when the Council of Indigenous Peoples overruled the township government's decision, that the dispute finally came to an end.

Land disputes remained in sharp focus during the Review of the Initial Reports of the Government of Taiwan on the Implementation of the International Human Rights Covenants.[152] The Review's panel of experts closely examined Taiwan's compliance with the ICCPR and ICESCR. They became particularly concerned that lands of indigenous peoples, such as those in Orchid Island, have been designated by the government for the permanent disposal of nuclear waste, without the agreement of the indigenous owners. Other indigenous-owned lands are designated as possible candidates for nuclear waste sites as well. The Review's experts therefore endorsed a public referendum for indigenous peoples to weigh in on the the issue.[153]

As a result of historical discrimination, indigenous peoples who once owned the island have now become marginalised in Taiwan's industrialised democracy, despite a series of reforms that have worked in tandem with the progress of democratisation and rights awareness. Recently, the Constitutional Court has displayed an increased willingness to enhance the rights of indigenous peoples. Notably, in *JY Interpretation No 719*, a recent dispute regarding a controversial provision of the Government Procurement Act—requiring winning bidders of government procurement contracts that employ more than 100 people to recruit a certain percentage of indigenous people—the Court upheld

---

[151] Simon, above n 129, 229–30.

[152] For further details, see the following section.

[153] Review of the Initial Reports of the Government of Taiwan on the Implementation of the International Human Rights Covenants, 'Concluding Observations and Recommendations Adopted by the International Group of Independent Experts' (1 March 2013), para 30, at www.humanrights.moj.gov.tw/public/Attachment/33516305719.pdf.

the Act's constitutionality. The Court reinforced the rights of indigenous peoples by referring to the United Nations Declaration on the Rights of Indigenous Peoples and the Indigenous and Tribal Peoples Convention, and reiterated the justifiability of granting preferential treatment to indigenous people. The Court held that its interpretation accorded with international standards, and was calibrated to maximise public interest in the plight of indigenous peoples.[154]

V. THE INCORPORATION OF INTERNATIONAL HUMAN RIGHTS

Elsewhere I have identified transitional and transnational constitutionalism as the two most distinctive features of constitutionalism today.[155] Taiwan's constitutional development is no exception to these two trends, though it has also been influenced by indigenisation.[156] In the development of transnational constitutionalism, constitutional incorporation of international human rights has been one of the key ways that international norms have crossed sovereign boundaries and become entrenched in domestic constitutions.[157]

Unlike in other recent democracies that have incorporated international human rights in a new constitution or through constitutional amendments, the ROC Constitution and its post-1990s constitutional revisions have not attempted any such incorporation. This has left Taiwan with only two options for incorporation: through the judiciary and by statute. The judicial strategy of incorporating of international human rights was covered in chapter 6. Therefore, this chapter will focus on the activities of civic groups, as they have engaged in building institutional capacity and effecting incorporation by statute. Indeed, due to its bottom-up nature, there is much distinctive about the development of Taiwan's transnational constitutionalism.[158]

---

[154] *JY Interpretation No 719* (2014).
[155] Yeh and Chang, 'The Changing Landscape', above n 4; Yeh and Chang, above n 3.
[156] Yeh and Chang, 'A Decade of Changing Constitutionalism in Taiwan', above n 4.
[157] Yeh and Chang, above n 3.
[158] W-C Chang, 'An Isolated Nation with Global-minded Citizens: Bottom-up Transnational Constitutionalism in Taiwan' (2009) 4 *National Taiwan University Law Review* 204.

Along these lines, the movement to abolish the death penalty stands as a prime example.

A. International Human Rights and Institutional Capacity-building

As discussed previously, in 1971 the United Nations expelled the ROC, an event which significantly affected the protection of human rights: none of the ROC's signatures or ratifications of UN international human rights treaties were recognised any longer. Since expulsion, the ROC remained incapable of joining new treaty regimes. This isolation, had it not been handled with care, could have led to Taiwan's withdrawal from the tremendous development of international human rights over the past few decades.

In response to this difficult situation, Taiwan aggressively promoted, through civil action and legislation, the development of an international human rights regime strengthened by domestic discourse. The 1990s witnessed calls for the harmonisation of international human rights with the national legal system. In that era, several human rights organisations pushed the government to ratify or join new human rights treaties. To further endorse their ideas, these organisations proposed the creation of a national human rights institution that might be able to help bring international human rights to Taiwan.[159] The specific plan was to organise a human rights commission that could effectively redress human rights violations. The commission could provide a public forum for dialogue about human rights, which in turn would effect the amendment of domestic laws that at the time fell below international standards with respect to their incorporation of human rights.[160]

To promote this idea, scholars took the first step by writing essays to be published by the media. On 6 December 1999, non-governmental organisations led by the Taiwan Association for Human Rights established a 'Coalition for the Promotion of a National Human Rights Commission in Taiwan', advocating that international principles and the experience of

---

[159] FF-T Liao, 'Establishing a National Human Rights Commission in Taiwan: The Role of NGOs and Challenges Ahead' (2001) 2 *Asia-Pacific Journal on Human Rights and the Law* 92.
[160] Ibid, 155–56.

other countries be consulted in designing a national human rights commission. While the Coalition's working group drafted the bill, another working group began efforts to lobby the then-incumbent government and the candidates in the 2000 presidential election.

In response, the Office of the President set up an Advisory Committee in 2000 to plan for the formation of a human rights commission.[161] However, the Executive Yuan opposed the idea of such a commission and only agreed to support the Advisory Committee if the commission's scope were limited to providing information about human rights. For its part, the Control Yuan contended that it was the proper body to protect human rights and that a new commission was unnecessary. Some scholars argued that a constitutional amendment would be needed to establish the commission.[162] At the time of this writing, the debate remains unresolved. Yet, in an important way, it reflects the bottom-up nature of Taiwan's civil society's institutional capacity-building.

Apart from proposing the formation of a human rights commission, an important step towards the incorporation of international human rights has been taken by citizens and NGOs advocating for statutory incorporation.[163]

Significant progress on the path to statutory incorporation was made in 2009 by the ratification of ICCPR and ICESCR and the passage of the act implementing the two covenants. To faciliate this development, the Presidential Consultative Human Rights Committee was established in 2010. However, this approach was by no means Taiwan's first attempt at internalising international human rights law. For instance, in 1993, without the prompting of any other state or international organisation, the Taiwanese government voluntarily announced its full compliance with the CRC, which had recently been enforced (in 1990). In 2007, Taiwan's accession to the CEDAW was passed by an overwhelming legislative majority and was formally announced by the President. In 2012, the Enforcement Act of CEDAW was passed, rendering CEDAW's women's rights and gender equality provisions applicable to domestic law. Most recently, the Implementation Acts of the CRC and the Convention on the Rights of Persons with Disabilities were passed in June 2014 and August 2014 respectively.

---

[161] Ibid, 101.

[162] Ibid, 104.

[163] Chang, 'An Isolated Nation with Global-minded Citizens', above n 158.

Mere accession to or ratification of international human rights conventions would not be sufficient for the United Nations, and citizens and NGOs continued to push the Taiwanese government towards domestic compliance. For example, after being pressed by NGOs, the Presidential Consultative Human Rights Committee agreed to draft initial state reports on the ICCPR and ICESCR, which would then be reviewed by independent experts. Both reports were released in 2012 and, in the subsequent year, 10 international experts, each with exemplary international human rights practices, were invited to review them. On 1 March 2013, the experts adopted the Concluding Observations and Recommendations; the government has also pledged full compliance and implementation.[164] In the case of CEDAW, the government released two state reports—one in 2009 and one in 2014. Independent experts were asked to review these reports and provide recommendations as well.[165]

In the march towards statutory incorporation, the influence of certain activists and NGOs has proved pivotal.[166] The international campaigns of the End Child Prostitution in Asian Tourism (ECPAT) and its affiliated Taiwanese organisation were able to introduce the CRC to Taiwan. In the CEDAW movement, women activists utilised their personal and professional connections to gain access to transnational collaborations, which was a factor critical to the successful introduction of the CEDAW to Taiwan. By helping to adopt domestic and transnational norms, these NGOs have only strengthened their capacity for continued human rights advocacy.

Furthermore, the incorporation of international human rights has had a significant effect on the design of government institutions. The debate about the establishment of a human rights commission, although bearing no real fruit, was instrumental in prompting the Office of the President to form the Advisory Committee in 2000. In 2003, the Advisory Committee managed to pass a draft of the Human Rights Fundamental Act, although, regrettably, this bill never became law.

---

[164] The state reports of ICCPR and ICESCR, along with information regarding their unprecedented international review, are available at www.humanrights.moj.gov.tw/np.asp?ctNode=33565&mp=200.

[165] For the government's compliance with the CEDAW, see www.ey.gov.tw/gec_en/.

[166] Chang, above n 158.

In 2008, following a change in Taiwan's governing party, the Advisory Committee was replaced by the Presidential Consultative Human Rights Committee, whose mission is to incorporate international human rights (and specifically those represented by the two covenants).

Aside from the Advisory Committee, the Committee for Human Rights Protection under the Executive Branch was formed in 2001 to research and promote international human rights. The formation of such committees has been driven by the statutory incorporation of each international human rights convention. For example, the Gender Equality Committee of the Executive Yuan was formed to handle the matter of the CEDAW and other conventions; and the Implemetation Acts of both the CRC and the Convention on the Rights of Persons with Disabilities called for the establishment of new committees under the Executive Yuan.

Institutional design has shown significant progress. However, a general lack of co-ordination has persisted, along with other issues. The largest unresolved matter is the debate over whether a human rights commission should be established—one that could facilitate inter-agency co-ordination. In their review of the implementation of the ICCPR and ICESCR, the panel of experts recommended that a new commisison be created.[167]

B. The Death Penalty Debate as Example

Of all Taiwan's human rights issues, the death penalty debate has the potential for the largest domestic and global ramifications. The Constitutional Court has thrice adjudicated the constitutionality of the death penalty. In *JY Interpretation Nos 194* and *263*, the Court held constitutional the concept of a mandatory death sentence.[168] In *JY Interpretation No 476*, the Court focused on the constitutionality of the death penalty itself.

---

[167] Above n 154, para 8.

[168] *JY Interpretation No 194* held that Art 5(1) of the Drug Control Act during the Period for Suppression of the Communist Rebellion is not contrary to either Art 7 or 23 of the Constitution; *JY Interpretation No 263* held constitutional Art 2(1)(9) of the Robbery Punishment Act, a special criminal law that imposes a mandatory death penalty on those who commit kidnapping with the intent to obtain ransom, regardless of the details and results of the crime.

The Court found it to be constitutional, on condition that the imposition of all death penalties must comply with due process, pursuant to Article 8 and Article 23 of the Constitution.

The historical backdrops of these death penalty interpretations are instructive. *JY Interpretation No 194* came down in 1985, when Taiwan was still under the Martial Law Decree. *JY Interpretation Nos 263* and *476* were released in the 1990s, at which time over 50 different offences were punishable by mandatory death sentence.[169]

As the movement towards democratisation progressed, some NGOs began to promote the absolute value of life and human dignity, including the abolition of the death penalty—especially as a mandatory sentence. To this end, the Taiwan Alliance to End the Death Penalty (TAEDP), a coalition of NGOs and research institutes, has been an influential advocate.[170] In September 2003, the TAEDP was launched by the Taiwan Association for Human Rights, the Judicial Reform Foundation, the Taipei Bar Association, and a number of other groups. At the time, the DPP government sought to distance Taiwan from its authoritarian past, in the hope that the nation would gain a new identity as a state committed to human rights.[171] In April 2006, with momentum building from the support of civil society and the DPP government, Taiwan finally removed the last mandatory death penalty provisions from the Criminal Code and other laws. Remarkably, Taiwan did not execute a single criminal from 2006 to 2009.

After the application of the ICCPR to the domestic legal system in 2009, the TAEDP saw a key opportunity to submit a constitutional petition. In the TAEDP's view, while the ICCPR did not demand the immediate abolition of the death penalty, it did provide for stricter guidance in the imposition and enforcement of the death penalty.[172] Regrettably, however, the Constitutional Court dismissed the petition in May 2010.[173] Nevertheless, the Court recognised the domestic applicability of the ICCPR, stating that the rights enshrined by the covenant

---

[169] J-P Wang, 'The Current State of Capital Punishments in Taiwan' (2011) 6 *National Taiwan University Law Review* 146.

[170] For more information on TADEP, see www.taedp.org.tw/.

[171] B Kennedy, 'Restraint and Punishment' (2004) 54 *Taiwan Review* 24.

[172] Art 6 International Covenant on Civil and Political Rights (1966).

[173] The dismissal was made in the 1358th Council meeting on 28 May 2010. *JY Dismissal of Petition No 9741* (2010).

should bind all levels of government, including the judiciary and the Constitutional Court.

Despite the efforts of NGOs from 2010 to 2013, 21 individuals were executed during those years.[174] In 2013, the Concluding Observations and Recommendations issued by the panel of international experts found the executions to be clear violations of the ICCPR's Article 6. The experts strongly recommended that Taiwan's government intensify efforts to abolish capital punishment.[175] They advised that until the final abolition was achieved, the government should ensure that it adhered scrupulously to all procedural and substantive safeguards related to the imposition and enforcement of capital punishment.[176] Unforunately, the review was ignored and, in 2014, five death row inmates were executed.

Taiwan's current policy on capital punishment risks violating international human rights and runs counter to the global trend of abolition. It is evident that further and bolder steps are needed. NGOs are ever ready to fight through the various avenues of constitutional review, legislative enactment and political leadership. And of course, not only constitutional but international human rights hang in the balance.

VI. CONCLUSION

As described above, the trajectory of Taiwan's protection of human rights illustrates the effectiveness of underpinning rights with institutional and societal forces—as opposed to mere texual enumerations—against a backdrop of democratic transformation. Human rights have been advanced in Taiwan by applying a social dialectic, in which courts, the legislature and civil groups play indispensable roles in constitutional/legislative reforms and in many landmark adjudications.

---

[174] W-C Chang et al, *The Death Penalty in Taiwan: A report on Taiwan's legal obligations under the International Covenant on Civil and Political Rights* (London, The Death Penalty Project, 2014) iv.

[175] Above n 153, para 56.

[176] Ibid, para 57.

Notably, the human rights guaranteed by the Constitution focus mainly on civil and political rights, whereas social, economic and cultural rights—not included in the human rights chapter—are incorporated in the policy directives of the Additional Articles of the Constitution. Advancing these rights means relying on the passage of statutes or governmental policy guidelines. A similar situation applies in the case of indigenous rights. The policy directives incorporated the protection of indigenous peoples via a series of constitutional reforms, yet legislative enactment and adjudication by the courts have made possible significant advancements in this area.

This phenomenon points to a valuable observation. Historically, the text of the Constitution has, especially in its rights chapter, changed very little. Even so, progress is achieved in practice, in tandem with the process of democratisation. This is due to the efforts of the various actors striving to bring about democratisation and constitutional reform. From an institutional standpoint, the Constitutional Court has been considered a chief influence of Taiwan's human rights transformation.[177] As most individual petitions involve human rights issues, Taiwan's protection of these rights has expanded with each decided case.[178] Moreover, especially with respect to the recognition of new rights and the incorporation of international human rights, civil groups and NGOs have played a pivotal role in this discourse.

In essense, Taiwan's protection of human rights is still a work in progress. Though enriched with human rights content, finding a way to institutionalise these rights' protection has not been without its troubles. For discourse to continue into the future, therefore, Taiwan must take the major step of establishing a human rights commission.

---

[177] FC-c Lin, 'The Implementation of Human Rights Law in Taiwan' in R Peerenboom, CJ Petersen and AHY Chen (eds), *Human Rights in Asia: A Comparative Legal Study of Twelve Asian Jurisdictions, France and the USA* (Oxon, Routledge, 2006) 301–03.

[178] Ibid, 302.

FURTHER READING

Chang, W-C, 'Public Interest Litigation in Taiwan: Strategy for Law and Policy Changes in the Course of Democratization,' in PJ Yap and H Lau (eds), *Public Interest Litigation in Asia* (New York, Routledge, 2011) 136–60.

Law, DS and Chang, W-C, 'The Limits of Global Judicial Dialogue' (2011) 86 *Washington Law Review* 523–77.

Rubio-Marin, R and Chang, W-C, 'Sites of Constitutional Struggle for Women's Equality' in M Tushnet, T Fleiner and C Saunders (eds), *Routledge Handbook of Constitutional Law* (New York, Routledge, 2013) 301–12.

Wang, J-P, 'The Current State of Capital Punishments in Taiwan' (2011) 6 *National Taiwan University Law Review* 143–75.

8

Conclusion: Challenges and Prospects

Constitutional Footprints: What Taiwan Has Achieved – Facing the Future – Conclusion

AIWAN'S TRANSITION TO democracy was made pos-
sible by incremental constitutional revisions, courts responsive
to changing dynamics and, most importantly, a civil society
engaged in the project of constitutional transformation. These changes
ushered in the unprecedented development of a transitional and transnational constitutionalism, and will no doubt continue to bring additional transformation over time—although the prospect of continuing
development will hinge on the consolidation and entrenchment of this
deep constitutional transformation. In short, the transformative constitutional practices listed above constitute the foundation for Taiwan's
future constitutional development.

Incremental constitutional reform, however, has not come without
a price. Brought about in response to immediate political crises and
short-term corrective measures, reform has left a few fundamental
issues unresolved, if not untouched. As it faces the future, Taiwan will
have to navigate these remaining challenges while making credible constitutional choices in the era of autochthonous development, regional
(dis)integration and global networking. This final chapter includes two
sections. The first discusses Taiwan's constitutional footprints: what the
nation has been able to achieve constitutionally in recent decades, with
a focus on the emergence of transformative and civic constitutionalism.
The second and final section lays out the constitutional challenges that
Taiwan must deal with in the future, including: (a) the infeasibility of

further change due to the extremely high threshold that constitutional amendments must pass over; (b) a system of government that is prone to stalemating on questions of constitutional reform; and (c) a fragile constitutional sovereignty susceptible to the nation's cross-Strait relationship with the PRC.

I. CONSTITUTIONAL FOOTPRINTS: WHAT TAIWAN HAS ACHIEVED

Taiwan's constitutional gains have been profound, though they were attained incrementally. Democratisation, indigenisation and globalisation all drove the transformation of an externally imposed constitution into an internally embraced, vibrant constitution—one that embraces the liberal democratic tradition while cultivating the salient features of a transitional and transnational constitutionalism.[1] Step by step, the nation has undergone unprecedented changes, including institutional shifts from a cabinet system to a semi-presidential system (chapter 3); from three parliaments to one (chapter 4); from three levels of government to two, with an increasing number of mega cities, and from manipulated central–local relations to a functional federalism (chapter 5); from a Constitutional Court that merely rubber-stamped to one that is responsive and supports dialogue (chapter 6); and from a short list of constitutional rights to a burgeoning rights-based discourse engaged by civil society (chapter 7).

Of the changes discussed in previous chapters, two stand out as the highest achievements of Taiwan's constitutional development via democratisation. The first is what I call 'transformative constitutionalism', according to which the Constitution has become a routine source of support for political resolutions and even projects of social capacity-building. The second achievement is 'civic constitutionalism', which describes the strength and resilience of civic engagement—even after the constitutional transformation—as it pushes towards democratic transition and constitutional reform.

---

[1] For a discussion of features reflecting transitional and transnational constitutionalism, see ch 1.

A. Transformative Constitutionalism

Taiwan has attracted much global attention for its 'economic miracle' of growth alongside equal distribution in the 1980s, as well as the 'quiet revolution' of political democratisation in the 1990s. The fascinating transformation in economics and politics was not simply the product of political leadership or naked power struggles. Rather, these unprecedented changes were deeply embedded in the context of constitutional transformation. With the benefit of hindsight, one comes to the realisation that, in the pursuit of profound change, constitutional issues have been invoked often, and constitutional solutions resorted to regularly. In other words, transformation has been carried out in accordance with the constitutional order and argued in constitutional terms with heavy constitutional footprints, as reflected in constitutional revisions, judicial decisions, and public discourse. Change has come at the expense of various constitutional struggles and has been codified in constitutional provisions or interpretations.

As illustrated in previous chapters, the process of democratisation and transformation has occurred along with a parallel track of constitutional change. In other words, the Constitution set the goals, generated the issues and guided the process of ongoing political change. Once changes were made in constitutional terms, they became part of the constitutional scheme that further steered—substantively and procedurally—the next rounds of change. Evidently, Taiwan has embraced constitutionalism as the primary rule for providing political and social solutions in times of crises of legitimacy, political gridlock, or civic campaigns for human rights recognition.

It is not difficult to trace these constitutional footprints at major junctures of Taiwan's constitutional change. Examples abound, as illustrated in previous chapters. Even a powerful leader like Chiang Kai-shek resorted to constitutional revision to extend his presidency beyond the two-term limit. By the same token, the direct elections of Presidents and national representatives were made possible through various rounds of constitutional revision. Constitutional solutions for divisive policy issues followed a similar path. For example, in order to resolve the nuclear installation controversy that threatened to tear society apart, the Constitutional Court was called upon to interpret the Constitution in its search for all possible solutions. Furthermore, the policy change from hostility with the Chinese mainland to peaceful engagement was made via constitutional delegation and based upon a special law. Such regular resort to and heavy reliance on constitutional practices and articulations have made Taiwan's dynamic transitions work for constitutionalism, in both substance and form, albeit with transitional and transnational characteristics.

B. Civic Constitutionalism

Taiwan's liberal constitutional order was established in the course of its democratic and political reforms. It is important to understand the nature of such a constitutional enterprise: either elite-centred and top-down, or society-engaged and bottom-up.

In comparative perspective, democratic transition and constitutional reform are usually aimed at building democratic institutions and adopting electoral mechanisms. Nevertheless, democracy entails much more than political representation and elections. With the installation of representative institutions, attention should also be paid to civil society and its roles during and after transition. All too often, political institutions such as the President, legislature and state apparatus are the foci of constitutional order, gathering nearly all attention on the process of transition. In such a power-centric model, civic engagement may gradually diminish and civil society become stifled, creating a crisis for a fledgling democracy.[2] A few newer democracies in Eastern and Central Europe have fostered such crises, as their democratic transitions and constitutional reforms occurred in contexts in which political institutions and courts—rather than civil society and rights agendas—occupied centre stage.[3] By contrast, Taiwan's democratic transition has had the fortune of retaining a civil society that is very much engaged and continues to be watchful.

Constitutional reform in Taiwan is not the product of party initiatives; nor has it depended on the mercy of benevolent, reform-minded leaders. Rather, it has resulted from strong civic engagement within

---

[2] See, eg, DC Williams, 'Civic Constitutionalism, the Second Amendment, and the Rights of Revolution' (2004) 79 *Indiana Law Journal* 379, 380–81.

[3] P Blokker, *New Democracies in Crisis? A Comparative Constitutional Study of the Czech Republic, Hungary, Poland, Romania and Slovakia* (New York, Routledge, 2014).

a process of dramatic change. Incremental and fragmented as it has been, Taiwan's constitutional reform has nevertheless generated a more representative legislature, a popularly elected President, and more reliable courts.[4] These power-centric institutional reforms, however, did not prevent civil society from increasing its engagement in the constitutional order. Indeed, Taiwan has displayed a pattern of strong civic engagement in support of constitutional reform, championing a model of 'civic constitutionalism', beyond representative democracy.[5]

Civic constitutionalism honours constitutional institutions such as representative bodies and the courts, but enhances the visibility of engaged citizens and civic groups as they relate to these institutions. In civic constitutionalism, citizens and civic groups exert a great deal of influence on public matters, such that they have an impact on the dialectical interpretation, form and shape of the Constitution. The general public values periodic elections by going to the ballot and honours representative institutions, which reflect public opinion, while insisting that these institutions involve citizen participation and submit to strong civic oversight. Even after successful constitutional reform, civic groups and engaged citizens remain alert to public policies and agendas of further reform.

The emergence of civic constitutionalism in Taiwan has not gone unnoticed. As illustrated in chapter 7, a robust civil society had already formed prior to democratisation in the 1990s. The student movement in the spring of 1990 was critical to the constitutional ruling that ordered the first national representatives to leave office and a second election to be held.[6] In the rounds of constitutional revision that followed, civic groups and human rights organisations actively pushed for an agenda of reform on rights and human rights institutions, in addition to an undertaking of strategic constitutional rights litigation. Such rights advocacy has been welcomed by the courts, and judicial decisions have become increasingly receptive to social consensus and keen to be in dialogue with civil society. Judicial review now functions as a strong check on political institutions, while leaving some space for political solutions

---

[4] J-r Yeh, 'Democracy-driven Transformation to Regulatory State: The Case of Taiwan' (2008) 3 *National Taiwan University Law Review* 31–59.

[5] See J-r Yeh, '*Marching towards Civil Constitutionalism with Sunflowers*' (2015) 45 *Hong Kong Law Journal* 315–29.

[6] See ch 2.

by adopting pro-dialogue strategies.[7] Stronger judicial checks on representative institutions—applied on behalf of the people—suggest that at least two sources of civic constitutionalism are the civil distrust of political institutions and the failures of parliamentary supremacy.

II. FACING THE FUTURE

The journey of Taiwan's constitutional development has been fascinating, if not completely successful. It has entailed the battle of constitutional indigenisation and transformation against the imperfection of constitutional text, institutions and politics. The Constitution's constructive resilience has helped Taiwan navigate political crises and other difficult moments. However, incremental constitutional revisions have left unresolved a few issues and structural challenges that need to be addressed. Facing the future, Taiwan must confront the following three major constitutional issues: (a) the infeasibility of further constitutional change; (b) a stalemate-prone system of government; and (c) a fragile constitutional sovereignty.

A. The Infeasibility of Constitutional Change

Taiwan's democratic transition and constitutional reforms have been neither a normative enterprise nor merely a political manipulation. In times of turbulent political transition, a new Constitution may not be achieved immediately, but may evolve over time. Initial changes may breed additional changes in a rather progressive fashion. In contrast with a traditional understanding of constitutions as stable and long-lasting, Taiwan's Constitution is transitory and susceptible to further transformation over time.

Incremental constitutional revisions were made strategically as democratic transition progressed step by step.[8] However, the very last

---

[7] J-r Yeh, 'Presidential Politics and Judicial Facilitation of Political Dialogue between Political Actors in New Asian Democracies: Comparing the South Korean and Taiwanese Experiences' (2011) 8 *International Journal of Constitutional Law* 911–49.

[8] J-r Yeh, 'Constitutional Reform and Democratization in Taiwan: 1945–2000' in P Chow (ed), *Taiwan's Modernization in Global Perspective* (CT, Praeger, 2002) 47–77.

constitutional revision, in 2005, imposed an extremely high procedural threshold for new constitutional amendments—so high that many believe any future constitutional revision to be almost impossible. Indeed, since 2005 there has been no constitutional revision, or even proposal of such, which is a dramatic departure from the incrementalist pattern of the past. Stringent procedural requirements—an affirmative vote by three-quarters of the Legislative Yuan out of a quorum of three-quarters, followed by more than half of the eligible voters casting their ballots of approval—demand no less than a national consensus for the passage of any constitutional amendment. In the absence of such a consensus, it is difficult to imagine that the present version of the Constitution will ever change.

Although the 2005 constitutional revision put an end to the previous transitoriness of the Constitution, it nevertheless represented a precious historical moment at which Taiwan's constitutional reform could be shaped in three new directions: the comprehensive, the periodic, and the citizen-centric.[9] Given the considerations of cost related to the extremely high threshold, future constitutional revisions will be held infrequently, and must be comprehensive—not piecemeal—in their coverage of issues, carrying a strong potential to obtain national consensus. Looking forward, constitutional change may be far less dependent on formal constitutional revisions than it has been in the past, but it will more heavily depend on the constitutional politics of multiple actors and, above all, on courts and an already burgeoning and empowered civil society.

B. A Stalemate-prone System of Government

A well-functioning democracy requires a clearly defined institutional structure that will empower the government to deliver public goods and constrain it from abusing power, thus allowing the private sphere to flourish. For societies experiencing political and economic transition, and which are anxious about global competition, it is even more

---

[9] J-r Yeh, A draft paper for the presentation at the 'Taiwan in Dynamic Transition' International Conference, 24–26 May 2013, University of Alberta, Edmonton, Canada.

important to establish an effective and impartial judicial system to protect human rights and business activities.[10]

To guarantee good and effective governance, constitutional clarity is important, both procedurally and substantively. Unfortunately, many studies have shown that political compromise and incremental reform—common in the third-wave democratisation process—are likely to create the kinds of constitutional vagueness and institutional inconsistencies that lead to political deadlock and instability.[11] It is not until constitutional clarity is achieved—either through comprehensive constitutional re-engineering or strong judicial intervention—that constitutional stability can be attained.

Taiwan's constitutional revisions exemplify the problems of muddling through reform. Only once short-term political crises had dissipated did long-term institutional weaknesses surface. At its inception, constitutional reform was intended to address the legitimacy crisis of three institutions—the National Assembly, the Legislative Yuan and the Control Yuan—which arose as a reaction to the nearly 40-year tenure of their members. Reform brought electoral accountability to these offices. Once democratic elections were established, however, other more intricate difficulties—specifically, those concerning the checks and balances among the three bodies—began to emerge. As discussed in chapter 4, the battle between the National Assembly and the Legislative Yuan did not cease until the former's abolition in 2005. The power struggle between the Control Yuan and the Legislative Yuan, and especially their competing claims for oversight of the administration, is unresolved even today.

The most notable reform has been the introduction of direct presidential elections. Although this development is one of the major achievements of constitutional reform, there has been a simultaneous neglect of important institutional arrangements that have contributed to an increasingly powerful presidency. It was generally anticipated that the introduction of a directly elected presidency would also provide for

[10] A Lijphart and CH Waisman, 'Institutional Design and Democratization' in A Lijphart and CH Waisman (eds), *Institutional Design in New Democracies: Eastern Europe and Latin America* (Boulder, CO, Westview Press, 1996) 6.

[11] JJ Linz and A Stepan, *Problems of Democratic Transition and Consolidation: Southern Europe, South America, and Post-Communist Europe* (Baltimore, Johns Hopkins University Press, 1996).

a triangular relationship among the President, premier and Legislative Yuan. Regrettably, however, without a firm consensus on how the system of government should be designed, even a minor alteration in the triangular relationship creates more problems than it solves.[12]

Today, Taiwan's President is directly elected by the people and enjoys full power, without legislative approval, to appoint the premier; thus, the President effectively controls the administration. Under Taiwan's structure of government as designed, the premier was supposed to be responsible to the Legislative Yuan. This means that, now, there are no effective checks and balances between the Legislative Yuan and the President. Although the Legislative Yuan can issue a vote of no confidence with respect to the President-appointed premier, the President can dissolve the Legislative Yuan. Fears of dissolution and the high costs of re-election effectively dissuade the Legislative Yuan from initiating a vote of no confidence. In this way, any semblance of a check on the President's power is lost. Some argue that the revised institutional arrangement resembles the French semi-presidential system, but it is clear that the French system employs stronger checks and balances to constrain presidential powers.

This ill-designed institutional arrangement has destabilised Taiwanese politics since 2000, when the first regime change occurred and the incumbent President did not enjoy a legislative majority. It reflects a structural problem that, in many respects, has limited for quite some time the government's ability to function, as illustrated in chapter 3. Thus, the prospect of reforming the system of government is caught between two competing claims. One claim pushes for a parliamentary system that, among other things, would re-introduce legislative approval for the premier's appointment and abolish the direct presidential election. The other claim seeks a pure presidential system that places the President on the top of the executive branch and directly checks him or her against the legislature. Either of these two options would be superior to the current system, but the vested interests of political parties and cumbersome constitutional revision requirements make any change extremely difficult to accomplish.

---

[12] J-w Lin, 'Transition Through Transaction: Taiwan's Constitutional Reforms in the Lee Tenghui Era' (2002) 20 *American Asian Review* 123.

Institutional flaws certainly will require a thorough constitutional re-engineering. Until that happens, the institutions of Taiwanese government will continue to find it difficult to deliver the good and effective governance so desired by a society facing delicate cross-Strait relations and intense global competition.

C. A Fragile Constitutional Sovereignty

Compared with the problems of representation and legitimacy, which were resolved in the early stages of constitutional revision, the issue of national sovereignty remained somewhat off-limits and has continued to haunt Taiwan.[13] Throughout the process of constitutional revision, Taiwan's framework of national identity—Republic of China or Taiwan in contrast to the People's Republic of China—received little attention. Similarly, the questions of what to do about the national flag and the national territories went unremarked. This lacuna resulted from the political compromise between the KMT, which sought to remain in power and satisfy its mainlander members, and the DPP, which lacked power but strived for substantial breakthroughs in reforming democracy. Tellingly, the forewords to the Additional Articles to the Constitution state that the purpose of constitutional revision is 'to meet the requisites of the nation prior to national unification'.

The closest Taiwan came to challenging the sensitive issue of national sovereignty was the demand for the Constitutional Court to rule on the status of Mongolia. Ironically, there was still a government agency of Tibetan and Mongolian affairs in Taiwan, which requested annual budget approvals from the Legislative Yuan. A group of legislators appealed to the Court for clarification on whether Mongolia was still part of the ROC. To nobody's surprise, the Court shrugged off a ruling by claiming that the determination of national boundaries is not subject to judicial review.[14]

Although not addressed during the democratic transition, the issue of national sovereignty as an ultimate problem continues to surface in Taiwan's politics. Above all, the China policy remains at the centre of

---

[13] Yeh, 'Constitutional Reform', above n 8, 47.
[14] *JY Interpretation No 328* (1993).

political debate and has become the source of much political confrontation, as has been demonstrated since the first regime change in 2000. Indeed, the problem of national sovereignty affects not only Taiwan's relationship with China, but also (and thus) its relationship with the international community.

Confounded by its uncertain statehood since the 1971 loss of its UN membership, Taiwan has had a difficult time participating in the international community. However, the nation has seized upon every chance to build its relationship with the international community and to contribute to it in every way possible. Though ruled out of most opportunities for treaty-making, Taiwan nevertheless makes good use of domestic institutions and mechanisms in connecting to prevailing international norms. Thus, international law and similar mechanisms have been ever-present in the development of Taiwan's constitutionalism, as illustrated in chapter 7. The reconstruction of a constitutional identity in tandem with democratic transition has offered a dynamic display of constructive constitutionalism.

In 2008, the KMT won back the presidency, completing Taiwan's second regime change. Confronting Taiwan's unprecedented economic downturn, President Ma Ying-jeou decided to seek closer co-operation with China. He took a dovish approach by rebuilding cross-Strait relations and resuming bilateral negotiations that had been suspended during the previous DPP administration. This belief in 'reaching the world through China' has been intensified by the reality of international politics. China's twenty-first century rise has become a burning issue for the world, and especially for Taiwan, as the non-stop growth of China's economy seems to herald a future of close economic co-operation between the two nations—and possibly even interdependence.

Taiwan's execution with China of the ECFA brought another significant development. After several rounds of cross-Strait talks, the ECFA was signed on 29 June 2010. It is a preferential trade agreement aimed at reducing tariffs and commercial barriers between the two nations. But although touted as the most important advance in relations since the 1949 split occasioned by the Chinese Civil War, the ECFA has not proceeded without controversy. Advocates celebrated the ECFA as a panacea that would help stabilise and eventually increase Taiwan's presence in the Asian market. Some said that the ECFA would help normalise the relationship between Taiwan and China so that businesses could prosper. Others argued that the ECFA would prevent the marginalisation of

Taiwan, making it easier for Taiwan to arrange trade agreements with other countries. However, concerns also existed regarding the potential derogation of sovereignty and the lack of transparency and public participation in the ECFA negotiations. Critics contended that while the ECFA may present short-term opportunities for certain businesses, it was questionable whether in the long run, or in other ways, it would bring any benefits.[15]

The signing of the Cross-Strait Service Trade Agreement, a major follow-up to the ECFA, turned into a constitutional crisis in March 2014. In order to expedite the ratification process, the Legislative Yuan performed a ruthlessly fast-tracked review: it allegedly approved the agreement in 30 seconds. To protest this irresponsible legislative action, a large crowd of citizens, led by students, occupied the Legislative Yuan and demanded that the Ma Administration withdraw the agreement and restart negotiations with China, and that the Legislative Yuan make laws supervising and reviewing future negotiations with China. The protestors made an attempt to occupy the Executive Yuan but were forcefully expelled by the police, injuring more than 100 people. Dubbed the 'Sunflower Student Movement', it was the largest student-led protest in Taiwan's history.

While the cross-Strait relationship has become closer than expected, no emerging consensus on national identity is in sight. Taiwan will continue to juggle competing claims of political allegiance and constitutional identity while balancing economic gains and political risks both outside and within.[16] Political rhetoric about the future status of Taiwan, as compared to that of China, has been divisive in words and actions, but there may still exist a wide spectrum of possibilities within the constitutional framework. Developments across the Taiwan Strait may be highly fluid for both sides, with many possible outcomes. Should the Constitution play a major role in this process, a large range of nuanced options will become available—beyond those of independence, unification, and the one-country-two-systems formula.

---

[15] See C-A Chou, 'A Two-Edged Sword: The Economic Cooperation Framework Agreement Between The Republic of China and The People's Republic of China' (2010) 6 *Brigham Young University International Law and Management Review* 1.

[16] Y-h Chu and J-w Lin, 'Political Development in 20th-Century Taiwan: State-Building, Regime Transformation and the Construction of National Identity' (2001) 165 *The China Quarterly* 102.

III. CONCLUSION

Taiwan's constitutional development offers one of the best examples in the world of constitutional indigenisation via incremental and negotiated change. More important, the end result of this journey has been fruitful, as witnessed by Taiwan's successful transformation into a full democracy committed to the protection of human rights and the rule of law—towards capacity-building in economic, social and environmental resilience. The legacy of incremental change leaves some structural issues unresolved and suggests that some challenges may lie ahead. But a constitutional foundation and a vibrant civil society have provided—and will continue to provide—a solid ground for this constitutional endeavour for decades to come. All told, the fascinating development of Taiwan's constitutionalism carries tremendous significance for the Chinese world, Asia and far beyond.

FURTHER READING

Chu, Y-h and Lin, J-w, 'Political Development in 20th-Century Taiwan: State-Building, Regime Transformation and the Construction of National Identity' (2001) 165 *The China Quarterly* 102–29.

Yeh, J-r, 'Constitutional Reform and Democratization in Taiwan, 1945–2000' in PCY Chow (ed), *Taiwan's Modernization in Global Perspective* (Westport, CT, Praeger, 2002) 47–77.

Yeh, J-r, 'The Cult of Fatung: Representational Manipulation and Reconstruction in Taiwan' in G Hassall and C Saunders (eds), *The People's Representatives: Electoral Systems in the Asia-Pacific Region* (Sydney, Allen & Unwin, 1997) 27–37.

Yeh, J-r and Chang, W-C, 'A Decade of Changing Constitutionalism in Taiwan: Transitional and Transnational Perspectives' in AHY Chen (ed), *Constitutionalism in Asia in the Early Twenty-first Century* (Cambridge University Press, 2014) 141–68.

Index

abortion policy   220–21
accountability, and separation of
    powers   10
Administrative Procedure Act (1999)   85
admonitory declarations *see under* judicial
    review
agencies *see* ministries and agencies
aims and structure of book   19–20
Alliance of Taiwan Indigenous
    Peoples   227
American Convention on Human
    Rights   18
Asia-Pacific Economic Cooperation
    (APEC), accession   6–7
Asian integration   151–52
assembly, freedom of   209–11
audit control   118–19
Austronesians *see under* indigenous peoples
    rights
authoritarianism
    constitutional   30–36
    Constitutional Court, functions   171–73
autonomy, legislative *see under* legislative
    functions and constitutional control
Awakening Foundation   202

Basic Code Governing Central
    Administrative Agencies Organisations
    (Basic Code)   72, 76, 77, 78, 82
Berlin Wall   5
branches, *Yuans see Yuans* (branches)
budgetary control and devolution   134–35
budgetary expenditure increases,
    limitation   117–18
Build-Operate-Transfers (BOTs)   84,
    85–87

Cabinet Meeting   70–71
Central Election Commission   108–9
central-local relations   131–35
    budgetary control and devolution
        134–35
    elections and accountability   131–33
    key issues   131
    local government system,
        structure   132–33
    multi-level governance   150–52

offshore islands   148–50
pre-emption/regulatory supremacy
    133–34
regional and global perspectives   148–52
state v province models *see* Taiwan,
    state v province models
Chen, Shui-bian, President   55, 66, 67,
    82, 143
Cheng family   225
Chiang, Ching-kuo, President   37, 61, 215
Chiang, Kai-shek, President   35, 37, 61, 63
Child, Convention on the Rights of the
    (CRC)   17, 204, 234
children's rights   204
Chinese Communist Party (CCP)   2, 4, 23
civic constitutionalism *see under* constitution
    for Taiwan
Civil Associations Act (1992)   110
civil and political rights   205–13
Civil and Political Rights, International
    Covenent on (ICCPR)   17, 229,
    234–36, 237
civil service and Examination Yuan   87–89
Civil Service Protection and Training
    Commission   89
civil society, rights in *see under* rights
    discourse
Co-ordinative Councils   75
commercial speech, protection   212
Confucian Analects   40
congressional reform   46–47
constitution for Taiwan
    achievement   242, 242–46
    aims and structure of book   19–20
    background/summary   1–3, 253
    civic constitutionalism   244–46
    constitutional sovereignty   44–48,
        250–52
    constitutional supremacy   7–12
    democratic constitutionalism   2–3
    democratisation   4–5
    driving forces for transformation   3–7
    feasibility of change   246–47
    future issues   246–52
    globalisation   6–7
    incremental revisions   12–13, 241–42
    indigenisation   3–4

post-World War II history   1–2, 23–24
stalemate-prone features   247–50
transformative constitutionalism
    243–44
transitional features   12–16, 241
transnational features   16–19
see also Republic of China (ROC)
    Constitution
constitutional authoritarianism   32–36
Constitutional Court   2, 9–10, 19
    constitution-amending process   116
    constitutional authoritarianism   35
    content-based/content-neutral (freedom
        of expression) restrictions   211
    and Control Yuan   95–96
    dialectical judicial review   13–15
    electoral system   106–7
    financial control   118–19
    five-power government scheme   54, 57
    global convergence of institutions   18
    independence   11–12
    legislative autonomy   115–16
    Mainland China, authorised agreements
        with   121
    manipulation of representation   33–34
    and National Assembly powers   45–46
    personnel appointments   122–23
    political parties, accountability
        issues   110, 111–14
    and president's powers   68
    privileges and immunities for members
        of Legislative Yuan   117
    reconstruction of representation   38
    Taipei City Government, disputes with
        Central government   143–46
    tenured representation   39–41
Constitutional Court, functions
    adjudication procedure   165–67
    appointment process   160–62
    authoritarian context   171–73
    contextual changes   171–74
    Council of Grand Justices   156, 157–67
    and democratic transition   155–56,
        173–74
    functional transformations   167–74
    historical phases   156
    institutional changes   157–67
    issuance of opinions   167
    judicial guardianship role   155–56
    as Judicial Juan   156, 157
    jurisdiction   164–65
    number/term of justices   160
    Organic Acts etc   158–59
    organisational evolution   157–59

political parties (appointment)
    cooperation model   162, 174
    powers   162–65
    procedure   165–67
    qualifications for appointment   161
    quorum rules   166
    review powers   163
    and ROC Constitution   158
    statistics of performance   168–71
    submissions, written/oral   165–66
    summary   191–92
    transformations   167–74
    see also judicial review
constitutional democracy   8–9
constitutional indigenisation   3–4
Constitutional Interpretation Procedure Act
    (1993)   159
constitutional sovereignty   44–48,
    250–52
quasi-constitutional statutes   15–16
content-based/content-neutral (freedom
    of expression) restrictions   211
Control Yuan   53, 55
    censure/correction powers   123–24
    financial control   117, 118–19
    and five-Yuan system   95
    impeachment proceedings   124–25
    and Legislative Yuan   95–97
    members, appointment/powers
        123, 125
    nominated appointment   94
    as ombudsman-like body   94
    powers   123–25
    reform proposals   125–26
    three to two parliaments   95
    transformation   94–97, 123–26
Convention on the Elimination of All
    Forms of Discrimination against
    Women (CEDAW)   17, 234–36
Convention on the Rights of the Child
    (CRC)   17, 204, 234
Convention on the Rights of Persons with
    Disabilities (CRPD)   17
Council of Grand Justices *see under*
    Constitutional Court, functions
counties (*hsien*)   132–33
cross-strait policy   64–65

death penalty debate   236–38
declarations, variety of *see under*
    judicial review
defamatory statements   212
democratic constitutionalism *see under*
    representation and legislative process

Democratic Progressive Party (DPP) 2, 13, 14–15, 109
  as competing/cooperating party 42, 43
  and Constitutional Court 162, 174
  National Assembly, abolition 45–46, 99
  National Communications Commission (NCC) 80
  offshore islands 149
  pan-green alliance 15–16
  referenda 208
  special municipalities 147
  streamlining of government 82
  votes and seats held by 102–4, 106–7
democratisation 4–5, 36–48
  key issues 36–37
  multi-level governance and devolution 129–30
  negotiated change 37–38
devolution *see* multi-level governance and devolution
dialectical judicial review 13–15
Disabilities, Convention on the Rights of Persons with (CRPD) 17
disability groups 199–200
Dutch rule 23

Economic, Social and Cultural, International Covenent on (ICESCR) 17, 229, 234–36
economic social and cultural rights 200
election rights 206–7
electoral districts *see under* electoral system
electoral rule changes *see under* electoral system
electoral system
  electoral districts 105–6
  electoral rule changes 102, 104–7
  key phases/issues 100
  legislative seats, changes 100–101
  neutrality 107–9
  political participation right 206–7
  political parties *see* political parties, accountability issues
  SMD system 104–5
  votes and seats held by parties 102–4
Electronic Toll Collection (ETC) system 86
employers' rights 218
environmental protection groups 196, 199
European Convention on Human Rights 18
evolution of constitution
  democratisation *see* democratisation
  externally imposed constitutions 24–30
  historical background 1–2, 23–24

indigenisation *see* constitutional indigenisation
  key issues/summary 24, 48–49
  manipulation and authoritarianism, constitutional 30–36
evolution of presidency and executive
  Executive Yuan *see* Executive Yuan
  five-power government scheme *see* five-power government scheme
  governmental structure 51
  incremental reform 51–52
  key issues/summary 52, 89–90
  premier, appointment/role 69–71, 90
  reform *see* government reform
  see also President/presidency (ROC)
Examination Yuan 53, 55
  and civil service 87–89
Executive Yuan
  basic role 68–69
  Cabinet Meeting 70–71
  composition/function 70
  financial control 117–19
  ministries *see* ministries and agencies
  premier, appointment/role 69–71, 90
  and president's powers 63–64, 68
  Taiwan Provincial Government, organisational restructuring 141
  see also evolution of presidency and executive
Executive Yuan Council (Cabinet Meeting) 70–71
expression, freedom of 209
externally imposed constitutions 24–30

family structure changes 218–21
Far Eastern Electronic Toll Collection Co. (FETC) 86–87
Fatung concept 30, 33
Five-Five Draft Constitution (1936) 28
five-power government scheme 51, 52–59
  basic features 52
  development 52–57
  inequalities between powers 55–56
  interactions between powers 54–55
  mediation powers 54
  revolutionary model 53–54, 55
  semi-parliamentary government 51, 52–57
  semi-presidentialism 57–59
  separation of powers 56–57
  Yuan structure 53
foreign relations, shared powers 120–21
foreign workers 223–24
Formosa 25–26

free speech rights   208–13
freedom of assembly   209–11
freedom of expression   209, 212–13

gender equality   218–21
Ginsburg, Tom   172
global convergence of institutions   18–19
global perspectives   148–52
globalisation   6–7
Government Information Disclosure Act
    (2005)   85
government reform   80–89
    Examination Yuan and civil service
        87–89
    key issues   80–81
    public-private partnership   83–87
    streamlining of government   81–82

health insurance   143–45, 214–16
health rights   200
Hong Kong's handover   42, 43
hsien (counties)   132–33
Hu, Fu   37
human rights
    constitutional authoritarianism   32–36
    see also international human rights

immigrants
    and equality   222–24
    foreign workers   223–24
    Mainland
        restrictions on rights   208
        spouses   222–23
impeachment proceedings   124–25
imposition *see* externally imposed
    constitutions
incremental constitutional reform/
    revisions   12–13, 241–42
    and representation, reconstruction
        of   38–39
    see also evolution of constitution;
        evolution of presidency and executive
independence of courts   11–12
independent regulatory commissions   19
independent regulatory commissions *see*
    under ministries and agencies
indigenisation *see* constitutional
    indigenisation
Indigenous Peoples Basic Law   229
indigenous peoples rights   200, 224–32
    assimilation   226–27
    Austronesians   224–25
    collective/individual rights   229
    cultural rights   230

Han culture   225
historical discrimination   224–27
implementation   229–32
indigenous movement   227–29
land disputes   230–31
language use   229–30
preferential employment   231–32
shou-fan/sheng-fan groups   225–26
Indigenous and Tribal Peoples
    Convention   232
International Covenant on Economic, Social
    and Cultural (ICESCR)   17, 229, 234–36
International Covenent on Civil and Political
    Rights (ICCPR)   17, 229, 234–36, 237
international human rights
    conventions/treaties, incorporation   7,
        16–17, 18, 234–35
    death penalty debate   236–38
    government institutions' design   235–36
    incorporation   232–38
    institutional capacity building   233–36
    international treaties, incorporation   7,
        16–17
    judicial review   186–89
    statutory incorporation   235
    transnational judicial dialogues   17–18
    see also human rights
International Labour Conventions   18
international law, incorporation (judicial
    review)   186–89

Japanese colonisation   23, 25–27, 226
Judicial Juan *see under* Constitutional Court,
    functions
judicial review
    admonitory declarations   179
    concurring/dissenting opinions   189–91
    declarations, variety of   178–83
    foreign law references   186–89
    international law, incorporation
        186–89
    limited constitutionality or
        unconstitutionality declarations   180
    pro-dialogue/dialectic approach   13–15,
        175–78
    proportionality principle   184–86
    prospective declarations/rulings
        181–83
    statutory delegation   176–77
    statutory reservation   177
    strategy/style of judgment   174–75
    summary   191–92
    unconstitutional declarations   178–79
    see also Constitutional Court, functions

Kaohsiung City 43, 144, 147
Kinmen island 149
Kuomintang (KMT) 1–2, 4–5, 13, 14–15,
  23, 48
  budgetary control and devolution 135
  constitutional authoritarianism 34–36
  and Constitutional Court 162, 171, 174
  Control Yuan 97
  democratisation 36–37
  as dominant party 109, 111, 113–14
  external representation crisis 43–44
  five-power government scheme 55–56
  full suffrage to Taiwan's residents 41–42
  incorporation of Taiwan 28–30
  indigenous peoples, assimilation 226–27
  Mainland China, authorised agreements
    with 121
  manipulation of representation 32–34
  National Assembly, abolition 45–46, 99
  National Communications Commission
    (NCC) 78–80
  negotiated change 37, 38
  offshore islands 149–50
  pan-blue alliance 15–16
  public insurance 214–15
  public-private partnership 86
  referenda 207–8
  special municipalities 146–47
  streamlining of government 81–82
  Taiwan, state v province models
    137–38, 142–43
  votes and seats held by 102–4, 107

Lee, Chen-yuan 197
Lee, Teng-hui, President 32, 37–38, 42,
  43, 215
legislative functions and constitutional
  control
  audit control 118–19
  citizens' petitions for legislation 114
  financial control 117–19
  foreign relations, shared powers 120–21
  key issues 114
  legislative autonomy and limitations
    114–17
  personnel appointments 122–23
  shared powers and conflict resolution
    120–23
Legislative Yuan 30, 32, 69
  and Control Yuan 95–97
  electoral system *see* electoral system
  financial control 117–19
  five-power government scheme 55–56,
    57, 58

foreign relations, shared powers 120–21
legislative functions *see* legislative
  functions and constitutional control
  and National Assembly, abolition
    44–46, 98–99
  offshore islands 150
  political parties *see* political parties,
    accountability issues
  and president's powers 64, 68
  privileges and immunities for
    members 116–17
  Taiwan Provincial Government,
    organisational restructuring 141
legitimacy issues 32–34
Lien, Chan, Vice-President/premier 45, 59
limited constitutionality or
  unconstitutionality declarations *see under*
  judicial review
Lin, Shan-tien 197
Linz, Juan 34
Liu, Xia 206–7
Local Government Act 16
local government system, structure *see under*
  central-local relations
local self-government, constitutional
  recognition *see under* Taiwan, state v
  province models

Ma, Ying-jeou, President/Mayor 80, 113,
  143, 162
Mainland China 2, 8, 16, 23–24, 29, 37
  authorised agreements with 121
  and Constitutional Court 171–72
  cross-strait policy 64–65
  immigrants *see under* immigrants
  offshore islands 149
manipulation and authoritarianism,
  constitutional 30–36
  manipulation of representation 32–34
marriage disputes/protection 203–4
martial law, and constitutional
  authoritarianism 34–36
Martial Law Decree (1949) 1, 2, 35–36, 37,
  195–96, 209
Meiji Constitution 25–27
ministers/ministers without portfolio
  (MWPs) 70, 71
ministries and agencies 71–75
  designated independent
    commissions 75
  discretionary expansion 71–72
  8 Co-ordinative Councils 75
  fixed framework 71
  14 ministries 74–75

independent agencies 75–76
independent regulatory commissions
    76–78
  National Communications Commission
    (NCC) 78–80
  reform/reorganisation 72–73, 73–74
    Table
  special-mission-orientated
    commissions 77
Moustafa, Tamir 172
multi-level governance and devolution
  central-local relations *see* central-local
    relations
  democratisation *see* democratisation
  historical background 129
  key issues/summary 130, 152–53
  state v province models *see* Taiwan,
    state v province models
Multi-Level Reservation Structure 177

National Academy of the Civil Service 89
National Affairs Conference 38
National Assembly, abolition 44–48,
    97–100
  and Legislative Yuan 44–46, 98–99
  local self-government, constitutional
    recognition 139
  President/Vice-President, direct
    election 65–66, 98
  two parliaments to one 97–98
National Communications Commission
    (NCC) 19, 78–80
National Health Insurance programme
    (NHI) 143–45, 215–16
National Security Council (NSC) 63–64
Nationalist Party, Kuomintang (KMT) 1–2
nuclear power plant controversy 67–68,
    175–76

obscene speech 213
occupation, freedom of 216–18
Offshore Islands Development Act 150
Old Thieves
  and manipulation of representation
    32–34
  tenured representation 39–40
Operate-Transfers (OTs) 84

pan-green/pan-blue alliances 15–16
parliamentary reorganisation 8–9
Penghu island 149–50
People's Republic of China (PRC) 4, 6,
    24, 30
Political Donations Act (2004/2008) 111

political gender equality 221
political participation right 205–8
political parties, accountability issues
    109–14
  constitutional importance 110
  number of registered parties 109
  statutory regulation 110–12
political rights *see* civil and political rights
pre-democratisation era *see* manipulation and
    authoritarianism, constitutional
premier, appointment/role 69–71
President/presidency (ROC)
  ceremonial role 60
  Control Yuan appointments 123
  cross-strait policy 64–65
  direct presidential elections
    65–66, 98
  evolution 60–68
  executive role 62
  foreign relations, shared powers 120–21
  intermediary role 61
  key features 59–60
  National Security Council (NSC) 63–64
  personnel appointments 122–23
  and political conflicts 65–68
  powers/accountability 10
  role/powers 60–62
  see also evolution of presidency and
    executive
Principle of the People's Livelihood 135
privacy rights 204
proportional representation 206
proportionality principle *see under* judicial
    review
provinces 132, 133
Provisional Constitution for the Period of
    Political Tutelage of the ROC (1931) 28
public office, holding right 208
Public Officials Election and Recall Act
    (1991) 101, 112
public referendum 47–48
Public Service Pension Fund Supervisory
    Board 89
public-private partnership *see under*
    government reform

Qing Empire 23, 53, 134, 225
quasi-constitutional statutes 15–16

recall (electoral) right 206
referenda 207–8
Referendum Act (2004) 114, 207
regional and global perspectives 148–52
regulation, independent regulatory
    commissions 19

representation and legislative process
democratic constitutionalism 2–3, 91
electoral system *see* electoral system
historical development 8–9, 91–93
key issues/summary 93, 126–27
legislative functions *see* legislative
functions and constitutional control
political parties *see* political parties,
accountability issues
representative institutions,
transformations *see* Control Yuan;
National Assembly, abolition
representation manipulation 32–34
representation, reconstruction of
congressional reform 46–47
constitutional sovereignty 44–48,
250–52
external representation 42, 44
and incremental constitutional
reform 38–39
internal representation 39–42
key phases/summary 38–39, 48–49
National Assembly, abolition 44–48
provisional government status/
downsizing 42–44
public referendum 47–48
rounds of revision 38
tenured representation 39–40
Republic of China (ROC)
indigenisation 3–4
relocation to Taiwan 1–2, 23–24, 43
UN representatives, expulsion 6
Republic of China (ROC) Constitution 1,
2, 24, 48
Additional Articles and seventh revision
(2005) 12–13, 116
budgetary expenditure increases,
limitation 117–18
central-local relations 131–35
constitution-making process/
promulgation 28–29
constitutional authoritarianism 32–36
constitutional sovereignty 44–48,
250–52
democratisation 36–37
five-power, semi-parliamentary
government 51, 52–57
freedom of expression 209
implementation in Taiwan 29–30
local self-government, constitutional
recognition *see under* Taiwan, state v
province models
manipulation of representation 32–34,
39–41

National Assembly, abolition 44
national representation structure 30
pre-War framework 28
quasi-constitutional statute 16
representation and legislative
development 91–93
and rights discourse 197–201
see also constitution for Taiwan
rights and freedoms
civil and political rights 205–13
human rights *see* human rights;
international human rights
indigenous peoples *see* indigenous peoples
rights
key issues/summary 9–10, 193–94,
238–39
socio-economic rights 214–24
in transformative society 194–95
rights discourse 194–204
in civil society 195–97
and constitutional reform 197–201
demonstrations/protests 197
incorporation by judiciary 202–4
non-governmental organisations
196–97
policy directives 200–201
rule of law 11–12

separation of powers *see under* five-power
government scheme
separation of powers, and
accountability 10
shou-fan/sheng-fan groups *see under* indigenous
peoples rights
social rights 200
socio-economic rights 214–24
Soong, James CY, Governor 43, 141
Spanish rule 23
special municipalities *see under* Taiwan,
state v province models
statutory declaration/reservation *see under*
judicial review
streamlining of government *see under*
government reform
student movement reform agenda 38
Su, Nan-cheng 45
Sun Yat-sen's model 51, 53, 92
Sunflower Movement 121

Taipei City Government, disputes with
Central government 43, 142–46
election postponement dispute 145–46
National Health Insurance programme
(NHI), financial allocation 143–45

as special municipality   147–48
transitional politics, significance   142–43
Taiwan
  in multi-level governance   150–52
  and offshore islands   148–50
  post-World War II history   1–2, 23–24
Taiwan Alliance to End the Death Penalty
  (TAEDP)   237
Taiwan Association for Human
  Rights   196, 202
Taiwan High Speed Rail (THSR)   85–86
Taiwan Provincial Government
  historical obsolescence   139–40
  organisational restructuring   140–42
  as symbolic body   142
Taiwan, state v province models   135–48
  background   135–36
  constitutional amendment and legislative
    action   137–40
  democratic transition   138–39
  as geopolitical change   147–48
  key phases   136
  local self-government, constitutional
    recognition   139–40
  special municipalities   146–48
  Taipei *see* Taipei City Government,
    disputes with Central government
  Two Capitals/Six Capitals systems   136,
    147–48
Taiwanese council, petition (1921)   27
Takeno, Takenori   25
Temporary Provisions for the Period of
  Mobilisation to Suppress Rebellion
  (Temporary Provisions) (1948)
  1, 31–32, 35–36, 37, 38, 39, 62, 63,
  171–72, 195–96
Tiananmen Square   5

transnational judicial dialogues   17–18
Two Capitals/Six Capitals systems   136,
  147–48
228 Incident   28

unconstitutional declarations *see under*
  judicial review
United Nations Declaration on the Rights
  of Indigenous Peoples   232
United Nations General Assembly,
  resolution (1971)   6
United States
  Administrative Procedure Act and
    Freedom of Information Act   7
  Supreme Court   157, 160
Universal Declaration of Human Rights
  (UDHR)   18

Vice-President, direct election   98

Wang, Jin-pyng, Speaker   113–14
Weber, Max   33
Weng, Yueh-sheng, Justice   160
Women, Convention on the Elimination
  of All Forms of Discrimination against
  (CEDAW)   17, 234–36
women's groups   199, 202–3
women's sexual freedom/reproductive
  rights   220–21
work, right to   216–18
World Trade Organization (WTO),
  accession   7

Yeltsin Effect   141
Yuans (branches)   30*n*, 53
  see also Control Yuan; Examination Yuan;
    Executive Yuan; Legislative Yuan